STRAIGHT
FROM
THE HEART

STRAIGHT FROM THE HEART

A LOVE STORY

ROD AND BOB JACKSON-PARIS

WARNER BOOKS

A Time Warner Company

Warner Books, Inc., 1271 Avenue of the Americas, New York, NY 10020

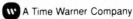 A Time Warner Company

Printed in the United States of America
First Printing: February 1994
10 9 8 7 6 5 4 3 2 1

Library of Congress Cataloging-in-Publication Data

Jackson-Paris, Rod, 1961–
    Straight from the heart / Rod and Bob Jackson-Paris.
      p.   cm.
    ISBN 0-446-51748-8
    1. Jackson-Paris, Bob. 2. Jackson-Paris, Rod, 1961– . 3. Gay men—
United States—Biography. 4. Gay marriage—United States.
I. Jackson-Paris, Bob. II. Title.
HQ75.8.J33A3   1994
305.38'9664'092—dc20   92-51029
                                                        CIP

I dedicate this book to the gay, lesbian, and bisexual youth who must struggle so hard to find their place in this world, and to those who never made it due to emotional, spiritual, and physical abuse. I also dedicate this book to my brothers and sisters who have died of AIDS or who are living with HIV or AIDS. You fought for the right to live and die with dignity. In doing so, you taught the rest of us how to stand with our heads held high, hungry for justice and equality. Martyrs and heroes, one and all. And, of course, for Bob.

—ROD JACKSON-PARIS

To everyone who fights darkness, hatred, and ignorance everywhere. Warriors of peace, we go hand in hand toward a world where all people can live as brothers and sisters. It is the beauty of our differences that gives us so much in common. But most of all, with love for Rod.

—BOB JACKSON-PARIS

ACKNOWLEDGMENTS

We wish to acknowledge and thank several people for their support and belief in this project. To our literary agent, Basil Kane, who believed in this book, even when many others did not. To Rick Horgan, who initially sold Warner Books on what most were seeing as a very controversial book. To Eric Marcus, our collaborator and co-author, for the patience and hard work editing, organizing, and helping us to put this book together. To Kathy Prata for transcribing our words. To Darryl Peterson for the cover photo. To Michael Denneny, for his enthusiasm and friendship. And to our editor, Karen Kelly, for her sensitivity, creativity, and excitement for this project.

To all of those who have played such an important role in our lives but are not acknowledged here, thank you! You know who you are.

To all those who work in the gay and lesbian media whose work and words are so necessary—truly a matter of life and death. To those who work in the mainstream press who help to break down unjust and false myths about gay and lesbian people and their families.

Finally, to all the women and men who pioneered the homophile movement, we gratefully acknowledge the bricks you laid in the road that we and millions of others are now able to travel.

"The reason that fiction is more interesting than any other form of literature to those of us who really like to study people is that, in fiction, the author can tell the whole truth without hurting anyone—or humiliating himself too much."

—ELEANOR ROOSEVELT

INTRODUCTION

Straight from the Heart is the story of two people who love each other passionately, who are deeply committed to their shared life, and who are willing to sacrifice everything for one another. It's a love story—our love story.

We're a little hesitant to call *Straight from the Heart* a memoir or an autobiography, because you might think we're looking back from the end of our lives, recalling our many years together. But we're still in our early thirties, so *Straight from the Heart* represents the beginning of our story. It's the early chapters of what we hope will be a long life together, about the love that first drew us to each other, the past that shaped who we are, and the exciting and often challenging life we've shared for the past seven years.

By nature we're very private people, so writing about our lives, and our relationship in particular, is something that by nature we would be reluctant to do. We've already had the experience of talking about our lives and our relationship for newspaper and magazine articles, at college speaking engagements, and on television—from *Oprah* to *Donahue*. That might sound very exciting, but sometimes it's made us feel that we don't own our lives. It's hard not to wonder, "What's ours to keep? What isn't

Bob and Rod at
Niagara Falls, 1987.
Just another pair of
visiting lovebirds.

Bob and Rod
at the beach
in California.
(*Art Zeller*)

public property? Why are we doing this to ourselves?" And now a book.

So why *are* we doing this to ourselves? We believe that at this stage of our lives we have an obligation—a responsibility—to live our lives so that we leave the world a better place for the generation that follows. In real terms, this means leading a life we can be proud of.

We want our story to show that it's possible to find someone you can love and who loves you in return. We want you to know that, despite the challenges we all face, there's hope for a better future, that gay and lesbian people can live the American dream, that we can all have both romance and love in our lives.

In addition to being our love story, *Straight from the Heart* is also about survival. It's about surviving difficult childhoods and about surviving against impossible odds in a society that so destructively condemns gay and lesbian people. Through our example we hope you'll see that it's possible for all people, both gay and non-gay, to overcome the odds, to live with pride, to stand up and have dignity, and still succeed—even thrive.

When we started speaking out publicly about our lives, we didn't think in terms of giving people hope, but then after the first magazine articles and television appearances we began receiving tens of thousands of letters from all over the country. Many people have written to tell us how they were inspired by our example to live their lives with pride, to confront the challenges they face, and to pursue their dreams. Both of us have been overwhelmed by what people have written, which in turn has inspired us to continue our work. We especially draw strength from these letters when we're feeling dispirited by the prejudice and ignorance we encounter in our day-to-day lives and as we travel the country.

We knew from the start that telling our story would mean being as honest as we could about our lives together. We haven't sugar-coated anything, because we want to paint a true picture of ourselves. Our life together hasn't been perfect and easy; it's not that way for anyone. Unfortunately the truth can be difficult

With Phil Donahue at the 1993 March on Washington.

to tell, and it isn't always what people want to hear. But we want to be sure that the people who look to us and our lives as examples know that while it's possible to find both dignity *and* love, a relationship is far more complex than a paperback romance novel.

Straight from the Heart will not be easy for our families. Like us, they're very private, so we're sure it will be painful for them to see in print family experiences they wouldn't consider talking about even behind closed doors. By talking about those experiences and about how our families have handled the fact that we're gay, we don't mean to suggest that our parents and families are any different from many other American families. We love them dearly, but we want other families to learn from our experiences so the vicious cycle of denial and alienation can be brought to an end.

We were pretty sure that doing this book would be a challenge, and we were right. Neither of us likes to dwell on the past, and having to dredge up memories that were often painful was rough.

When it came to our shared memories, there were two of us to fill in the details, but we didn't always agree on what happened or the reasons why one of us did one thing or the other. In the end, we both agreed that *Straight from the Heart* was worth the effort, because, beyond the challenge, doing this book has been a positive experience for us. What we've learned about ourselves, each other, and our relationship has helped open new doors in our lives. We hope that *Straight from the Heart* will enrich your life as well.

—ROD and BOB JACKSON-PARIS
May 1993

When you're lovers in a dangerous time
Sometimes you're made to feel as if your love's a crime
But nothing worth having comes without some kind of fight
You got to kick at the darkness 'til it bleeds daylight.

—BRUCE COCKBURN

1

The first time I saw Bob Paris, I was living in Denver working part-time managing a gym, doing social work, and modeling all at the same time. Bob was in town to do a bodybuilding seminar at my gym, and I was behind the counter taking tickets. I didn't know much about him, but I knew that he was Mr. Universe, and I also knew what he looked like because we had used a photo of him for the poster announcing the seminar. I thought he was okay-looking and had a fantastic body, but I didn't think he was my type since I wasn't into overly muscular men. Then I saw Bob get out of the car. There was a big picture window in front of the gym right where the car pulled up. About fifty people were waiting around when he walked in the door. He looked right at me and my heart went *woo-ooh*. It was like, *Where have you been?* It wasn't, *Oh, he's hot.* It was, *Oh, my God, I've been looking for you all my life. I didn't think you existed, and here you are!*

As I walked through the doors to the gym, I saw Rod standing behind the counter and locked eyes with him. It was like the wind was knocked out of me. My heart was racing. There were people milling around and a lot of activity at the gym, and people were trying to get my attention, but everything else in

Rod doing body work for *Muscle and Fitness* magazine.
(*Dan Arsenault*)

Bob and Rod are the first openly gay couple to grace the cover
of a sports magazine in North America.

the room just disappeared as I focused on Rod's eyes. I didn't even realize how extraordinarily good-looking he was until later on. I just knew this was something that was meant to be. I knew from that instant on that I would spend my life with this person. I was already picking out dish patterns within the first half second.

Ironically, this was going to be my very last seminar. I'd been retired from professional bodybuilding for almost a year, but I kept doing seminars and guest appearances to pay for acting school. After this one I was going to stop working for a while and concentrate on studying.

I'd just come from a month working in Australia and a ten-day visit with my family in Indiana. I was extremely depressed at the time. Even though I was moving ahead in my career and setting goals, life seemed worthless to me. Then I saw Rod, and I felt like we had known each other for a very long time but had to catch up for all the years that we'd missed so far.

It was a truly cosmic moment, absolutely magical. But what made it even more magical was that it was so unexpected because I didn't believe I could have love in my life, although that's really what I wanted. I thought it was all bullshit, especially for a gay person in America in 1985. Sure, gay people could have relationships, but really falling in love? I didn't think that was possible in this society. But here it was happening. I looked in his eyes. It was the first time I ever fell into anyone's eyes. I didn't see anything around us. I saw the past and then the whole future. It scared the hell out of me. That's why when the owner of the gym brought Bob over to meet me, I thought, *I've got to get rid of this guy.* I was afraid I was going to fall in love. So I just got busy sorting through the membership cards. And when the owner introduced Bob to Linda, the other manager, who was standing next to me, she elbowed me so I'd look up from what I was doing.

Rod was always chased, so I think he immediately felt vulnerable and didn't want to open himself up to being hurt. Love is a messy thing. It's fantastic and it's horrible all at the same time, but that's what makes it such a desirable thing.

I was leaving for L.A. in three weeks, and I didn't want to complicate my life. But mostly I was scared. I'd never really been in a romantic situation where I felt vulnerable. I didn't want to get hurt. Nobody can hurt you like a lover, and it scared me. So Linda elbowed me, and the owner introduced Bob to me. My knees went *woo-ooh* and my stomach did little butterflies, because I felt Bob could look straight inside me. I felt naked and very excited, all at the same time.

As soon as Bob walked off to meet some other people, Carol, a friend of mine, came over to me and whispered, "You guys will make a great couple." And I said, "What are you talking about?" She said, "I've never seen you do that with anybody before. You're going to go after him." And I told her that I wasn't going after anybody, and she said, "You always get what you want," and walked off.

Bob went to the back of the gym to do his seminar. There were over a hundred people sitting on benches watching. After he started, I went back and sat down on the floor in the front row. I was supposed to go out on a date later that evening, so I was going to try to get out of there early. But Bob stared at me the entire time—two hours! It was like no one else existed. So I stayed through the whole presentation. Afterward the gym owner and Linda asked if I wanted to go with them and Bob to dinner. I said that I had a date, and Linda looked at me like, *Oh, you've got to be kidding.* I made a call and changed the date.

During my seminar, Rod sat there the whole time taking his Topsiders on and off. I noticed he had sexy feet. I remember he was wearing blue jeans and a purple tank top. And he had bleached-white punk hair. I kind of knew he was crazy about me because of how he was trying not to look interested. And

Bob and Rod training together, from *BodyPower*, a British magazine.

I was a bit spoiled myself. It's not ego, but I just figured, why wouldn't he be interested? But I have to admit that he was pretty poker-faced through the whole thing. I was giving him his own private seminar in the presence of a hundred strangers.

Now keep in mind that neither of us up to this point had said that we were gay. I'd heard rumors about Bob before he got to the gym, but sexuality didn't come up right away. It was a primal, millions-of-years, soul-mate type of thing.

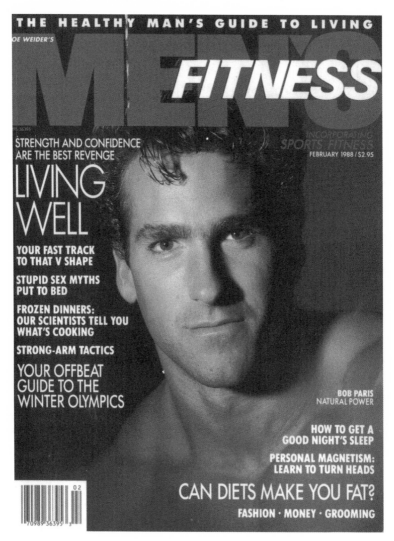

THE HEALTHY MAN'S GUIDE TO LIVING

JOE WEIDER'S

MEN *FITNESS*

INCORPORATING SPORTS FITNESS

FEBRUARY 1988 / $2.95

STRENGTH AND CONFIDENCE ARE THE BEST REVENGE

LIVING WELL

YOUR FAST TRACK TO THAT V SHAPE

STUPID SEX MYTHS PUT TO BED

FROZEN DINNERS: OUR SCIENTISTS TELL YOU WHAT'S COOKING

STRONG-ARM TACTICS

YOUR OFFBEAT GUIDE TO THE WINTER OLYMPICS

BOB PARIS NATURAL POWER

HOW TO GET A GOOD NIGHT'S SLEEP

PERSONAL MAGNETISM: LEARN TO TURN HEADS

CAN DIETS MAKE YOU FAT?

FASHION · MONEY · GROOMING

Bob on the cover of *Men's Fitness*.

So four of us—the gym owner, Linda, Rod, and I—went to the Metropolitan Grill in downtown Denver for dinner. Right away Rod and I started talking about politics, and we got off on social issues and starving children and what novels we liked. The other two kept trying to butt into the conversation.

I was used to boring acquaintances to death by talking about politics, current events, and the condition of the world. And here I was able to talk about these things with someone who was passionate, gorgeous, intelligent, and sensitive. By this time Rod's cold front had crumbled away.

The really nice thing for me about that dinner was that I've always been such a socially conscious person and here was someone I shared that with—and he was also good-looking, smart, and successful. And he had so much compassion. He told me that he read six newspapers every day, and that he liked to keep up on what was going on. We got into discussing all the social ills plaguing the world.

I was so impressed that he was really pulled together and self-educated. All through dinner I was on edge and very infatuated. I already felt like I was in love. I had never, ever felt like that in my life.

To me this was proof of reincarnation beyond all shadow of a doubt. I knew that Rod and I had been together many, many times before. I felt that way from the very beginning. Early on we were able to finish each other's sentences. We had dreams in common. We went to places we knew we had been to together before. There was just too much history for it to be any sort of accident.

I had never really thought anything about reincarnation. But when Bob walked in, I knew that I'd never met him in this life, but I knew everything about him instantly.

This photo, advertising a seminar at a Denver gym, was the first Rod saw of Bob before meeting. (*Mike Neveaux*)

A work shot of Rod for a fitness magazine.

Rod knew I had a lot of skeletons in my closet. He knew that I had had a really hard life. And I knew immediately we came from the same place. We come from very similar backgrounds. I could relate to him instantly.

I think Bob was kind of unnerved by the intense conversation and impressed at the same time. He was used to people trying to please him, trying to bullshit with him. And I didn't bullshit him on anything. I was just saying things the way they were, and he wasn't used to it.

Well, I was this little budding star living in Hollywood. Everyone was trying to get close to the fire all the time, kissing ass, and trying to play their cards right so that if I became this big star, they would be on the inside. So I wasn't used to hearing a lot of honesty.

After dinner, we went down to the parking garage. As we walked toward my car, Bob said, "Here's my card. Give me a call when you get to L.A."

My first impulse as we were leaving was to kiss Rod, but I knew I had to play this very carefully. It was like encountering a deer in the forest. If I took any wrong steps, he was going to flee, never to be seen again. So I played it cool, gave him my card, and told him to give me a call if I could help him with anything when he got to L.A. I didn't say anything insinuating, like let's go out or let's jump in the sack. I just wanted to cherish the romanticism of the moment.

Then Linda asked me if I was going to work out the next day, and I asked Rod if he would be working, but he said he wasn't. I told him I planned to work out at about nine o'clock. I was hoping he'd show up.

Bob (*left*) competing in Italy in 1988.

I purposely didn't go at nine. I didn't want him to think I was chasing him, but I was hoping he would be waiting for me to show up. I thought if he wanted to see me, he'd be there at ten. If he wasn't there, then I had nothing to worry about. So I got there at ten, and he was in front of a mirror doing side raises. I was wearing these cheesy red running shorts with white stripes and a red tank top. I was coordinated for the first time in my life. I guess I wanted to get Bob's attention, but I was very professional. Bob calls it "friendly efficient." I was feeling very vulnerable, and I wanted Bob to chase me, and at the same time I didn't want him to chase me because I didn't think I could handle it. I was very conflicted. So I said hello to Bob, and then went to do some work. It was my day off, but when you're a manager at a gym, you always wind up working when you go in to exercise.

By the time I got through, Bob had gone upstairs to do the stationary bike. So I went upstairs and got on the bike next to his. There were only two bikes available. I put on my headphones and immediately turned up the volume. I was just looking straight ahead and Bob kept trying to talk to me.

We were both trying to play it as subtle as possible. But it was frustrating—humorous and frustrating at the same time. I wanted him to take the damn headphones off and talk to me. I wasn't accustomed to being ignored.

Now, I wasn't the kind of person who would go to the gym to meet people. I went to the gym to do my work and get out. Striking up a conversation was a completely alien thing for me to do. So I asked Rod how long he had worked at the gym, about his social work job, and when he was moving to Los Angeles, dumb things like that. I knew this was the person I was going to spend my life with. He was a tough cookie, a really tough cookie, but I wasn't going to let him go.

I didn't want him to let me go, but I didn't know how to react. I wasn't being calculating or anything like that. But every time he asked a question, I turned down my Walkman, answered the question, and turned it back up. Finally, after the first few questions I just took my headphones off because he obviously really wanted to talk to me. The whole time I was thinking, *Oh my God, he's interested in me.* And then, *Oh, he's not interested in me. Oh my God, he's interested in me. Oh, he's not interested in me.*

It's not like I didn't know what was going on. I had a reputation for being a big flirt. I knew when people were making a move, but this was the first time I *wanted* someone to make a move, so I didn't know if I was imagining things.

He wasn't imagining anything, but it was like fly-fishing. I was trying to figure out how to play the fish, for both of us. It was a mating dance.

We talked for about twenty minutes, and I asked Rod if I could tan. I had to do a bodybuilding guest posing exhibition at a contest that night, so Rod arranged for me to use the

A standard model shot of Rod from his pre-workout years.
(*Alfred Garcia*)

tanning bed. I asked him if he was still going to be there when I got done, but he told me he was leaving. So again I told him to give me a call when he came to L.A. Besides being head over heels in love, I knew what a tough city L.A. was.

Oh, Bob didn't care about that. He just wanted to see me again. And I wanted to see him, so I told him that I wanted to take him to lunch when I got to L.A. because I really didn't know that many people there. And then I left. I could have seen Bob at the contest that night, but I didn't want to go. I just thought that if this was meant to be, then it would be later. I didn't want this to happen right then. I couldn't deal with it.

Before I left Denver, I picked up a copy of a local gay magazine, and there was this ad for the gym where Rod worked, and there was a photograph of him. I tore the picture out and took it back with me to L.A. I was like a little kid who was head over heels in love, going around saying to people, *I met the most wonderful, neatest person in Denver, and here's a picture of him. Here's what he looks like.*

I moved to L.A. about three weeks later, and I called Bob and left a message for him on his answering machine.

I returned the call and left a message for Rod.

And I never called him back.

2

I was going to return Bob's call, but before I had a chance, something strange happened. Well, I thought it was strange. This was the first week I was in town, and I had already started working at the Athletic Club in West Hollywood. I was at the counter checking people in and this really good-looking man, who was a well-known TV actor, came up to me and asked if I was Rod. I wasn't quite sure who he was, but I knew he was "somebody," and I said, "Excuse me?" And he said, "I'm David so and so, and I'm a good friend of Bob Paris's and I've heard all about you." Right away I thought, *Bob is talking about me because he's trying to put another notch on his headboard.* So I shut off. I never wanted to speak to him and didn't call him back.

Part of me really didn't care if I ever saw Bob again, but over the next six months our paths kept crossing. For one thing, I became friends with that TV actor, who was already a friend of Bob's. Then Bob and I wound up going to the same acting conservatory, although we weren't in the same class. And then I started going to the hairstylist who cut Bob's hair. I didn't know that until I was sitting there one day and the stylist told me that he'd heard all about me from Bob Paris. Well, then I got really mad.

I had never even talked to this guy about Rod. Rod was the new man in town and people were talking about him. Somehow the hairstylist had made this connection. Then it got back to Rod that I'd warned our mutual friend, the TV actor, to stay away from him. I was getting jealous because I knew David was spending time with Rod, and I wasn't. I wanted Rod all to myself, so I told David, "Rod's too good for you. Leave him alone."

When I heard that, I was so pissed, and I told David, "You can tell Bob Paris to mind his own business. I don't even know the man, and if he's got a problem with my life, you can tell him to call me."

I got the message, so I didn't call Rod, but I still wanted to see him desperately. Finally, a couple of months later, I was in a car with David driving back from Malibu, and we were back in the city right across from the Beverly Center shopping mall, and I saw Rod. I told David to pull over. I rolled my window down and yelled, "Rod!" and waved wildly. Rod squinted in my direction. I couldn't tell if he was squinting or scowling.

I vaguely remember somebody yelling my name, but I didn't have my glasses or my contacts on, so I was almost blind. I just kept walking.

I didn't know that and figured Rod was ignoring me. I remember thinking to myself, *God, what is with this person?*

Rod wasn't much warmer the next time I saw him, which was a month or two later at a Christmas party. I hadn't been there very long, but I only knew a couple of people and I wasn't into parties anyway, so I was about to leave. Then Rod walked in with a couple of friends. I stayed, but I was very tentative about approaching him. Eventually I got up my courage and walked over and said hello. He was very cold and efficient, and said, "Hi Bob, how are you doing?" That was it until I left the party and ran into him in the hallway. We talked a little back and forth, and said good-night.

By this time I had heard that Rod was moving into my neighborhood or had already moved. So when I went out running, I would try to get a glimpse of him. Then a couple of weeks after the party, on Christmas Day, I was driving back from buying some stuff for Christmas dinner and I saw Rod's red Jeep go down Fountain Avenue with a mattress on top of it. I tried to turn around quickly to follow him, to try to catch up with him. I just wanted to say hello, to wish him "Merry Christmas." But by the time I turned around I couldn't find him. I was starting to think that we were going to bounce off each other forever, that this was one of those things where sixty years from now I was going to look back and see Rod as the great unrequited love of my life.

This whole thing had become some kind of pissing match. I wanted to see Rod, but my pride kept me from calling him. And, I found out later, he really wanted to call me. But neither of us wanted to reveal our vulnerability. And I think both of us wanted to be chased by the other.

It wasn't like I didn't want to see Bob, but part of me was disgusted with him. I was mad that I was the topic of his conversations, yet he couldn't call me himself and talk to me. And I wasn't about to call him even though I was in love with him. I was so depressed.

The next semester at acting school I saw Bob again. I had just finished class and was talking with my friend Brian, when I spotted Bob coming up the block. I turned my back to him, but he came right up and stopped, and said, "Hi, Rod." And I went, "Uh, uh, Bob, right?" I don't know what I was thinking to put on such an act, as if I couldn't remember his name.

That was really a turning point for me, because that was when I knew he was as mad for me as I was for him. Why else would he have been so ridiculous as to pretend he didn't know who I was? This just showed me it wasn't dead after all, and that I was being played with more than just a little bit.

I wasn't playing games with Bob. I was just trying to protect myself because I didn't know how to deal with the situation. I wanted Bob and I didn't want him.

We only talked for a minute, but realizing that Rod felt about me the same way I felt about him was all the encouragement I needed to lift my spirits. I'd been going through a very rough time in my life, which was made even more intense by having this person so close to me yet impossible to reach. I would wake up during the night wondering what he was thinking about, wondering what he was doing, wondering if he was okay. I was so worried that Rod would get chewed up in the mill—L.A.'s a tough city. Rod looked like he had just come off the farm, and I didn't want to see him go through all the bangs and bruises that I'd been through.

Bob didn't know me. He saw that I was fresh, honest, and young—I was twenty-four—but he didn't understand that I was pretty street-savvy with people.

So about a month later, as I was leaving class, Bob came up to me again to talk to me. He asked me if I'd like to go to dinner sometime and could he have my phone number. I guess my guard was down a bit, and I said okay and wrote my number down for him. I think I surprised both of us.

I called Rod that night after I got back home from my class, which ended pretty late. The first thing I said when we started talking was to apologize about telling David to stay away from him. And then I said, "Would you mind if I fixed dinner for us at my place instead of going out to a restaurant?" Rod said that was fine. I was absolutely elated. I was through the roof and over the moon.

I really let my guard down during that conversation, because for the first time Bob was being *really* human. When we'd talked before, when we first met, I knew he was bullshitting me some of the time. When I say bullshit, I mean he was enhancing everything. But that night he was being totally vulnerable and really being himself. So I said, "You're great when you're really being yourself." He asked me what I meant, and I said, "Well, you're a bit full of it sometimes . . ." and we just started talking and talking. At some point Bob asked if he could read me a poem he had written.

I didn't tell Rod until later that I'd written the poem for him. I took my life experience and what I was seeing in Rod and crafted it all into a poem. It was nothing unusual for me to write poetry, but no one ever read my work. So reading that poem to Rod, whom I was so in love with, made me very nervous. The poem's called "Wood and Stream."

> *Wood and stream,*
> *oh come and take me.*
> *Take me to*
> *your heart of gold.*
> *Give me breath*
> *to see my life now*
> *as I never did before.*
>
> *I went in*
> *to urban masses*
> *seeking love*
> *and maybe gold*
> *But instead*
> *I looked around me*
> *and in time*
> *I found my soul.*

But to face it
meant to challenge
everything
I knew before
so I must
go to the woods now
giving myself
a chance to grow.

When I got there
I discovered
what I'd missed
for all those years
so I started
to uncover
that infant strength
which knew no fear.

And in time
understanding
what it meant
to be set free
and I learned
to let the flower
open on the tiny tree.

Just beginning
then to realize
that the flower
would not last
but the tree
would grow in splendor
thru the seasons
which would pass.

So the tree
would come and go too
while the earth

kept turning around
I just stood
with my new knowledge
uttered not
a bastard sound.

Far beyond
the pomp and dogma
see the spark
that lights our soul
know that tree,
bird, beast and man
do dwell, oh heaven
inside us all.

And the spark
which lives inside me
will not die
but shall go on
joining with
the mighty forces
flower, child
and sparrow's song.

Wood and Stream—Oh,
come and take me, take me
for I have no fear
for this body once so proud
will feed the earth
and all she'll bear.

I was very moved by the time Bob finished the poem, and I told him that it was beautiful, that it was brilliant. I told him how glad I was that he had shared it with me because it really showed there was a fantastic person inside him. Then Bob said, "You're just saying that."

And Rod said, "Don't you ever call me a liar again," and hung up. I pleaded, "But, but, but . . ." It was too late.

I'd heard this beautiful poem, and it had me crying. It spoke to me. It said everything that was in my heart. And then he had the nerve to basically say that I didn't know what I was talking about. In L.A. Bob was so used to people saying, "Oh that's great, fabulous, fabulous . . ." that he didn't trust me to be honest. It especially pissed me off because I had just finished saying that I didn't like people who put up a false front. So I hung up.

I knew right away that it was a stupid thing to say, and I called back immediately. Rod let it ring a few times before picking it up. I said, "I'm so sorry. I'm so sorry. Please forgive me. Did you really like my poem?"

Of course I liked his poem. I loved the poem and I told him again. But then I said, "Look, I'll never tell you anything if I don't mean it. If we get to be friends or get to know each other better, there will be times that you'll wish I would, but I won't. I'll always tell you the truth." And then we continued talking for about three hours. As we talked, I thought, *This is the person I've been dreaming of.*

While we were talking I was sitting in my apartment in front of a window, in a wood chair, leaning back, and I took my toe and I drew a little heart on the window, which had condensation on it. I never did things like that. I wasn't a romantic person, but there was actually love in my heart. It was the first time I really let myself feel that way about someone.

We talked about all kinds of things—the poem, life, and the rampant corruption in the Reagan administration. And I told Bob that he came off as so fickle sometimes, somebody who moves through relationships, someone who glosses over everything, someone who manipulates the facts. I explained that before the poem and our conversation I really didn't think he was a person who would know how to sustain a relationship, that I thought he was this person who just wanted the infatuation and the thrill of it.

I knew from our three hours on the phone that my assumptions had been wrong. I was in love, and I remember telling myself that I was going to get hurt, but that was okay.

I put the phone down and was feeling totally head over heels in love. But then I started thinking about what Rod had said during our first conversation when we met in Denver. Rod told me how he was really anti-drug and that he could never be in a relationship with someone who did drugs. He said that he'd done a lot of work with drug-addicted kids who were from drug-addicted parents and knew firsthand what it could do to someone's life. I didn't know what to do, because I was having trouble getting through a day without getting high. I was severely addicted to marijuana, really off the deep end. I was high all the time, from the minute I got up until the minute I went to bed, and sometimes I would wake up during the night and get high. This was Wednesday and Rod was coming over on Friday.

3

When we first met, Bob and I got into talking about how I'm anti-drug, and my feelings about any addiction. And Bob asked me, "How do you deal with your friends who do drugs?" I said, "I can deal with my friends who do drugs, as long as they're not over the top, but I would never get involved with anybody who did drugs." Of course, I had no idea that Bob was so addicted.

I wasn't just addicted. It was totally self-destructive, because when I couldn't find it anywhere else, I was buying pot on the street in a place called Pot Alley in L.A. People were getting arrested there all the time, so I was putting myself in a totally vulnerable position.

I'd been smoking pot for a long time, although I'd stopped for a while when I first started working out and when I came to California. I was on a real health kick then, but after I began dealing with being gay, when I was twenty-one, I started getting high again. It kind of helped me keep my mind off the struggle with my sexuality.

I faced a serious decision about what to do. Rod and I spoke on Wednesday night. He was coming over for dinner on Friday. I knew I had a little bit of pot left, so on Thursday I smoked all the rest of it and said to myself, *This is it. That's the end of that.*

That's *so* like Bob. I would have thrown it down the toilet. He had to smoke it. We had been together six months and Bob was talking about his drug addiction, and I asked him, "Well, when did you stop getting high?" He said, "The night before we got together." I said, "You went through that all alone and you never even told me!" I thought, *Wow.*

I didn't tell Rod because I was afraid I'd lose him. So Rod was coming over the next day, Friday, and I busied myself with preparations. I was madly in love and too busy making a shopping list to notice that I was missing out on my daily habit of getting stoned. I was in heaven. (I still have that shopping list, as a matter of fact.)

Then I went to Arrow Market and bought enough groceries to feed a dozen people. I bought pasta and pesto, steak, sourdough bread, wine, Brie and crackers, stuff for salad, and flowers. It was going to be a feast!

I was so excited that I was delirious. I couldn't wait. I cleaned and scrubbed the apartment. I set the table and put out candles, and I watched the time all day.

When I got everything done, then I had to decide what I wanted to wear. I thought, *I need to be myself.* I put on a white T-shirt and a pair of baggy blue chinos, and I was barefoot. I said, *This is it. He's got to see me the way I am, because this is who I am.*

I didn't stop thinking about Bob the whole time from our phone conversation until Friday evening when I went over to his apartment. But I was nervous, because I was still thinking, *Is he going to be able to be a real person with me all the time or is he going to get stuck trying to put on some sort of persona?*

On Friday I went to the gym, and I tanned double the normal time because I wanted to look good. Instead I wound up looking like a lobster. I also spent time trying to figure out what I was going to wear. I didn't want to look like I was trying to impress him. I didn't want to dress a part. I'm very, very casual, so in the end I just wore blue jeans and a polo shirt.

No, Rod didn't wear a polo shirt. He wore a white T-shirt with a Colorado logo on it. And he had on those Topsiders again.

Before Rod got there, I went out on the balcony that ran the length of my apartment. It fronted on the street, and I watched him park his Jeep, get out of it, and walk up to the building. He was a vision, just a total vision.

I still didn't know at this point whether Rod had the sense that this was a date. I just didn't know.

The doorbell rang. I took a deep breath, let it out, and said to myself, *Here goes nothing*. I opened the door and said, "Hi. Come on in."

4

We didn't talk much before we ate because Bob wanted to get dinner out of the way. He made gobs of food, but I couldn't indulge myself because I was on a diet. My agent had told me I had to lose twenty pounds if I was going to get any work, because I was too muscular and bulky. I didn't really have a choice because I had to work.

I ate hardly anything either because I was also on a weight-loss diet, to try to get down to a more normal body so I could get parts in plays.

We were both a little uptight during dinner. We were still trying to get comfortable with each other. But once Bob got me onto social issues, I got more relaxed and so did Bob.

I knew Rod couldn't be that uncomfortable, because when he first came in and saw how I was dressed and saw that I didn't have any shoes on, he asked, "Can I take my shoes off?" I said sure, so he took them off and left them at the door. I knew then that it was going to be a pretty comfortable evening.

After we finished dinner, I moved over to sit on the couch, and Bob lay down on the floor about eight feet away, with his hands behind his head. We talked for a couple of hours and Bob kind of inched a little closer, and inched a little closer. I wasn't comfortable talking down to him so finally I moved off the sofa and sat down on the floor.

We talked for a while longer, and Bob said, "You know, we're meant to play some kind of a role in each other's lives." I'm normally such a practical person and not at all into going along with this kind of talk. But this was really odd, because I couldn't help but agree with him.

Rod told me that he didn't know what that role was right now, but that there was something drawing us together, that it was destiny. Then I asked Rod, "Can I touch your hand?" I just kind of held it and time was suspended.

It was wonderful. It was so romantic and sweet. Then he asked if he could kiss me. I said, "Please do." It wasn't a long kiss the first time, but it was really wonderful. Then we kissed again, this time for longer. The fireworks were so intense for me that it was like a half dozen Fourth of Julys, and then some. At some point we stopped, and Bob said, "I love you." I thought, *Am I hearing things?* but at the same time I thought, *How can he say this so soon?* It was so magical and I loved it, but then there was this nagging voice that kept saying, "Does he do this with everybody?"

I hadn't planned to tell Rod that I loved him. It just came out. I'd been head over heels in love for months, the steam had just been building up with no vent, and all of a sudden here was a vent, and it just came out. I knew it sounded a little wacky to Rod, but that's what I was feeling.

We kissed for quite a while longer on the carpet and then I asked Rod if we could go in the bedroom—not to have sex, but just to be more comfortable. Well, I was just gone. I could have died at that moment and it would have been just fine with me.

We kissed for hours, with no talking. There could have been a fire in the building and I don't think either of us would have gotten up. We could have burned to death and never known the difference.

It was so transcendent that we were already in heaven.

After a two-hour kiss—by now this was four in the morning—Bob got down on one knee on the floor and took my hand. Oh, but first he took the family photo on the dresser next to his bed and turned the frame toward us. He said, "I want my family to witness this." I had no idea what he was doing. Bob took my hand and said, "Will you marry me?" I told him he was crazy, that this was ridiculous, that this was just too soon. It scared me, but inside I felt like I was hitting the jackpot and I loved it.

My tendency is to go from heart to thought to filter to mouth. This came from heart to mouth—no thought or filter in between. It didn't occur to me not to ask him to marry me, because I already knew that we were going to be together forever, so I figured there's no time to waste here.

You know, I wondered if Bob was just hitting on me, so I asked, "How many times have you used this line?" He told me that he had never proposed to anyone. I knew that, but I just wanted to hear him say it. So I pulled Bob back on the bed and we started kissing again. After a while, we fell asleep in each other's arms. We didn't have sex that night. We wanted each other badly, but it went unspoken that we would wait for a while.

I had to leave early the next morning for a business trip. I considered canceling because we didn't want to leave each other. We both felt like we were dreaming and we didn't want to wake up. We didn't want to stop looking into each other's eyes. But I really had to go, and finally we said good-bye and Rod went downstairs.

When I closed the door behind Rod, I ran out to the balcony. Rod left the building and walked down the sidewalk, and all of a sudden a gigantic crow flew up right behind him, hovered, made a circle over him, and then flew away. To me that was the sign that Rod was the one. It just reinforced everything that I already knew.

I know it will sound funny to some people, but the crow had special meaning to me because of a spiritual event I had when I was nineteen. I'd been in California for just a short time and was basically homeless, when I decided on the spur of the moment to take a trip back to Indiana.

On the train from California I started a conversation with this guy who had long hair and glasses and was with his girl-friend and their little daughter. We started talking, and he told me that he was a shaman. We got into a conversation about Don Juan and Carlos Castaneda. At some point he told me that they were getting off the train in New Mexico and would be going with a Native American friend, who was also on the train, to take part in a peyote ceremony. Peyote is a hallucinogen that some Native Americans use as part of sacred religious ceremonies.

So we all got off the train near the reservation in New Mexico, and we drove in a beat-up old pickup truck out into the desert to the reservation.

The ceremony was an incredible experience, and I just went into another world. During that spiritual journey, I found out that my spirit guide was a crow. I wasn't surprised, since I'd always found big birds fascinating and had always dreamed of flying. This was really the beginning of my understanding of my place in the world, because my spirit guide revealed to me that I was a holy man and had a mission in life. I learned that my destiny was to somehow make a difference in people's lives. I didn't understand then what that role would be.

I woke up two days after the ceremony. They'd been taking care of me all that time and I was wrapped in blankets. (During those two days my physical body was passed out; I was sweating, convulsing and could have stopped breathing, so someone had to take care of me.) As soon as I was up to it, my friends and I left the reservation and got back on the train. I said good-bye to them in Chicago and they told me I should read Carlos Castaneda if I wanted to understand more about the Yaqui Indian ways of becoming a man of knowledge.

As soon as I got to Indiana I went to a bookstore. It was so strange because Castaneda talks about spirit animals and how powerful the crow is. This is why the crow circling over Rod had such meaning for me.

After Rod left, I went to work, and as soon as I could get away, I called Rod. He was so happy to hear from me. I told him that I missed him and that I'd be back Sunday night. It was all very lovey-dovey.

Bob asked me if I wanted to come over when he got back. Of course I said yes. It seemed like forever before Sunday night came, but finally I walked up to his door, and there was a little scroll attached that said, "Read me before you come in." Well, I'm not great with following directions, so I pulled it off the door and rang the doorbell. Bob opened the door, and I said, "I have to read this." He said, "You were supposed to read it before you came in." So Bob made me go back out and closed the door, and I read a very romantic poem he had written. It was wonderful.

Rod rang the bell again and when I opened the door he flew into my arms.

It was probably three years before we spent the night apart.

5

The next weekend we decided to go hiking in the mountains above Santa Barbara. We drove along the coast highway to the trail head and then climbed up the side of the mountain through the woods. It was so much fun because we were pointing out little details to each other, like the shapes of the leaves and the colors.

When we reached the summit, we turned around and there was an incredible panoramic view of the coast and the ocean. It was so wonderful to be able to share that with someone I loved.

We were like teenagers in love for the first time, but because we were gay, we never had that experience when we were that age. Here we were in our early to mid-twenties, courting each other, infatuated with each other, and in love. It was definitely Aladdin's magic carpet ride.

We went camping and hiking almost every weekend those first few months after we got together. The most incredible of the trips was a day trip to Joshua Tree, which is a desert national monument. It was a place I'd been to by myself many times

Bob and Rod on the cover of *Genre*. The publisher/editor-in-chief gave us credit for helping to inspire the launch of this magazine from our *Advocate* interview.

before. I went there to hike and think. It's a magical place, and I wanted Rod to see it.

As we made the two and a half hour drive, I told Rod my entire life story up to the time we met. Well, I told him almost everything. There were things I was afraid to tell him.

We may have been head over heels in love, feeling like teenagers, but we weren't teenagers. We each had a past.

I wish Rod and I had been high school sweethearts, but that was obviously not meant to be. I gave Rod a slightly edited version of my life. I was afraid to share some things with him because I thought he would judge or reject me. Nonetheless, a lot of what I shared was very painful for me, and Rod shared in that pain. So it was very emotional for both of us.

Later, when Bob revealed those things to me, I was disappointed because I wanted to think of him as my perfect knight in shining armor. Of course, he still was, but I had to grow up and realize that armor can dent, and God knows Bob had been through his share of battles. If Bob had told me everything in the first place I would have been upset, but it would have been easier to get over because it felt dishonest learning about them later.

So we talked all the way to Joshua Tree, and Rod shared his life with me as well, especially some things he'd done that he wasn't too happy about. We pulled off the road and hiked into the desert under a full moon. That hike was part of the inspiration for the poem I wrote three years later for our wedding: "We were walking through the desert, moonlight bright, nightshadows dance, holding hands, whisper secrets. God's wondrous gift this sweet romance." I don't know how to explain it but we sailed away that night. We walked to the other side of the looking glass.

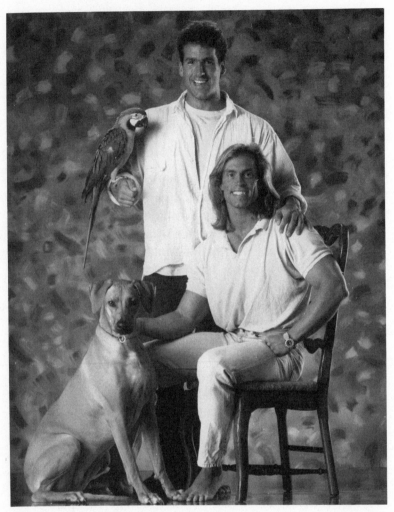

Our first family shot, used in the *Iron Man* interview as well as on our wedding invitations. (*Mike Neveaux*)

A publicity photo of Bob and Rod.
(*Art Zeller*)

It *was* like Alice through the looking glass. As we walked through the completely dark desert with only the moonlight to guide our way, we stepped into a different world.

The sky was a black that I didn't know could exist. And the rocks were a strange color, like a negative of a photograph.

There were voices in the wind, it was blowing so hard. And we could hear the coyotes. We walked and walked, holding hands. All along the way we brushed up against these jumping cactus, which have really nasty needles, and nothing happened. And there were rattlesnakes out there and scorpions, but nothing could hurt us. I felt that God was telling us to walk where we wanted because we were protected. It was the most magical night of my life. I felt that I could have taken Bob's hand and flown into the sky.

Rod's eyes were shining like a wolf's. We'd removed every piece of baggage, everything that kept us separate, and we were two, pure, intertwined animals walking through that primitive land.

We were completely in the moment because the past didn't count and the future was unknown. We had let our guard down totally, so we were both absolutely ourselves.

We got to a wonderful rock, which is where I'd gone many times to contemplate life. I looked at Rod, and his hair was wild, his teeth were shining, and his eyes were incredibly bright. It was frightening in all the best ways. And once again I asked him to marry me. In my heart, that was the moment we were married.

We left the desert that night with a much greater sense that this was a very special relationship and that we were destined to be together for the rest of our lives. For me it was God saying, "I've sent you thirty signs that this is it. And each time you've questioned these signs, calling them coincidences. Now here is an experience you won't be able to question."

Rod's 6 Story

During our trip to Joshua Tree, when I told Bob about my life, I started at the very beginning.

I was born Rodney Lynn Jackson on July 18, 1961, in Kimball, Nebraska, to Robert E. Lee Jackson and Neva Jane Jackson. I have one brother named Robert Jeffrey Jackson, whom I call Bob. I've always hated my name, and when I was seven or eight I asked my mother why she named me Rodney Lynn. She explained that she and my father had fought over the name, but in the end it was my father who won out. He was a typical macho guy, who insisted that his son had to have his initials, which were R.L.J., and that's how they settled on Rodney Lynn Jackson.

I lived in Kimball with my mother and brother on and off, depending on who was winning in the custody battle; my parents were divorced about a year after I was born. When my mother had the upper hand, we lived with her in Kimball. When my father was winning, we lived with him wherever he was stationed. Kimball is a small farming community in the foothill plains, not too far from Wyoming and Colorado. It's totally flat. It has a small main street, and we actually had a five and dime with old wooden floors, where I loved to go to get penny candy.

I never considered Kimball my hometown because we moved

Rod at one year—yes, I'm still this messy!

Rod (age four), wearing his favorite sweatshirt, and brother Bob.

Rod at five.

in and out so much, but I'll never forget the first place I can remember living in Kimball. It was a trailer, which everybody gave us grief for, primarily because it was pink. We were what people in our town called trailer trash. But to me it wasn't a bad place to live. My mother landscaped the yard and planted Chinese elms. She tried to make it home. Inside it was actually nice, with paneling all over. My brother and I shared a bedroom and bunk beds, and my mom had a bedroom at the other side of the house.

There was more than enough room in the trailer for the three of us, although it got crowded when my mother brought a college student in to live with us and take care of us. Vicki was a demon on wheels, and we weren't exactly easy kids; we were pretty free-spirited and undisciplined. For example, Vicki insisted we put our socks on a certain way, but it was torture to me, so when it rained or snowed, I wouldn't put my shoes on and just wore my galoshes to school. I also didn't like to wear underwear and didn't zip my pants, so I got sent home all the time.

I also got in trouble at school because I was left-handed. In third grade, in Dix, Nebraska, I had a teacher who was convinced that normal, good kids didn't write with their left hand. She believed that the left hand was against God. The right hand was good and God-like. It was put in exactly those terms. I just refused to write with my right hand, and finally my mother had to call up and tell my teacher that it was okay for me to use my left hand.

My favorite times growing up were spending the summers at my grandparents' ranch. I loved my grandparents dearly. These were my mother's parents, who were land-owning farmers and ranchers. They had a house in town and a big ranch out in the country. Actually, this is my mom's mother and stepfather. My mom's father was killed in an accident when my mother was fourteen. My grandmother was left with three girls and ranch land. The man next door was a widower with boys to raise. He married my grandmother and they merged their land. After that they had two kids of their own.

My grandma taught me all kinds of things, from respect for other people to basic skills like how to cook and sew. When she baked cookies, I was always in the kitchen helping. I would never miss warm cookies right out of the oven. Later on, when my grandparents found out I was gay, I know my grandma felt very guilty because she had taught me what were considered effeminate things for boys to do. She comes from the generation where people thought you could make a boy gay by teaching him traditionally female skills and letting him play with dolls. I'm sure she thinks that she made me different; I don't think it ever occurred to her that her behavior toward me had no influence over my being gay.

My grandmother also showed me how to garden and gave me a real appreciation for living things. She gave me my own plot of land and I had my own garden. Nothing thrilled me more than to watch a pumpkin vine grow a foot in a day. It was magic. The farm was a calm place in my childhood, the only place I felt

Rod (*right*), age six, and a cousin on Daisy.

Rod on his eighth birthday, wearing his favorite Snoopy shirt.

Rod as a freshman
in high school.

safe. And it was where I could get the positive attention I craved. I didn't get it from my parents, but I got it from my grandparents, especially my grandmother, so I was with her whenever I had the chance.

My favorite day in summer was always July 18, my birthday. I was a kid who believed in magic. It was my escape from what was going on between my parents. On my birthday morning, I'd get up early. I'd go out to my part of the garden and make three wishes just as the sun was coming up. It was a ritual for me. I believed that God would grant me three wishes on my birthday. One wish was that my garden would grow. The second was that my parents would get back together. And the third was for world peace. I don't know why, but the the world always weighed very heavily on my shoulders.

I also used my imagination as an escape. I wanted more than

anything to fly, and imagined that I could. On snowy, windy days, on the way home from school in Kimball, I'd open my coat and run as fast as I could, and imagine that the wind picked me up and carried me away. I really thought I was flying and—considering the winter winds in Nebraska—I probably was.

I respect my mother so much because she worked as a secretary to support two babies, and she also went to night school to learn shorthand. She was only in her mid-twenties when she and my father split up. My dad could have made things easier, but as I learned when I was older, he didn't even do the minimum. He made really good money, but he thought that paying child support was giving money to my mother. He wasn't thinking about my brother and me. I was too young to understand any of this. All I knew was that they argued all the time, which was awful. They treated each other terribly, and my father often cussed out my mother. But—on the plus side for me and my brother—my father breezed into town with gifts for us one weekend a month.

My mother couldn't compete with my father, because she couldn't afford to buy us gifts. She's embarrassed to admit this, but there were times we barely had food. We never actually went hungry, and I know my mom is proud of that. She said to me years ago, "I fed you boys. You never went without anything, and Spanish rice went a long way." To this day I can't eat Spanish rice.

My grandparents would have helped us out, but my mother was very self-reliant; she would have been too proud to accept anything from them or anyone. My mother and I are a lot alike in that regard. I know that my grandparents did everything they could that my mother would allow. Most of what my mother got she got on her own, and she passed that attitude on to me as well.

One time, when I was six or seven years old, I was at the center of a tug-of-war between my parents. My dad had taken us for the weekend to his parents. It said in the court papers that we were supposed to be home at 6:00 P.M. on Sunday evening. But my

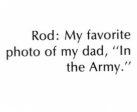

Rod: My favorite
photo of my dad, "In
the Army."

father, being the big man, decided to bring us home at 7:00
P.M.

We pulled up in front of the pink trailer and the cops were
there. I know this sounds extreme, because we were only an hour
late, but my parents were going through a power struggle, and
my mother had just had it. So she put her foot down and called
the cops, which was nothing new because my parents' divorce
was ugly from the beginning.

When we got out of the car, my mom was standing in front
of the trailer with about a dozen of her relatives. She told us to
come over to where she was standing. My brother, Bob, stood
by Dad. He was older and understood better than I did what was
going on, and he didn't want to get in the middle of anything.
I didn't know what to do because I couldn't figure out what was

happening, so I didn't move either. At this point my dad had me by the arm, and then my mom stepped over and grabbed me by the other arm. The next thing I knew, they were both tearing at me.

My brother and I were just objects in the middle of this huge love/hate game. And here I was literally being pulled on from both sides. I was horrified. It was one of the scariest things that happened in my childhood, because here were the two people I loved the most, and I was nothing more than a piece of meat, a piece of property, for them to fight over. I don't remember it hurting physically, but it was the emotional trauma that really killed me. They might not have torn my body in half, but my heart was split right down the middle.

As a kid I had a lisp, and I was sent to a speech therapist for a long time. It took until fourth grade to get rid of it, but while I had it other kids made fun of me. I wasn't ostracized, but it was clear to me that the lisp was a terrible thing. I had no idea that it was part of a homosexual stereotype. I just knew that it was imperative that I correct it.

But the lisp—and I also bit my nails—were nothing in comparison to the bed-wetting. That was a frightening thing for me. I'm willing to bet that the bed-wetting goes back to my parents' divorce, which left me feeling insecure and unloved. That day when they were literally pulling me apart is only one example of why my childhood left me feeling so unsafe and unwanted. I'm sure they wanted me and loved me, but that wasn't the impression I got.

I spent the night a lot at my Aunt Sharon's house, and the joke with all my cousins was that you had to be Moby Dick to sleep with me. One time, when I was about seven, I spent the night at my aunt's house. I was sleeping with my cousin Roxy and I wet the bed. I woke up terrified, because I knew everyone would make fun of me and my mother would be very angry. Back then the doctors and family told my mother that she should make a big deal of the bed-wetting to make me self-conscious because if I was self-conscious enough I would just stop. That really helped my sense of self-esteem. So I rolled Roxy to the edge of the bed and took off the sheet and rolled her back. She didn't wake up the whole time. I took the sheet downstairs and washed it and dried it. Before I put the sheet back on I covered the wet spot in the bed with a towel—it was one of the only times my mother didn't bring a rubber undersheet when we went to visit overnight. There must have been twelve kids sleeping around the house and three or four adults, but no one heard. So I put the sheet back on, got into bed, and just lay there until seven in the morning. I was too frightened of wetting the bed again to fall asleep.

My parents were very frustrated with me over the bed-wetting, so my mother took me to our local doctor in Kimball. He said that the opening to my urethra wasn't big enough and that if the opening was bigger, I could empty my bladder faster. I don't know what that had to do with my wetting the bed, but that was his theory. So with three or four nurses holding me down, the doctor used a scalpel to widen the opening in the head of my penis, which he sliced open without any anaesthetic and then sewed back up on both sides. For two days afterward I couldn't even touch my penis it was so painful, and peeing was excruciating. My mother actually had to help me when I had to pee. The operation didn't do anything, of course, and I continued to wet the bed for a few more years.

Sleeping over with friends was even more of a nightmare than with my family, because none of them knew about my bed-wetting, and I was determined to keep it a secret. So I would have to stay awake all night long. I'd keep my friends awake as long as possible, just talking, and when they finally crashed I'd just lie there, trying to stay awake because I couldn't wet the bed in my friend's house. It was terrible, but finally when I was ten, I went to sleep over at a friend's house and I just decided that I couldn't wet the bed. I didn't wet the bed that night or ever again.

For a long time I thought I was the only bed wetter, but later

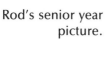
Rod's senior year picture.

in life I discovered that some of my friends, including my best friend in high school, had been bed wetters. In high school I remember hearing about Michael Landon's life story. He said the most traumatic thing that happened to him growing up was that he was a bed wetter until he was in his teens, and that his parents would hang the dirty sheets out on the lines. The way my parents teased me around their friends, I felt they were doing the same thing to me. When Bob and I got together, I found out that he, too, had wet his bed until he was ten. It was nothing unique.

It wasn't until I'd been in a relationship with Bob for a few years that I came to grips with the fact that my father physically abused me. My father would tell me, "I'm going to beat you until you're so sore that you can't sit down for a week." That's usually just a saying, but not with my dad. He meant it.

My father whipped me only nine or ten times, but when he did, boy, I never forgot it. My brother, Bob, didn't forget it either, because my father's policy was that if one kid got beaten, they both got beaten.

The worst beating my father ever gave me was over something my brother and I did. We used to do very dangerous things like point loaded guns at each other, and we'd do things to hurt each other. Now some people may think that pointing guns at each other is an odd thing to do, but where we lived it was a pretty typical macho thing for boys. It was playing chicken at its worst.

When we were living with my father in South Dakota, my brother went after me with a deer antler. Not that I didn't deserve it. I used to pick on him a lot—like I'd whack him in the head with a spatula. Our relationship wasn't complicated. We just didn't like each other.

My brother is two and a half years older than I am. He was totally antagonistic, the epitome of a macho creep. When we were kids, he'd go out and shoot a sparrow with his BB gun and then call me out of the house so I could cry over it and bless it and bury it. My brother also couldn't stand how I always said what I believed and never backed down, even if I was wrong, and even when he'd kick the shit out of me. I was always very headstrong; I could be really ornery and stubborn. But that's how my parents raised me, to stand up for what you believe in.

So one time my brother ran after me with a deer antler and pinned me down on my father's new and very expensive couch. He had the antler pointed right at my head, and I goaded him on, saying, "Go ahead. I dare you." He plunged it toward my face, and I jerked my head out of the way just in time. He grazed my ear and put a hole right into the brand-new couch, which had been delivered only the day before. We made a deal that I wouldn't tell Dad if Bob gave me his allowance for the next four weeks. (I was clearly a capitalist in the making.) So we flipped the cushion over and pretended that nothing had happened.

Things were fine for a couple of weeks, but then my father discovered the hole. My brother broke down and told him the

Christmas 1966. My dad breezed into town loaded with gifts.

whole story. So I got the shit kicked out of me for blackmailing Bob. My dad had this cowboy belt with a big buckle with "Robert" tooled into the leather. He was out of control, which happened only when he'd been drinking, and he hit me probably forty times. At school the next day, when I was changing for gym, the other kids couldn't believe what they saw. There were several bruises all the way down my back, and you could clearly read the imprint of my father's name from the buckle in several places. As severe as the beating was, I didn't think there was anything odd about how I got disciplined because I thought that was how all kids got punished. I know it might sound like my dad was a terrible person, but he wasn't. It's so easy to see someone in a story like this as one-dimensional, but I would be failing his memory if I didn't also tell you that he taught me, in his own way, compassion for other people.

Once he took us out for dinner at a Los Angeles coffee shop. A street person outside who was very drunk asked my father for money. My father said, "I won't give you money because I work hard for everything I earn and I like to know where it goes, but we're going in for dinner and you're welcome to join us." The man was shocked, but he came in and sat with us. My father told him that he could have anything on the menu.

The man began to sit up straight, and he got light back in his eyes. He looked as if he had regained some sense of pride in himself. He told my father it was kind of him to give him dinner. My father replied, "I'm not being kind. Everybody goes through hard times in life, and it's up to all of us to help each other out." It impressed me that my father didn't have him sit at the counter but asked him to sit with us and treated him as part of the family, not as a second-class citizen.

The reason my brother and I were living with my father in South Dakota was because we pestered my mother so much that she sent us to live with him permanently. My mom handled us pretty well until I was about nine, but after that my brother and I got increasingly angry and defiant, which shouldn't have surprised anyone given how we were treated in the community. The kids at school looked down on us and teased us because our parents were divorced. Divorce just didn't happen in Kimball, Nebraska. Also the church ostracized us. My mother's own sister told her that she was going to hell if she ever married another man because the Bible says you have to marry one person and stick with it. And then when we would visit with my father's mother for the weekend, she'd tell us terrible things about our mother.

Living with my mother was hard. She worked all the time and didn't make much money. So when she told us we were going to move to Windsor, Colorado, where she'd gotten a new job, we told her we weren't going to leave Kimball, and that if we left, we were going to move in with our dad. It's funny how I never wanted to leave Kimball, and now I never want to go back, how growing up and seeing the world gives you another perspective on where you came from. We were at my grandparents' ranch when we had this discussion, and my mother cried. My grandparents encouraged her to let us do what we wanted, and finally she gave in. A couple of days later we were on a plane to our father. Of course, what my brother and I didn't realize was that we'd have the same problems with my dad that we would have had with any parent. But all we knew at the time was that whenever he came to visit us he was lots of fun and brought us gifts.

I had hoped life would be easier with my father. I always kept thinking that there had to be a silver lining somewhere, but there wasn't. My dad worked long hours, so we had to be very independent. We did our own laundry and cooked our own meals. The things my grandmother taught me came in very handy. But things were especially difficult because of my father's drinking. My father came home drunk all the time, and sometimes he was really trashed. If he were alive today, he wouldn't say he was an alcoholic, because back then drinking after work was the standard thing to do. He just drank more than most. And when he'd been drinking, you had to be careful with him because he could lose his temper. When he was sober, he was pretty calm and collected.

I don't mean to give the impression that I didn't like being with my dad, because despite everything I did love him and I liked living with him, but it was hard because of his drinking and because I missed my mother.

After my brother and I moved in with my father, we lived all over, from North Dakota to Missouri. My dad was a contractor for H. C. Smith Company, which worked in conjunction with Boeing. He went around the country refurbishing nuclear missile silos, and he took us with him.

My brother and I got really tired of moving, and we urged my father to try to get a transfer closer to Nebraska, where our family was. So when my father was offered a transfer to either Montana or Colorado, we begged him to take the transfer to Colorado because that was within striking distance of home. We wound up moving to Dix, Nebraska, which was only nine miles from Kimball. It was a town of about a hundred people. We'd lived there once before with my mother, about three years earlier, so we'd already gone to school there. I liked going to school in Dix very much because there were only a few kids in each class. The whole school, kindergarten through high school, had only sixty kids, so each one of us was important. Even better, you only had to beat out five other kids to be valedictorian. You just didn't tell anyone that there were only five other kids in your graduating class and all you needed was a B average.

For my father, the only problem with living in Dix was that he had a very long commute by car. But he gave in, and we moved to a huge five-bedroom house, with two kitchens. My best friend, Allen, lived in the house before we did. His brother hanged himself in the trailer behind the house, so Allen never came to see me because his parents couldn't handle it.

One of the things I loved to do during this time was play the piano. My father bought me my own piano for Christmas so I could pursue my love of music. It was my dream, from childhood until my mid-twenties, to be a professional singer and to be on Broadway. Growing up, my favorite singer was Tammy Wynette. I just loved her. And for the past twenty years I've been a huge fan of Tanya Tucker. But I love all kinds of music, and I didn't just sing and play the piano. I also played saxophone in high school, as well as the accordion, which my mother made me play. I gave up on my desire to be a professional singer only in the past few years. I looked at my priorities and realized that while I loved to sing, I wanted to make an impact on the world and I didn't see singing as my way to do it. But when I was young I put my musical skills to good use, singing in nursing homes and playing the piano for all the residents.

I had regrets on and off about leaving my mother and moving in with my father. But after my father was killed, I realized that living with my dad the last years of his life gave me an opportunity to get to know him better. I wouldn't have had that chance if I'd stayed with my mother.

I was eleven years old when my father died. It was the night before Thanksgiving, and my dad was late coming home from work. There was a school play that night, and my brother and one of his friends were going into town. I asked them to drive me because I didn't know if my dad would get home in time.

About ten minutes before we were supposed to leave, my dad arrived. He asked me if I wanted to go have dinner with him in Kimball, but I told him that I wanted to go to the school play. My father said, "I want to talk to you and spend some time with you." My dad didn't say things like that. I told him that I wanted to go to the play and suggested we go to dinner the following night. So he offered to drop me off at school to see the play.

We got in the car and started driving—it was about six miles on a gravel road to school—and my father asked me if I was happy. I said that I was, especially because moving back to Dix I had friends from the last time I'd lived there. Then my father asked, "Do you know how much I love you guys?" I said that I did, and he said, "Don't ever forget that." I was beginning to wonder what was going on because this wasn't like my dad.

When we got to the school parking lot, my dad just sat there and looked really sad. He said, "Just remember I'll love you forever. Take care of yourself and take care of your brother. Take care of each other." I thought it was crazy talk. Then he said, "Hang tough, because you're special. I know you've had a hard time and that a lot of times you don't feel like you fit in, but you're very special and you need to hang in there because you'll understand everything later in life." He kissed me, which my dad didn't do very often, told me again that he loved me, and said good-bye. Then he drove off. I felt really, really weird.

My brother and his friend drove me home after the play. I went into my dad's bedroom, got into his bed, and crawled under the covers because I liked the smell of his body. I loved when my father would let me sleep with him. I would sleep against his belly, and he put his leg over the top of me. I felt so safe there because it was warm and wonderful. It wasn't sexual and had nothing to do with being gay. It was just that I felt so safe, that nobody could hurt me, not even my father because this is where he was vulnerable.

I turned on the television and watched *Love Story*. I cried and cried through the movie. I'd seen it three times before and I'd never cried, so I couldn't figure out why I was crying. After the movie I went to bed.

At about four in the morning I was rocked awake, and my dad's parents were standing in front of me crying. I said, "He's dead, isn't he?" The odd thing is that before they woke me up, I'd had a dream that my father was in a fiery crash. I already knew what had happened.

There are two ways to look at my father's death. I know it may sound like a suicide, but suicide never crossed my mind at the time, because my dad wasn't the kind of person who would do that, although I guess nobody really is. Other than being sad that evening, he wasn't despondent. He was actually hopeful at the time that he and my mother could get back together. My personal belief system is that a lot of people are given an opportunity to know before they move on. Part of me has always believed that God said to him, "You've got a couple of days left. You've made a mess out of so many things, Robert, and here's a small opportunity to right some of the wrongs." I think that's why he had that conversation with me. To this day, I hold that conversation close to my heart. It sustained me through many difficult times, especially for several years after he died. I felt reassured and loved every time I thought of his words.

We won't ever know exactly what happened, but my dad probably fell asleep at the wheel. He was driving several hours a day commuting to and from work, and he probably had something to drink that night when he had dinner in Kimball. He drove right into a concrete bridge, going about 90 miles an hour.

After my grandparents woke me up and confirmed what I already knew, I ran into my brother's room and told him. He looked at me and said, "It's all your fault." We were always trying to take the blame for everything that went wrong in our family. It was our fault that our parents broke up. It was our fault that they weren't back together. But this was too much for my brother to handle, so he had to blame me.

We went to my grandparents' house and waited for my mother to come from Colorado. The next day, after my mother got there, they started making plans for the funeral. I was adamant that I wanted to sing "Onward Christian Soldiers," which was one of my favorite songs. They couldn't understand that this was my way of expressing my grief, a way to show my love for my father. I needed to sing, but they wouldn't let me do it.

I insisted on going with my family to the funeral home to pick out the coffin. We picked out a beautiful coffin with a pearl-gray finish. Later, after they put him in it, I insisted on placing things in his coffin for him to take with him so he would have part of me with him for all time. I chose a photo of myself, the last one I took in Rapid City before we moved, and some other photos of me with my dog Zipper. I also chose a big white marble cross with a gold chain. I placed the photo of me on his chest under his hand, and I put the other photos in the coffin beside him. Then I put the cross in his hand and wrapped the chain around his hand.

Just before they closed the coffin, I climbed up on the side and kissed my dad good-bye. Everybody freaked out, but this was the last time I was going to see him and I didn't care what anyone else thought.

From the time of the crash, I kept asking to see the car. My family thought they were protecting me by not letting me see it, but finally I talked one of my cousins into showing me. What they didn't understand was that I had to see it, that I had to know how it happened, had to see the wrecked car to make sense of it.

The car was impounded at a car lot for damaged cars. I'd already seen a picture of it on the front page of our local newspaper on Thanksgiving. There was a caption under the photograph that described the accident. After that, I knew I had to see the car for myself.

Of course, the car was totally crashed up, but I had to get inside. I crawled in and sat in the driver's seat. I noticed that there was dried blood all over the ceiling and on the door handle. I know this is going to sound morbid, but I remember thinking that the physical part of my dad was gone. I would never hug him again. He was gone. And here was his blood. So I scraped the blood off the ceiling and off the door handle and put it in the little Bible locket that I'd taken with me into the car. The locket contained the Twenty-third Psalm.

I knew that if my mother or grandparents knew what I'd done they'd never let me keep the dried blood, so I gave the locket, with the blood inside, to my Aunt Sharon, who agreed to keep it for me. I've never asked for it, but it was important to me to save some part of my father. Just knowing it was there was all that mattered. My Aunt Sharon has saved it for me until this day.

After my father died, even though he wasn't much of an angel in real life, I felt he became my guardian angel, that he would be on my right shoulder watching over me for the rest of my life. I still feel him near me.

The morning of the funeral, my mother had to take me and my brother to the local clothing store; there was only one in Kimball. I still can't believe it to this day, but my father's mother had taken all of our clothing and given it to our cousins because she felt that we had more than enough. I think she was trying to punish my mother, but instead she ended up hurting all of us, because my brother and I didn't even have clothes to wear to my father's funeral.

She also took all of my dad's clothes and gave them to her brother after I had told her that I wanted to keep a few things for myself, especially his cowboy boots. We have the same size feet and I could have worn them as an adult. Maybe it sounds

Family photo after Dad's death—Mom, Bob and me.

dramatic, but I still wonder if it would have been a way to step in and out of my father's boots. Most little boys imagine that they'll grow up and fill their father's shoes. I didn't have that chance, literally or figuratively.

Then there was my dad's horse. Blue was a racehorse from a famous racing line, and his coat was really blue. As executors of the estate, my father's parents were responsible for what happened to the horse. I wanted Blue more than anything else because he reminded me of my father. He was proud, stubborn, wild, and free. For me, he was the only living thing that represented my father. Dad was the only person who could ever ride him.

I called my grandfather shortly after the funeral and told him that I wanted Blue, but he told me that Blue had died. I knew it was a lie. They had sold him. I couldn't believe that they didn't care enough to realize how important this horse was to an eleven-year-old. But they were more concerned about making money than helping me get through a very tough period.

I was very angry with them for a long time, but prior to my confirmation, when I was fourteen, I forgave them. The minister told us that it would be a shame to confirm anyone who held a grudge or had hatred in their heart. Because I didn't want anything to come between me and God, I forgave my grandparents and invited them to my confirmation.

My father's death meant that we had to move yet again, this time to Windsor, Colorado, to live with my mother. Within a very short time after we moved there, my mother was convinced that I'd gone off the deep end because I was having dreams about my father, and I talked about how I was going to be with him soon. Everyone thought I was talking about killing myself, but I was just talking about how I would be with him again one day in the future. I was also just impossible for my mother to control, which mostly had to do with the fact that she couldn't say no.

My mother's solution for dealing with me was to send me to a therapist. I didn't want to go because I didn't need somebody sitting in a chair acting like he could solve my problems. I just needed somebody who would sit across from me at home and talk to me. My mother tried, but she wasn't able to reach me.

I cussed out the first therapist she sent me to, a woman, and she told my mother that she couldn't handle me. So off I went to a male therapist. He said, "How do you feel?" And I said, "How do you feel?" And he said, "No, I want to know how you feel?" And I said, "Are you too stupid that you can't figure out how you feel?" I just played games with him until he finally told my mother that he couldn't help me.

Despite how difficult I was being and all the inner turmoil over my father's death, Windsor quickly became home because I knew I was finally going to stay somewhere for good.

After I moved back with my mother, I brought her back into the church. Spirituality was always a big deal for me, and the church in Windsor was great, not at all like the one we'd belonged to in Kimball. This new one was Bethel Lutheran, and it was very open and embracing. I was so lucky that they didn't speak against sexuality, abortion, race, or divorce. Most important of all, the church youth group provided a good support system for me, which I needed right after my father died. The church reaffirmed what I'd been taught about compassion, to listen to people instead of judging them.

One day, Pastor Brokering, whom I loved, called me in and asked me if I had ever thought about going into the ministry. I was in eighth grade at the time and I laughed because, as I reminded him, I was such a difficult student in confirmation classes. He said, "I know, but you ask the hard questions. You've got a sharp mind, and a big heart—you want to help people." I told him that I'd thought about it a lot, but that it wasn't for me.

Pastor Brokering was an important person in my life, especially one time when I was thirteen. I was really struggling with my sexuality. My hormones were raging, and deep down I knew I was gay. I was in complete turmoil over what to do. I was afraid that my only choice was to kill myself because the alternative was to live, be hated, and be considered an evil person for the rest of my life.

So I was riding my bike around town, trying to figure out what to do, and I decided that I had to speak directly with God in his house. So I rode to the church, parked my bike, and walked inside. Pastor Brokering was working in his office, and I stopped and asked him, "Do you mind if I go in the church and pray because I have to talk to God about something that I'm struggling to understand." Pastor Brokering asked me if there was anything he could help me with. Given the place and time, I couldn't imagine talking to anyone but God about this.

I went into the chapel and knelt before the altar and prayed. I said, "Please God, don't let me be gay." Tears started spilling down my cheeks, and I felt so completely alone. I was sobbing so hard that I sank to the stone floor. I waited and waited and waited, but God didn't answer me.

After about fifteen minutes, I decided that God didn't love me enough to help me with this and I should just go home. I got up and turned around, and there was Pastor Brokering standing in the doorway. I realized that he had probably been standing there the whole time. As I walked down the aisle and got to the doors where he was standing, he looked at me. My face must have been wet and my hair was all matted. I looked at him and said, "I'm dealing with a very difficult thing. God won't answer me, and I don't know what to do." He said, "Sometimes it seems like God doesn't answer our prayers, but many times it's just that we're not asking the right questions."

During confirmation classes the next year, somebody in our discussion group asked what Pastor Brokering thought about homosexuals. He looked right at me and said, "I believe God loves everybody." And that was the end of the discussion.

Although I was raised in a church that considered homosexuality wrong, I feel fortunate that we were led by a man who was so compassionate. That one simple sentence from Pastor Brokering may have saved my life.

My faith is still very important to me, although organized religion is incredibly unimportant to me. My faith is in God, whether it's a he or she, black or white, a Buddhist, Jewish, or whatever. I refer to God as "he" only because that's what I grew up with, but I don't really think that God has a gender, whatever God is. My faith is simply based on the fact that I know life wasn't all an accident and that there's a reason for everything, even though I don't understand it. My faith gives me the ability to try to do the best I can with what I have and to understand that the world is sometimes a very screwed-up place and I can't fix it all. It's been hard for me to accept that while I can make a difference and can find my own joy and happiness in small ways, I'm only one person.

In high school I was very involved in athletics. I played football and was all-district my senior year. I had two football scholarship offers from small colleges—really, really small colleges. I was also an all-state swimmer and did track for a couple of years.

Everybody hated me because I was "Mr. Goody Two Shoes." I didn't drink much. I was anti-drugs. I was a jock. I was college prep. I mowed the lawn for my neighbor, an elderly widow. I really enjoyed helping her. I was in stage band and played lead tenor saxophone in the marching band. I was in all the school musicals. I was lead in the senior play. I was president of the choir. I was homecoming king.

Looking back now, I realize that I stayed incredibly busy running around in large part because I was running from having to deal with who I really was. I was running from my sexuality. I would leave the house at 6:00 in the morning for stage band. Then there was school all day. After school I had work, then I had sports, and after sports, drama, so I'd get home at 10:30 at night. That was my life. I was trying very hard to be the best little boy in the world. I had people convinced that I was this all-American kid, yet I was always afraid that somebody was going to discover who I really was.

If I'd been non-gay and born into my family looking the way I look, I would have been your typical arrogant high school jock. But because I knew deep down that I wasn't like everyone else, I went out of my way to be compassionate toward people who were different. Being gay gave me the perspective to understand that it's not right to be unkind to people just because they're different.

I don't want to give the impression that I was always good, because I wasn't. Not that I was a troublemaker, but I wasn't always the easiest student. I got into trouble all the time challenging teachers and talking out of turn. I was the cocky, popular kid with the big mouth. One time we had a substitute teacher for band. She was middle-aged and very timid, so we decided to play a trick on her. We whispered to each other that when she told us to play one thing, we'd play another, and play at full bore. Finally she ran out of the room in tears. Everyone thought it was so funny, but I felt terrible. I ran after her and told her I was sorry, that I didn't mean to make her cry. I took responsibility for the whole thing. When she asked why we did it, I explained that we thought it was funny, but that we didn't mean to hurt her.

I know I made a few enemies in high school, people who harbored resentment toward me because of all the things I was involved in and because I was popular. This one friend made that very clear right after I'd had a car accident. I was coming home late one night from doing a modeling job in Denver and hit a patch of ice. My head went through the windshield, and it took sixty stitches to close up all the cuts in my face. This was just before graduation, and my good friend, who I had grown up with, said to another friend of ours, "Good. Maybe it screwed up his face enough so he'll be a real person. Maybe now he won't think he's so perfect and won't act so high and mighty." With the stitches still in my face, and knowing that some friends were saying things like this about me, I had to get up in front of 2,000 people and sing the class song at graduation.

I never thought I was so perfect; I just tried to do the right thing. Maybe that came off as arrogant sometimes, but inside I just felt insecure, because I was afraid that if somebody knew who I really was, they would reject me. So I put on this facade, and maybe it looked arrogant, when in reality I just felt scared and alone.

By my senior year of high school I was eager to get the hell out of Windsor. In the end, it all came down to my sexuality. I was running from it as fast as I could, and I guess I thought if I ran from Windsor I could leave that conflict behind me. I also wanted to find a larger world where I could have some kind of impact. It turned out that I was too scared to get very far away. I don't know why, because I had a small trust from my father that could have helped me go anywhere I wanted to go. But I wound up going to Colorado State in Fort Collins, which was only fifteen miles from home.

I think if I could have come to grips with being gay while I was still in high school, I would have had the confidence to get away, to go to school out of state. And I would have avoided doing lots of the stupid things I did in college, but I had a long way to go before I dealt with my sexuality.

From the time I was a little kid, I was very curious about things that had to do with sex. I was notorious in my family for playing doctor with everybody and anybody. One time we had about twenty kids over at my grandmother's house for a double birthday party; I was turning six and my Aunt Margaret was turning five. My aunt and I decided to show everyone at the party what a boy and girl looked like. The two of us went to the top of the stairs and called down to everyone to come and look. There I was with my weenie hanging out, and there was Aunt Margaret with her panties around her ankles and her dress pulled up. We thought we'd educate everybody. My grandmother was horrified.

I had my first girlfriend when I was about five. She had long, curly brown hair. I used to walk her home and when she moved away I cried and cried and cried.

I did my best to keep my crushes confined to girls because having crushes on boys wasn't acceptable. But it's not like I was looking at boys, because I pushed those feelings down so deep.

The first "sexual" experience I had was with a cousin of mine when we were ten. He was apparently already experienced in how boys could play with each other and decided he would teach me. It was kid's play, but while we were in the middle of it, my brother walked in. I can remember the look of disgust on his face, and the shame rolled over me like fog through the Golden Gate.

I was terrified forever that my brother was going to tell someone what he saw, and he did tell one of my cousins, who didn't think it was any big deal because he had brothers and had walked in on them playing around. But I avoided that cousin for years because he knew what I did, and I knew instinctively from the signals society had sent me that whatever I had done was wrong, terrible, and disgusting. However, that did not stop me from messing around with one of my other cousins and some of my friends, because it was still fun and exciting. The key was not getting caught.

In high school I had a girlfriend who was a great kisser, although when I had fantasies I thought about men. I kept thinking it was a phase I would grow out of because I couldn't possibly be gay. It was relatively easy having girlfriends and being physical with them, because when you're going through puberty your testosterone is in full production. But, honestly, I had to force myself to direct my sexual energy toward women, because that wasn't the natural direction for me.

Part of our high school social ritual was to get together with your friends and cruise up and down Main Street. There were usually ten or fifteen cars, and you waved and honked every time you passed another car. At the red lights you'd rev your engines. Eventually everybody would stop and park and talk.

Sometimes we went to Fort Collins and Greeley, which were about fifteen miles away, and do the same thing. We were outsiders there, but that made it even more fun to try to pick up their girls. We drove up and down the street and catcalled the women, and all the girls were together catcalling all the guys. You'd pull up to a car filled with girls and say, "Oh, I get her, Joe gets her, and Ray gets her . . ." It's not like anything happened, but it was a heterosexual rite of passage, and it was fun. I liked the social part, being part of the crowd, and fitting in. It wasn't hard for me to fit in, to flirt, to give off attitude, to be a smartass, and to have a good time.

There was one particular time when my friend Ray and I met these two girls, Marla and Tammy. We were all about sixteen then. Marla was a very, very beautiful woman. She and Tammy came to visit us in Windsor. We knew they were coming to see us, so Ray and I camped out that night in a tent in the front yard, and they snuck into the tent without my mother knowing. That was the night I lost my virginity.

I'd dated girls before, and we'd made out and there was heavy petting and all that. It was titillating because I knew it was something you weren't supposed to do, but it wasn't thrilling.

With Marla, I knew it was something I was supposed to do as a man. And I thought that if I did it maybe I could save myself, maybe I could change from being gay to being straight. I thought if I just did it and it felt right, that all the hiding, all the worrying about who I was would be over.

When I left home for college, I didn't know what to expect. It turned out that I loved school and I totally hated it. I hated what a scam it was. I never felt challenged. I'm far from brilliant, but I could bullshit my way through class, take the midterm and final without ever buying the book, and get an A. (Then again, there was a time when I thought I could pull it off and ended up with a D.) But the main reason I hated college was that I didn't know what I wanted to do and everybody was taking everything so seriously, as if college was the real world. They also took fraternities seriously, as if it was a life-and-death issue. And the schedule drove me nuts, because my life wasn't my own. Someone else was telling me what to do and when to do it. I'm very independent, so I had a hard time adjusting.

After the first semester, I decided I needed a break, so I took off the next semester and went to work at a clothing store. I was miserable, but that's where I met Debbie. That's not her real name, but I don't want to hurt her any more than I already have.

This was early summer, and the store had hired her to work at the customer service counter. Debbie was beautiful; she had the best body and the most incredible legs that God ever gave a woman. I'll never forget the first time I saw her. She was wearing a peach-colored gauze dress, and she had an incredible tan. I thought that if there was a right girl for me, it was Debbie. I didn't think she'd go out with me—for one thing, I was nineteen, and she'd already graduated from college—but I got up my courage and I asked her out. The fact she was older made her even more enticing.

During the time leading up to when I met Debbie, I was still conflicted about my sexuality. I didn't want to be gay and was trying as hard as I could to ignore what I was feeling. I wasn't

Rod: Post *Saturday Night Fever* look; my first year lifeguarding, the summer before starting college.

always successful at keeping the feelings and my curiosity at bay. One time I actually bought a gay porn magazine at a truck stop on the way back to Fort Collins from Denver. I was shaking as I tried to pay for the magazine, and I didn't look up as I handed over the money. I couldn't. I paid and ran out of that place, jumped in my car, and drove a hundred miles an hour. In fact, I backed out so they couldn't see my license plate. I really believed that they might take down my license number, call the police or someone, and have me cornered. It made me feel so ashamed and dirty buying that magazine. And I thought, *If this is what it's like to be gay, the hiding, the shame, who could live this way?*

Looking back now, I realize that I wouldn't have felt ashamed buying that same kind of magazine if it had been for heterosexuals. In fact, many young men at that time in their life weren't exactly discouraged by their parents from buying *Playboy*. It was a rite of passage.

After I brought the magazine back to my condo, I hid it in my closet behind boxes and all kinds of stuff. Every time I had company I was terrified that someone would find it. Finally I got so disgusted with worry that I threw it away. I couldn't live with that kind of shame and fear. Ironically, with or without that magazine, I was still living with the shame and fear.

I was miserable and in major turmoil up until I met Debbie, because I felt deep down that I was gay, which in my mind was still a terrible thing to be. But with Debbie I felt sexual attraction. I thought that maybe she was my savior, that maybe I just hadn't met the right girl before. That's what everyone always said, and I wanted to believe it because I couldn't imagine the hiding and self-hatred that I thought being gay entailed.

I thought Debbie would say no, but she said she'd go out with me, and my heart jumped. This was major puppy love. So we set the date, and I went over to her house to pick her up. She met me at the door in really short jean shorts and a half shirt. We stayed in because Debbie made dinner for me. I liked Debbie a lot. Besides being beautiful, she was a good person and very complex.

After dinner, we went to her bedroom and started making out. We didn't go all the way that night because I was too nervous. On the one hand I wanted to do it, but on the other hand it didn't feel right because I was so conflicted about my sexuality. Besides, I was so nervous that I didn't think I would be able to do anything anyway. So I just kept things light that night.

Very quickly after that first date I was infatuated with Debbie, and we got sexually involved. We went out all summer, and I really thought that this was the answer. Looking back now, I was nineteen, so what did I know? The answer I wanted was that I wasn't gay, and the relationship with Debbie, which was genuinely exciting and fun, let me forget the conflict going on deep down inside me. Well, I didn't really forget, but the relationship with Debbie let me push away the feelings I had for men.

If ever there was a chance for me to be heterosexual, I thought this was it. Sexually it was wonderful; I really enjoyed it. Even though I was more attracted to men than women, sex with a woman was still great.

It was an incredible summer. I had a girl everybody wanted; my brother drooled over her every time he saw her. (My mother didn't like Debbie, so I knew she was perfect.) I left the job at the mall and got a job as a lifeguard and another job at the Kodak factory packing boxes. I was on a whole macho kick.

By the end of August I was on cloud nine because I thought I'd beaten it. I thought, *I'm cured! I'm safe! It's not a facade. I'm not pretending to be straight. This is me! I really am a jock. I really am a stud.* I rode that all summer long and into the fall, which is when Debbie and I moved in together.

I really wanted the relationship to work, and at one point I even asked Debbie to marry me. We set up a home together, and our sex life was still fine, but after a few months it felt emotionally and spiritually empty. I was having a hard time ignoring the truth about what I was. As much as I wanted to believe I was heterosexual, I knew I was playacting. It felt like the whole thing was a sham, so I began to pull back and distance myself from Debbie. After about six months I told her that I wanted to move back on campus, that the relationship had become too serious for me. Debbie was understanding, but I didn't tell her the real reason why I wanted out.

I joined a fraternity and moved into the frat house. By this time I thought that no one would guess the truth about me because of my relationship with Debbie. But I guess I wasn't finished trying to prove that I was a "real man" because I began having relationships with a number of different women. I was into conquests, and I wasn't always considerate of everyone's feelings. I know I hurt some people.

After I moved back to campus, and at the same time as I was dating different women, things began happening with men. One of the first men I kissed was a classmate. I'll call him Steve. We were at Steve's dorm room studying for quite a while, and I don't

Rod in a fraternity, junior year in college.

know how it came up, but he asked me if I wanted a back rub. I thought it was an odd suggestion, but it was also titillating, so I said yes. He gave me a back rub for two hours, and I could tell he was waiting for something else to happen, and I guess I was, too. Well, something else happened. He kissed me on the neck, and I turned around and we made out for a while, and one thing led to another.

I wasn't in love with this guy or anything, but there was some emotion in addition to the physical experience. It felt right and it felt like the most natural thing in the world, even though I felt dirty doing it. Given everything I'd learned about how sex with another man was wrong, there was no way not to feel dirty. It didn't help that he had even more shame than I did. Afterward he told me he did what we did because a girl he loved in high school married somebody else. I was an idiot because I knew it wasn't true, but I listened and it made me even more confused.

It was a long time before I got over the feeling that I had done something wrong, but nonetheless we had a few more back rubs. That never really developed into a relationship, although Steve and I remained friends, and I continued chasing women.

Another time, probably the next semester, I was on my way back to the fraternity after a dance, and I stopped off to visit my friend Jim. Again, that's not his real name. Jim was the kind of "straight" guy who ran around pinching all the guys' butts, pretending to be effeminate. He was trying to be funny and people would tease him about his fag routine, but he was going so far out of his way to act gay that everyone knew he couldn't really *be* gay. He was just playing up the stereotype.

Jim was getting high when I got to his room. He was all depressed and asked me to sit down. I didn't get high with him, because I was so anti-drug. Anyway, Jim said he wanted to talk about something, but he wanted to listen to music for a while first, which we did for a couple of hours, mostly Tanya Tucker albums. At some point Jim took off his headphones and kissed me. I was startled and pushed him back, and said, "Please don't do that." I wasn't mean and I didn't freak out. I said, "You don't have the right to come on to somebody like that." Well, he was terrified that I'd tell somebody. I told him that I wasn't going to tell anybody and encouraged him to talk to me. I told him that there was nothing wrong with being gay, and, of course, I was probably trying to convince myself as much as I was trying to convince him. He couldn't talk and started crying. I held him for about an hour as he cried and cried before he finally passed out. I put him to bed and then went back to the fraternity.

When I saw Jim the next day he was as cold as ice, and I found out later that he had started saying things to people about what a bad person I was and spreading rumors that I was gay. That was the first time I dealt with someone who was having a hard time coming to grips with his sexuality and not doing a very good job of it. I don't know what happened to Jim. He was a very macho kind of guy, and I imagine he wound up getting married and hiding the fact he was gay. I fear that he, like so many men and women, lived a secret gay life.

I know it's going to sound like this sort of thing happened to me all the time if I tell another story about a closeted gay man at school coming on to me, but it really only happened a handful of times. But there is one other story I want to tell because it's an example of how frightened people were of being found out.

This experience started with a formal at a sorority. There were twelve of us in all, including my date, whom I'll call Susan, and my friend Carolyn's date, Doug, who belonged to a different fraternity from me. (I've also made up these names.) Doug wouldn't take his eyes off me the whole time, and I was getting very self-conscious because he was being so obvious. It was completely inappropriate, not because this was a man interested in a man, but because I had a date and so did he. If he was interested, he shouldn't have been so obvious. What made it even worse was that I found him very attractive. I was trying to be good, so I just ignored him.

Almost everybody drank too much at dinner and got trashed. Susan passed out, and so I got up to put her to bed upstairs. Doug offered to help me, so we both carried her upstairs and got her tucked in. We were walking out of the bedroom, and Doug turned and put his arm against the wall, blocking my way. I turned to him and he wrapped his arms around me and kissed me. I have to admit, I let him kiss me for a minute because it caught me off guard and, I guess, because I found it exciting.

Then I pulled back and freaked, because if anybody caught us— Susan was ten feet away—it would have been a very hard thing to live down. So I told Doug that I didn't have any problem with what he just did, but I said that it wasn't the right place, that it wasn't appropriate.

A few days later I went over to Doug's fraternity and asked him if I could buy him a cup of coffee. He said yes and we walked to McDonald's. We sat down and I told him, "I don't want you to feel weird about what happened the other night. I just didn't think it was the appropriate place." This was actually my way of trying to come out, or at least letting him know that I knew personally what he was going through, and that maybe we *could* find the appropriate place and time. Unfortunately, he missed that hint. In fact, he didn't hear anything I said and just got upset. He said, "If you tell anybody, I'm dead." I told him that I wouldn't tell anybody and that I'd be just as dead if I did. He told me that if anyone found out he'd have to kill himself. I told him he needed help but that there was nothing wrong with being gay. It's not as if I didn't have my own problems over this issue, being closeted and all, but I had no intention of killing myself. I'd gotten over those feelings in high school.

Still, this was such a confusing time for me because I didn't know how I was going to fit my personality into my sexuality. I knew I'd have to do it one day, that there would come a time when I couldn't run from myself any longer, but I didn't know how I would do it. My plan was to run from who I was for as long as I could so I could at least enjoy my college years. I saw how difficult it was for gay people to live an honest and open life, so I didn't think I could ever live like that.

What it came down to for me was the simple difference between what felt normal and what didn't. It wasn't like I couldn't function with women, because I could. I got to be pretty good at heterosexual sex. And it isn't that it didn't feel good, because it did feel good. But it didn't feel normal. It wasn't me. So whenever I had sex with women it was like acting. Now, whenever I hear actors talk about the fantastic acting schools they've been to, I think, *I've been through the acting school of life.* I don't think I'm any different from most gay people in that regard. As soon as you realize that you're not like other kids, you learn to pretend to be like everyone else.

My real coming out—when I began to accept myself—started with a couple of trips to a gay dance club in Denver. The first time I went was with Steve, the guy who gave the back rubs. He asked me one time if I wanted to go to a gay bar in Denver, a place called Tracks. Of course I was curious, so I said yes. I was a little apprehensive, but once I make a decision, I don't look back.

So we drove into Denver one evening during the week. Tracks was located in an industrial area of downtown. It was a very big space with a long bar, two dance floors, and a balcony. The music was very loud, mostly disco music. It wasn't crowded because it was a weeknight. As soon as we walked in I felt perfectly comfortable and really liked the attention I got. At the heterosexual clubs, I liked the attention I got from women because it fed my ego. But that night at Tracks, when men looked at me, there was a lot more than ego at stake.

A few guys asked me to dance, but I wasn't yet comfortable enough to do it. I remember one guy who asked me to dance; when I turned him down, he said, "Oh God, another straight person seeing how the fags live." At the time I felt honored that a queer didn't think I was queer; I could pass for heterosexual. In my mind that was a good thing, to look straight, because I still had so much self-hate. To me, "looking gay" was still a bad thing, so to be told that I looked straight was a compliment.

A few months later, I went to Tracks again with another friend who was gay. He thought I was gay, but I hadn't said anything yet, and I didn't tell him that I'd been to Tracks once before. So we went and had a good time, and when I told him I wanted to go again, he said, "Straight boys usually aren't comfortable in gay bars more than one time." I told him that I was pretty comfortable and he started laughing.

By this time, I didn't care anymore if people knew that I was gay. I was getting ready to graduate at the end of the summer, so I knew I was going to move away and get on with my life. It was time to quit being what I thought I needed to be. It was time to be who I really was. So I started going out to Tracks regularly that summer. It was exciting and fun, and besides, I was tired of the hiding and the shame. Coming out of hiding was *the* most liberating thing I've ever done. For the first time in my life, I could be myself.

All summer long I went out dancing and actually had a couple of dates. Nothing much happened, but I discovered that men could be romantic. It wasn't what I expected in the gay world. Instead of hearing, "Wouldn't it be great to go home and have sex," this one man I went on a date with said, "You have beautiful eyes and I'd like to get to know you," and he read Shakespeare to me. Romance is exactly what I wanted, but I didn't expect it, so it was a nice surprise.

Still, I told people that I would never fall in love and that it was impossible to find a lasting relationship. From what I saw at the bars, and from the negative stereotypes that were ingrained in me, it didn't seem that it was possible to have what I wanted, so it was easier and safer to say that I didn't want it. At least that way I'd never be disappointed. But deep down I knew that I wanted to fall in love and eventually raise kids.

My mistake was thinking that I was seeing all sides of gay life at Tracks. When I went to straight bars I never thought that the singles scene was the only possible way of life, because there are all kinds of heterosexual role models. But, foolishly, I just assumed that bar life was the only gay life possible. I didn't know I had options, because I didn't have any role models. I didn't know any gay people in long-term relationships, and I didn't know any gay people who had kids.

At the end of the summer of 1983, I graduated with a degree in sociology and journalism, with a minor in psychology, and I'd also taken all kinds of business classes. But until the last year of school I really didn't know what I was going to do. What helped me decide on a career was all the volunteer work I was doing. I was a trainer for the Special Olympics, and I volunteered at the college as a big brother. I also worked on a peer-counselor crisis phoneline; it was an incredible experience the year I did it, and later I was responsible for training a new group of peer-counselor recruits.

I loved the volunteer work because it made me feel good about myself. I was doing it for the satisfaction it gave me. But that wasn't the only reason; it was also important to me to counteract all the bad things that happen in the world. I thought then, and still believe now, that you have to put your butt on the line and make a commitment to help other people in whatever way you can, even if it's not convenient for you. Since I was little, I've believed that it was up to me to make the world a better place. When I finished college, I thought the best way for me to do that was to get a job helping people as a social worker. It was the natural next step.

That fall I took a social work job in Denver at a private group home for thirty juvenile delinquent males. Most of them had been sexually and physically assaulted in their traditional heterosexual families. They had been drug abusers and had been pushing drugs for their families. Two had committed murder. And here I was from Windsor, Colorado, very idealistic and very Wonderbread. College could never hold a candle to the education I got there.

I was a basic counselor, which meant meeting with the kids and counseling them. In reality, that meant disciplining and yelling and shouting at the kids. We worked in eight-hour shifts, helping them buy shoes, getting them to school, and then keeping an eye on them once they were there to see if they were getting high outside school.

The whole experience was very disillusioning because the people who ran the group home really didn't care about helping the boys become productive citizens. The counselors tried, but the administrators were incompetent and seemed more concerned with punishing the kids than helping them turn their lives around.

Rod at twenty-two—doing social work, just started
training, and finally feeling good about being gay.

I have so many examples of what I mean by that, but the one
that upset me the most involved a kid I'll call Bradley, who had
been inserting a Pepsi bottle into his rectum. We had a house
meeting over this—the boys and the entire staff—and we all had
to sit there and listen as one of the administrators, who was a social
worker, explained how this was homosexual behavior, which was
abnormal to start with, and how inserting the bottle in his rectum
was inappropriate, and how we needed to help Bradley change.
The bottle business was obviously emblematic of something going
on with Bradley, so it was okay to talk about appropriate and
inappropriate behavior in that regard. What I objected to was
bringing in the homosexuality issue and linking it to inappropriate behavior. I also thought it was a mistake to discuss this in a

public forum, and the decision to punish all the kids for what Bradley did with a bottle made me crazy.

The way it worked at this group home was that if one of the kids was punished, they were all punished. After the discussion, which was really a lecture, all the kids were forced to sit on wooden benches for hours. While the kids were still sitting on the benches I went to the head of the staff, Jerry, and told him that what he was doing with Bradley was wrong. I told him it was sick. He told me that if I ever came to him to object to his policies, he would fire me. From then on I wasn't allowed to sit in on the rest of the sessions regarding Bradley. They kept him and all the other kids on benches for three days, as the kids yelled and screamed at Bradley, calling him a faggot and a pervert while the other counselors stood by and said nothing, giving these kids their tacit approval.

What made me really sick was that one of the head social workers was an extremely self-hating and closeted lesbian. Her attack of Bradley was a sick effort to throw off any suspicion that the director may have had about who she was. This was an incredibly strong example of what happens when you teach people to hate themselves. What they wind up doing is teaching others to hate themselves as well. But, of course, that's what society intends to do. This is where the Roy Cohns of the world come from.

About a year later I saw this woman at a gay bar in Denver. My gut was filled with disgust and anger. She saw me and I could see the terror in her eyes, and before she could look away, I spit in her direction. If people choose not to learn to love themselves, that's their prerogative, but when they take it out on children, it's unforgivable.

After three days of the bench treatment and screaming and degradation, Bradley finally said, "Yes, homosexual behavior is wrong and I wasn't trying to be gay. I don't know why I did it. I'll never do it again." Can you imagine? On a bench for three days? He would have said anything to get away from them at that point.

This made me angry and sad at the same time, especially since there was nothing I could do. I felt helpless and couldn't imagine how I could continue at my job. When I took the job I really thought I was going to help lead these boys out of the system and help them get on with their lives. But one thing I learned is that society can't rape and molest a kid most of his childhood, get him addicted to drugs and have him pushing drugs by the time he's five and on the street, and expect that at fifteen or sixteen anyone's going to help this kid very much. Where was society when he was three? That's when something should have been done. But even if this home had been well run by people who really cared about the well-being of the kids, I don't think it would have made that much of a difference. They had all been dealt such unfair and terrible childhoods.

So I got more and more depressed every day I worked there because I realized that I wasn't allowed to have an impact. I was disillusioned because I grew up believing all that Martin Luther King and John F. Kennedy stuff about changing the world. I went in there believing that and left with the knowledge that the problems were so complex and so deep that one person couldn't do everything—especially given the attitude of the people who ran the place where I worked.

I didn't give up entirely because I went to talk to Bradley even though I wasn't supposed to. I told him, "I just want you to know that what they did to you was horrible, that it was one of the most disgusting things I've seen in my life. I don't know whether or not you're gay, but I just want you to know that there's nothing wrong with it. Using the glass bottle was dangerous, and you shouldn't do that, but there's nothing wrong with being gay." I told him not to listen to the administrators, that they were wrong. He barely acknowledged what I said, but I know he heard me, because when I quit my job a short while later, Bradley told me that he would miss me. For a kid who would never look you in the eye and hardly ever talked, that was remarkable.

After the incident with Bradley, I didn't last much longer at my job. I got into a dispute with Jerry, who ran the home, over how much money was being spent on a dinner for contributors. At the same time he was planning the dinner, he was cutting back our budget to pay for it. So I confronted him at a staff meeting, which he hated because he never liked to deal with staff conflicts in a public setting, and he threatened to fire me. I'd had enough by then, so I quit. I didn't care if I had a job. All I knew at the time was that this guy had made me feel completely helpless, that I wouldn't be allowed to accomplish anything with these kids. And if there's one thing in life I hate, it's feeling helpless. Now all I wanted to do was walk out of there with my dignity.

Before I left I said good-bye to the kids. I explained to them that I couldn't take it anymore. I told them, "You know what some of the problems are here, but that doesn't mean you can act out, because it's just going to make your life harder. And just because there are problems doesn't mean that everything here is wrong. At least you're eating and have a roof over your heads." I told them that my leaving had nothing to do with them and that I loved getting to know them. Then I cleaned out my desk and left.

It was one of the best experiences of my life and one of the most aggravating. I wasn't done trying to change the world, but that was the end of organized social work for me. I think that social work is one of the most important, yet grossly underpaid, professions in the world. To me it's a sad reflection of society's misplaced priorities.

After I quit my social work job, I went to work full-time at a gym in Denver where I'd already been working part-time to help make ends meet. I met lots of gay people at this gym and got a sense of community and belonging that I had never felt. There was a lot of support and brotherhood there. I joined a frat in college and I never felt that. I was homecoming king and I never felt that. In my family, I never felt that. And in my church, I never felt that. But I felt that at the gym because this was a place where there were people who knew who I was and didn't hate me because of it. They supported me.

I also lived in a gay neighborhood, and went dancing a lot and spent time with my gay friends, so that whole time I was in Denver I got more and more comfortable with being gay. I was making friends, true friends, who really knew who I was. It was exhilarating.

I was always fairly vain, but now that it really mattered to me that I was attractive to men, I made more of an effort to look good. I dressed to get attention. I had my hair highlighted. And I was very lean because of all the aerobic training I was doing. It worked. Really it wasn't any different from the mating game in college, which I admittedly played. But then it was like acting. This was the real thing. It was great to finally have the adolescence I never had before.

I had two significant boyfriends while I was living in Denver. The first person I was involved with, Greg, thought I was about as mature as an adolescent. I'm afraid I wasn't very nice to him. It started out as total puppy love for months and months. Greg lived in Dallas, so we sent letters and had long phone calls.

Greg and I were set up by mutual friends. My knees didn't buckle when we met (although I did feel some butterflies in my stomach), and he wasn't my soul mate like Bob is, but he's beautiful, sweet, compassionate, and talented. I was taken with him, and he was wonderful to me. He wrote to me every day. He sent me gifts. He was great.

I shouldn't have been surprised when Greg told me he was moving to Denver, because I'd been telling him how much I missed him and how much I liked being with him. So how could he have known that I really didn't want a forever, live-in relationship with him? I should have been more clear with him, but when it came to relationships, I didn't have the maturity to be that responsible.

When Greg told me he was moving to Denver, I told him not to. He moved anyway, and it was obvious that he was doing it for me even though he denied it. This was only about seven months after we'd started seeing each other long distance, so I really didn't think I was ready to live with him.

The first night after Greg moved to Denver we had dinner, and I was very cold. I didn't know what else to do because I was scared. This man had dropped everything and moved halfway across the country to be with me, and I felt trapped. I was terrible, because I ignored him from that day on.

The second man I was involved with, Tom, was also very sweet and one of the most wonderful people I'd ever met. But he wasn't right for me either. I liked him and I enjoyed being with him, but I never had any expectations that it would be a lifetime relationship. To this day I care about them both very much and feel that I was fortunate to have them in my life. Tom and Greg taught me a lot about how to love myself and other people.

Greg and Tom helped make this the best time in my life—up to that point—because I had the freedom to be honest for the first time. I was with people who understood me and knew what I went through in life. You can walk into a room full of gay people and even though they're all different and the only thing you have in common is your sexuality, they still all know what you went through growing up. And that's so different from when I was younger and thought I was the only one.

By this time, I'd pulled back from all of my old friends. I'd been very popular in college, so I had a lot of friends, but I didn't want to deal with them anymore. Those friendships were based on who people thought I was. They reminded me of my self-hate, the hiding, the acting. So I left and made a very clean break and didn't look back, with a very few exceptions.

One of the friends I wanted to keep in my life was Jill, who owned the restaurant where I worked near school. She probably knew I was gay from the day she hired me, but we never talked about it, and I was afraid to bring it up because she used to make fun of one of the other waiters who was gay. I learned later that Jill made fun of him because he was funny and happened to be gay, not because he was gay. I didn't know all this, so when I called her and asked her to meet me in Denver, I was a little anxious.

I loved Jill and I wanted her back in my life. We'd been there for each other in the past, and I missed our friendship during the months since I'd left for Denver. But we couldn't be friends again unless I could be completely honest with her. I didn't want to hide who I was from the people I cared about, and I didn't have room in my life for anyone who objected to the truth about who I was.

Deep down I knew Jill would always love me, and I was right. When I told her I was gay, she said that she knew and didn't ask only because she felt it wasn't her place. She asked me if I thought she would think differently of me. I said that I didn't know. Jill looked at me like I was crazy and said, "You've done so much for me in my life, so much more than any friend I've ever had. How could I ever judge you like that?" The fact I was gay was never, ever an issue again.

There was one other friend from college who I came out to. We became friends during hazing for our fraternity and stayed friends all through college, although Darren left before graduation and moved to Washington, D.C. We hadn't stayed in touch, but after I moved to Denver I got a call from a mutual friend who told me that Darren was gay. I mean, here we were good friends and I was gay and he was gay and we didn't know it! So about a month later I called him. I wanted to tell him I was gay, but I didn't want him to know that I knew that he was gay because I suspected he was still at the point where he would freak out if he knew that people were talking about it. I had to be very careful. I said, "Darren, I want to talk to you about something." There was dead silence on the other end of the phone. Then he said, "Well, Rod, I don't know if I want to or can." I realized at this point that he was afraid that I was going to ask him if he was gay, but I just ignored his response and said, "What do you think of gay people?" He asked me what my point was, if I was trying to say something. So I came right out and said it, "Darren,

I'm gay." He said, "*What*? You're kidding me!" I told him I wasn't kidding him, and then he said, "Rod, so am I." After that we just laughed and laughed.

Looking back now it's amazing to me that here we were close friends in college and we could have been there for each other. We could have said, "Hey, we're okay, and if we're not, who cares because we've got each other." Instead, each of us thought he was the only one in the world. We were both so alone.

While I lived in Denver, I did a lot of work as a model. I'd been modeling in fashion shows since I was in high school. I did it on a dare and it was an ego thing. In college I signed with a Denver agency and modeled part-time doing runway work for shopping centers and photo-shoots for department store magazine layouts. I didn't like the work and I never saw this as a career path, but I kept doing it after I got the social work job just to help pay the bills.

Shortly before I left Denver for California, I had an offer from the Wilhemina modeling agency in New York. I wasn't looking for a major New York company, but it felt good to get the offer, to know that I could do it. The most important thing was to prove to myself that I was good enough to get the offer. I was a small-town, hick boy from Colorado. To have someone from an agency that signs the best men in the world tell me I had a great look, that I could work in New York and Milan if I wanted to, meant a lot to me, probably too much. But that's how I felt. The conflict, of course, was that I *was* a small-town, hick boy from Colorado, and I was scared of going to New York and competing with all the other models. But it was more than that. I was afraid that if I signed with Wilhemina, people would only see me as a piece of meat, that no one would know there was a real person with a heart behind the facade.

I know enough about myself to realize that if I based my entire life on my looks I was going to be incredibly screwed up. If, on the other hand, I stayed in Colorado, I could work when I wanted to. I got paid pretty well, so I had the time and flexibility to explore other interests because I knew that modeling alone wouldn't be enough. So I turned down the Wilhemina contract.

A short time after that, I got an offer from a California agency. I didn't sign with them, but I was already thinking about moving to Los Angeles, so I felt more secure knowing that I probably wouldn't have trouble getting modeling work there.

I left Denver because I decided it was time to take full responsibility for my life. Some people think I moved because I'd already met Bob and was going to California to be near him. But I'd already made plans to move when I met Bob and told him that. It was nice to know he was there and I looked forward to seeing him again.

Saying good-bye to my friends in Denver was very hard. These were people who had seen me through my coming out. But they were great and threw a huge going-away party for me. It had been an incredibly social period in my life, one during which I'd developed into a complete person and found the courage to accept myself.

In Los Angeles, I kept to myself because I was very focused on my career and wasn't comfortable. Not long after I got there, Bob and I fell in love, and our life together became my social life.

Bob's 7 Story

When Rod and I told each other our stories, I was amazed how much we had in common, from the fact our dads were alcoholics and physically abusive to the bed-wetting; I wet my bed until I was about ten years old.

Like Rod, I come from a Midwestern, rural family, one generation off the farm. And if you asked my grandparents, they would say we had traditional family values. Looking at the old home movies from Christmas, you would think we were a happy family and that my parents loved each other. There's my dad sitting in the chair and my mom sitting on the arm of the chair giving him a kiss. But it was all for show. They may have cared for each other at one time, but that didn't last very long. The truth was that our family was a mess.

My mom, whose given name is Constance Diane Clark, got married when when she was eighteen years old in the small town of Nashville, Indiana, to Robert Gene Paris, who lived in Columbus, fifteen miles away. My mom had been the high school cheerleader and beauty, and Dad ran cross-country. They were introduced by one of my mom's cousins. My sister Lisa was born ten months after they got married. I was born a year and a half later, on December 14, 1959. Leslie was born a

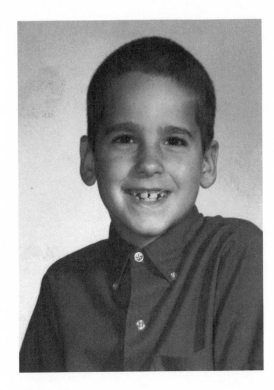

Bob in
first grade.

year after I was. She was a twin, but Todd died sixteen hours
after being born. And Jim, the youngest, was born a year after
that. It was pretty much bim, bam, boom, so Mom had her
hands full from the very beginning.

If you asked my mom about the time when she was married
to my dad, she would say that all the family problems were his
fault and that it was her duty to be obedient, to support her
man, and raise her family. It doesn't take much digging to get
her to remember that life wasn't so great, that in fact my father
treated her and us like dirt.

I know my mother tried to ignore what was going on and to
pretend life was perfect on the outside. But my dad's abusive
behavior and alcoholism overwhelmed her, and when I was
three years old my parents divorced. Mom, Lisa, and I moved
in with my mom's parents, Mam-ma and Pap-pa Clark, but we
weren't there very long before my parents remarried for the

sake of the kids. If they'd really been thinking of the kids, they would have stayed divorced. (I should explain here that Mamma and Pap-pa were what we called our grandparents. We called our great-grandparents Grandma and Grandpa.)

One of my earliest memories is waking up on a Saturday morning and seeing my mom washing their sheets in the bathtub. They were covered with orange-colored vomit. She said, "Dad's sick," which became a euphemism for "Dad's drunk." Most of the time they did the best they could to hide his drinking.

In addition to Dad's drinking, and in large part because of it, he was a violent man. Generally he picked on people who were weaker than he was, so his children and wife were ideal targets. One time—and this was one of many times—when I was in the fourth grade, in the middle of the night we heard all sorts of noise and things being slammed around the living room. Jim and I shared one room, and Lisa and Leslie shared another. When we tried to come out to see what was going on, Dad told us to stay in our rooms.

When we got up the next morning, I saw that the phone had been pulled out of the wall and was next to the basement stairs. And when my mother came to pick me up at school, she had on sunglasses, and when I put my arm around her waist, I could feel that she had on a rib brace. I found out later that Dad had thrown her down the stairs. I grew up thinking that this kind of violence was just a part of life.

My father beat me occasionally, mostly for minor things. I remember in eighth grade I got an hour of detention at school for talking out loud. We were having a debate in social studies class. I got excited and spoke out of turn, and the student teacher who was leading the class gave me an hour's detention. When I got home and told my parents what happened, I'd hoped they would come to my defense, but instead Dad took me into their bedroom for what started out as a paddling on my butt with a two-by-four. It turned into a beating all over my

Bob, age four,
with sister Leslie.

butt, legs, and back. It got pretty violent. The whole time I was
crying and I couldn't catch my breath, but I could smell the
scotch on his. He always said, "This is going to hurt me more
than it's going to hurt you," which was far from the truth. If
not for my mom's protection, he would have hurt me a lot
more than he did. I have to give her credit because she saved
me from a lot.

The physical torture my dad inflicted on me was pretty bad,
but it was the emotional torture that hurt the most. For example, he would constantly threaten to send me to reform school
for such trivialities as forgetting to mow the lawn or leaving a
wet bathing suit on the carpet in my room.

At that time, besides being a cruel, cold, and distant man,
my father tried to make sure I didn't have any friends. He was
always saying how horrible my friends were and tried to chase

them all away. It was as if they weren't good enough to be his son's friends, which was confusing to me because he treated me as if I wasn't good enough to be his son.

I don't think my dad and I ever had an in-depth conversation the whole time I was growing up. He never took any interest in anything I did. Even with the Boy Scouts, which I loved, it was my mother who took an interest, not him. My dad never understood how much I loved the outdoors and how much I would have loved for him to be a part of that with me.

I joined the Boy Scouts in sixth grade, and that proved to be my salvation. The scout master was like a surrogate father, the father I never had. Scouts got me out of the house for weekly

Bob protecting home and hearth, with weapon at the ready.

meetings and for trips. We went on long backpacking, camping, and canoeing trips. It was my introduction to the outdoors that spurred my love of nature, which is still strong today. Being in the outdoors was an adventure I wish I could have shared with my dad.

When I was young, I tried to do things that I thought my father would approve of. One time I was with my family at my Mamma and Pap-pa Paris's house. It was after church and we were all sitting out in the yard on a hot Sunday afternoon. I got up on one of the lawn chairs. I was still wearing my church clothes: black pants, white short-sleeved shirt, and little clip-on tie. My father was sitting on another chair smoking a Lucky Strike. I began to give a sermon, which I thought up on my own, inspired by what I'd heard earlier that day. I don't remember what the subject was, but I was great. I was being a ham, totally theatrical. I had the voice and the right arm gestures. I was even making sense. In the middle of my sermon, Dad looked over at me and said, "Why don't you shut up? You're embarrassing me."

It was such a big deal for me to overcome being shy, and I thought I was doing something my father would approve of. I was feeling so tall, and then Dad demolished me. I felt like nothing, and I vowed to myself that I would never, ever, let him hear me speak up again. I can't understand how a father could do that, because if this were my child showing interest and talent in something, I would want to nurture it. Why would a parent want to crush the spirit of his child? It was especially hard for me because deep down I wanted to be an entertainer of some kind, but it was years before I felt confident enough to try doing anything in public again.

The only thing my father encouraged me to do was play golf. Golf was the thing he loved most in the world. Later, after my parents divorced, my father frequently missed child support payments because he said he didn't have the money. But it

Bob, age five, with sister Lisa in the backyard, fall 1964.

was nothing for him to drive his Cadillac up to the country club with a new set of professional golf clubs in the trunk.

I withdrew more and more into myself. I badly wanted my family to be normal, but I always knew that it never would be, so I retreated into my imagination and conjured up all kinds of things. One thing I did was draw wonderful pictures of what I saw in my mind, everything from trees, to street scenes, to blueprints for houses that I wanted to build. I once even entered a drawing contest and was accepted into a program, but despite my mom's lobbying, my dad refused to pay.

Sometimes I imagined I was flying on my own without wings or a plane. I was incredibly attached to birds, and I could see myself flying alongside them. (Rod had the same fantasies about flying. It must have been the freedom of flying that

Bob in
third grade.

struck us so.) Also, I kept an imaginary horse in a ravine in the
woods behind my grandparents' house. I got all dressed up in
a makeshift cowboy outfit and went to play with my imaginary
horse in the woods. I also imagined all sorts of war games that
let me take out my frustrations and my own violent feelings. I
had lots of different kinds of toy guns, and I'd go out into the
woods and create battles and kill all my enemies.

Everybody knew about my imaginary wars. I played army
constantly. But I also tried to be the best little boy in the world.
I was very quiet as a child and was always afraid of saying or
doing the wrong thing, so I always kept my thoughts to myself.
But I had another side, which was very theatrical. So even
though I was a shy kid, at times I was also a cut-up and a clown.

I was also a very emotional and sensitive kid. I cried at the
drop of a hat, and I laughed and giggled over just about any-

thing. I also had a tremendously strong conscience. When I was nine years old, I threw a caterpillar into a trash fire and it burst into flames. For a long time I had nightmares about it and would wake up crying. I don't know why I killed that caterpillar, because I really loved living things. The desire to throw it in the fire came out of nowhere.

Given how different I was, or at least how different I thought I was, it's no wonder I felt like I never fit in. I always felt uncomfortable living my life, like a stranger looking in the windows of someone else's home. Everyone else was on the inside living life, and I was standing on the outside with no place to go. Even the words coming out of my mouth made me uncomfortable. I would watch myself in the reflection of store windows as I walked down the street and I'd trip over my feet, wondering who I was looking at.

I was so unhappy with myself and with life at home that from the time I was old enough to realize that I could get away, I began to plot my escape. The first time I decided to leave I was nine. I was in trouble for something, I don't remember what, and decided I'd run away to a piece of land my parents owned out in the country, about forty miles from home. When my parents were out, I packed a bag with clothes, stole a Kennedy fifty-cent piece from my little brother's piggy bank, and set out on my bicycle. It had two flat tires and I was riding on the rims, so by the time I got five or six blocks away, I was completely exhausted. I gave up and went home.

My parents managed to coexist until just before I started the ninth grade, and then they finally divorced for good. It took my older sister to push Mom to divorce Dad for the second time. She went to my mother and said, "Are you going to let him keep treating us like this? Are you going to get away from this man or not? You have to do something." And finally she did.

One night, my parents brought us together in the family room of the house. Dad sat in a reclining chair and explained that they had something to tell us, that it was going to be hard

Dad and Mom, still married, in 1967.

news. We weren't surprised when he said they were getting a divorce. They'd already been very distant from each other. My father had been sleeping in his den, and my mother was openly unhappy. And I knew about Lisa's pushing. More than anything, the news that they were getting a divorce came as a relief.

I thought I'd feel better after my parents divorced, but I started getting very depressed and self-destructive. I began smoking cigarettes and marijuana. Before my parents divorced I thought that smoking marijuana was terrible. My best friend in Boy Scouts told me about someone he knew who had smoked marijuana, and I told him it was awful, evil stuff. But after my parents got divorced, it didn't seem like such a bad thing, especially since marijuana made it so easy to escape. I was also trying to hide from something that cast a shadow across my life. I was beginning to have secret crushes on other boys when all of my friends were having crushes on girls.

My schoolwork suffered, and I went from being an almost straight-A student to screwing up in school big time. I was disappointing my teachers, which was really hard on me because it was still important to me to get their approval. I also grew my hair very long and bought strange, wire-rim glasses. It was an awkward time anyway because I was in the middle of puberty. I wanted to be good-looking and popular, and while I didn't believe it, everyone told me what a good-looking young man I was becoming, and people were really drawn to me because of my sense of humor. If I'd taken care of myself I would probably have felt better-looking, but it didn't matter because I was way too shy and thought I was too weird ever to be popular.

After the divorce, I moved with my mother and the other kids to a smaller house in an older neighborhood. Moving was no big deal, because when I was growing up we moved a lot. I went to four different elementary schools. The only place I remember as home was the house we lived in for the three years prior to my parents' divorce. It was a large house with a barnlike roof, in a picture-perfect middle-class neighborhood on Laurel Drive in Columbus, Indiana. That was the longest we lived in any one place. We just kept moving.

Right before I began my sophomore year of high school, when I was fourteen, my mom sent me to live with my father. She couldn't handle me anymore. It wasn't that she didn't try to discipline me, it's just that deep down I knew that she was weak, so I asserted my budding manhood by defying her at every opportunity.

The first time my mother sent me to stay with my father was after she found out that I'd asked a friend of mine—who was also a friend of hers—to buy me a bottle of wine. This friend, who lived in our neighborhood, was probably in her early twenties, an age between me and my mom. My friends and I used to go to the river and camp out. A close friend of mine and I thought she would be the ideal person to buy wine for

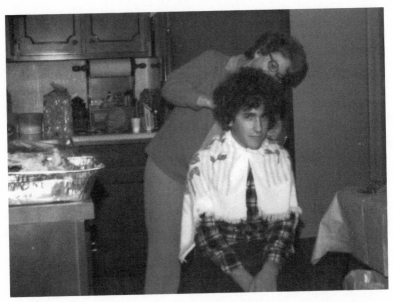

Bob getting his afro cut off by "Mam-ma Clark,"
Thanksgiving 1976.

us so we could take it with us camping. It turns out that she wasn't, although at first she said that she'd do it. I guess her conscience got the best of her, because she went to my mother and told her that I'd asked her to buy wine for me, and off I went to my dad's apartment. When I got there, Dad gave me a lecture about the evils of drink. He said, "You know why you're here . . ." and proceeded to tell me why I shouldn't have done what I did. The whole time he talked he had his highball glass in his hand. As he was popping ice cubes in his glass and pouring J&B scotch, he said, "I know what you're thinking. You're here because you were caught trying to buy alcohol and here I am drinking. What kind of example is that, right? I'll tell you what kind of example it is. I'm an adult, you're a kid. I can do whatever I want."

Dad was such a complete hypocrite. I can't believe my mom actually thought he was going to straighten me out when he needed more straightening out than I did. I stayed with him for about a week and then went home.

About a week and a half later I was in the grocery store with my friend, the one who had been in on the failed attempt to buy the wine, and I decided that I was going to steal a magazine. We took a copy of *National Lampoon* off the magazine rack and went into the bathroom to hide the magazine under my shirt. On the way into the bathroom we passed a man who looked at us but didn't seem to take any notice. I hid the magazine under my shirt and walked out of the store. Well, the guy who saw us on the way into the bathroom saw me go in holding the magazine and leave empty-handed. He caught me outside the store. He took me by my arm and dragged me up to the office inside the supermarket. The store manager called both my mom and my dad at work, and they came to pick me up. Mom gave me the "you're stabbing me in the heart" speech, and I was trundled off to live with my father for good.

My mother thought I needed a strong hand, which I did desperately, but my father didn't care to exercise it. I felt she was abandoning me to an abusive alcoholic. On the other hand, I thought that by moving in with my dad I might get his approval. I also thought I would have more freedom. I got freedom, and that was about it. My father was gone a lot for business and worked late, so I was on my own. I made my own meals, did my own laundry, and basically raised myself from that time on.

I don't blame my mother for sending me away. For one thing, I was an angry, hateful teenager, in the middle of puberty. In addition, she had no idea that I was beginning to consciously have unnerving crushes on boys. I was also developing a drug problem. I must have been impossible to deal with.

Mom really tried. She wanted to understand what was going on inside my head and she asked me, but I was very introspective and I didn't share a lot of what I was feeling. In my heart I knew that she couldn't possibly understand, because I didn't.

Bob as a junior in high school.

I know she was frustrated that I wouldn't confide much in her, but I didn't confide in anyone.

Mom also had tried to make me comfortable at home. She and my grandparents had built me my own room in the basement of our house. And she had tried to provide order; I had to check in with her and let her know where I was all the time. It wasn't like I could just run the streets. But I kept pushing the limits, and obviously I pushed beyond what she thought she could handle.

Later, as an adult, I confronted Mom about sending me to live with my father. I said, "You know, you sent me to live with a violent alcoholic." Her explanation was that he forced her to do it, that he threatened to cut off all child support unless she sent me to live with him. I think this is her way of not taking responsibility for what was really her decision, but I know she felt badly about doing it.

Then I discovered weight lifting at the end of my sophomore year in high school. I finally had something to focus on; it gave me a goal. My imagination really helped, because I could project ahead and imagine being very successful at bodybuilding. I didn't start out wanting to be a bodybuilder; I really wanted to play football. But the first day of football practice in eighth grade, I broke my leg after getting tackled. I didn't play in ninth grade, but I played again in tenth grade, although not very successfully. I was a very gangly kid, really too skinny for football. That's when I discovered an old Universal weight machine in the high school gym. It was a basic nine-station Universal gym, and there was also a set of free weights.

I started training right away and felt great. Well, not the first few times, because I'd go to the gym and do hundreds of repetitions of every exercise and then I couldn't lift my arm up to comb my hair. Training is something I had an instinct for, so I figured it out pretty quickly, and my body began to respond. I kept going back day after day and began developing a positive addiction, challenging myself to train more and more intensely as the months went by.

As I began to understand on an intuitive level that I could be good at bodybuilding, I could see that this might be my ticket out of Indiana. I was athletic and artistic, so bodybuilding allowed me to meld those two passions. With each passing day I was getting bigger and stronger.

Bodybuilding did two other things for me. First, it allowed me to focus on something that was goal-oriented and constructive instead of destructive. That would one day save my life. Second, I literally built a suit of armor around the fragile little sissy that I pictured myself to be. In spite of the armor, there are times when I still get a glimpse of that shy, googly kid staring back at me from across the years.

I focused completely on my training. Even after other guys at school got interested and were working out, I wouldn't talk to anyone else while I was doing it because training was a matter of total concentration. My method of escape grew more solid with each repetition. I was at the gym constantly, experimenting with different routines and doing endless sets. I was hooked. Very quickly, my body changed dramatically. I was becoming a muscle man, and people noticed.

During this time, I started buying *Joe Weider's Musclebuilder* magazine, which was the predecessor to *Muscle & Fitness*. I would take the magazines to school, and some of my friends teased me because bodybuilding was still considered weird. A lot of gay people may think I started buying the magazines because of a sexual thing, but for me there was nothing sexual about it. It was a sport in which I could use my artistry and athleticism to build a perfect suit of armor and be a real man.

This was in the years when *Pumping Iron* first came out, so bodybuilding was beginning to grow out of its fringe, cult status. I remember seeing an article in *Rolling Stone* magazine during my junior year in high school about Arnold Schwarzenegger and the making of *Pumping Iron*. The article was accom-

Bob, a senior in high school, with brother-in-law Doug,
Thanksgiving 1978.

panied by Annie Leibovitz photos of Arnold competing and
winning his seventh Mr. Olympia title in South Africa. I went
around telling everyone, "I'm going to look like this in six
months." My grandparents thought that was very strange and
complained to my mother that I was getting uppity, and that
maybe I shouldn't think so highly of myself.

Bodybuilding helped give me focus, but it wasn't enough to
keep me out of trouble. It seemed that my life was a total
contradiction. On the one hand I was this budding, goal-
oriented athlete; on the other hand, my life was completely
out of control.

During this time, I began hanging out with a group of seven
guys who were more or less party-jocks. We were the cool
guys. We played sports, got high, and raised hell. Straight A's
were not exactly a major priority. To get out of classes, we
would sneak into the dean's office, steal passes, and forge

them. By the end of the second semester of my junior year, I skipped out on about a third of my classes. I was getting high all the time. I failed chemistry. I was a mess.

Because I was screwing up so badly, I decided that I needed an excuse, a sickness of some sort, that would explain why I missed so many classes and why I did so badly in the classes I did attend. It had to be something that wasn't really visible, like leukemia. And leukemia seemed perfect for another reason as well. In my mind it was the ideal parallel to the invisible shadow that I could never outrun.

So I started hinting to teachers that I had leukemia. Once I started this idea, it took on a life of its own as people began talking about it. One of my teachers called the dean and asked if I really had leukemia. It got out of hand and I knew that I'd get caught in all my lies, so I began to think about how I could get out before the whole thing caved in.

My Pap-pa Paris had given me a double-barrel shotgun. I started thinking about using it on myself. I carried it around in my car; I had a beat-up blue 1967 Mustang Fastback. I also kept some other stuff in the back of my car, like clothes and a bong, just in case I decided to run away on the spur of the moment.

A month before the end of junior year, I was at a party where I'd gotten really drunk and high. I left the party and somehow managed to drive far out into the country, without killing myself or someone else. I stopped on a dirt road, beside a cornfield, got out, and took the shotgun with me. I staggered out into the field, loaded the gun, and put the butt of the gun down between my legs and the other end in my mouth. I worked a couple of sticks into the trigger and sat there with my hands on the sticks, ready to blow my head off at any time.

I must have passed out because I woke up the next morning on the ground. I was still alive, and there was the gun on the ground. I knew what I'd almost done. I thought about whether I should pick it up and just do it, but instead I got back in my car and drove home. The sun was hard and bright in my eyes, and I was in a daze. I got into bed and stayed there all day. I wasn't just hung over, I was also profoundly depressed, obviously suicidal.

When Dad got home from his accounting office that night and found me in bed, he must have figured out something was up because he went out and searched my car. He found the bong and the shotgun, and he found all my clothes and brought them in the house and set them down on the kitchen table. I was up by this time, and he wanted to know what was going on. He was extraordinarily upset about the pipe because he hadn't realized that I'd been smoking pot. And he said, "What's with the shotgun? Is that what I think it's for?" I said it was. I was at rock bottom and had nothing to lose, so I told him everything. I didn't tell him the details about the previous night or the true reason why I wanted to end my life, but I told him about skipping classes and how I had told everyone I had leukemia. I felt so badly because people were legitimately concerned and they cared about me. I realized later that they really cared because I was such a screwed-up kid.

What I didn't tell my father was that the primary reason I screwed up in school so badly, and the real reason I wanted to die was because I knew I was gay and couldn't imagine that I'd ever fit into the world. I feared that no matter what I did, no matter what I accomplished, I'd be miserable my entire life. At the time, I only knew that I was looking up from the bottom of a black hole and was simply trying to shut off the pain.

After I talked with Dad, he came with me to meet with the dean, the guidance counselors, and my teachers. They agreed to let me make up the work that I'd missed and sent me for counseling. I didn't want to go to a counselor, but I knew that if I agreed I'd be able to get out of some of the trouble I was in.

The counselor was very aloof, and I went in with an attitude—not a great combination for making any headway. My feeling was, "You're getting paid to get me to talk, so I'm not going to make it easy for you. You're the expert; *you* crack the nut." During the third session he asked me, "What would you do if a man ever made a sexual overture toward you?" I said that I'd beat the shit out of him. I was trying to be macho, which probably signaled to the counselor that here's a raging homo trying to pretend that he's not.

By the fourth session the counselor was fed up with me, and he said, "Since you're not telling me anything, there's no reason to continue. If what you've been trying to do is get out of the trouble you're in by coming to me, you've succeeded." I said, "Thank you very much. Can I go?" and I left.

Even though I told the counselor that I'd beat up someone who approached me, I really wasn't anti-gay as a young person, although I was very defensive about the whole issue. In junior high I had a teacher who I knew was gay. He was rather effeminate, and everyone knew that he lived with another man. Three or four of my friends and I would hang out in his classroom during lunchtime and talk about the work we were doing in class. He was a very respected teacher, and we felt lucky to be able to spend time talking to him.

During one lunchtime this teacher innocently put his hand on my shoulder, and I said, "What are you, gay or something?" The color drained out of his face, and he said, "Don't ever come back to my room during this time," and he left. Obviously I'd hit a button with him. The thing that's going to freak out a gay teacher more than anything else is to be accused of molesting one of his students. He'd done nothing, and here I was seeming to make an accusation. I felt terrible because I liked hanging out in his classroom, and now I was banished. So I apologized to him, and eventually he got over being angry and let me come back.

Besides my weight training, the other bright spot for me during this time was getting involved in high school theater. When I was in my early teens I went to a wonderful outdoor theater in our community. They produced young people's plays every summer, and I wanted to be in them so badly. I would fantasize about what it would be like to be up on stage performing, but I waited until tenth grade before I auditioned for the school musical. I also got involved with the speech team, the debate team, and all those kinds of public-profile activities.

The first show I got a part in was *How to Succeed in Business* during my sophomore year. It was a medium-sized part. I was overwhelmed with fear over the audition, but I had a surge of confidence and got through it pretty well. People had been telling me for a while that I should try out because my voice had changed by then. So I did well in the audition and got the part. The next year I got a role in *The Pajama Game*. I was in love with acting from then on and knew it was what I wanted to do. I loved creating characters. It gave me the opportunity to go outside myself, to escape the confines of who I was and become someone entirely different, at least on stage.

The day after I performed in the sophomore-year musical, I was on the cover of the school newspaper with one of the lead actresses. We were caught in a very theatrical moment, and I was glowing. It gave my confidence a real boost, and my party-jock head friends thought it was pretty cool. I began to make a whole new group of friends because of my involvement with the theater and the speech team.

It was expected that I start dating, especially because I was a football player, and now I had this body, and I was on the speech team, and in the high school musical. I would ask a girl out on one or two dates and then never ask again. There were a couple of times when girls I dated wanted to go steady, and I would avoid them. I wasn't at all interested in doing what the girls made pretty clear they wanted to do. It wasn't my cup of tea. All my friends could think about was going out or getting laid, and I didn't think I had any sexuality whatsoever.

I felt like a third wheel with my friends because I didn't fit in. I didn't feel normal. When I was sixteen I was trying to understand that I was gay. I thought about it day and night. One night I had a dream that I was standing in a place with light and magic. A voice that I assumed was God said to me, "You're different than many other people, and if you have the strength and the courage to hang in there, here is your destiny." And before me appeared a completely nude, perfect man who looked very much like Rod. I walked toward him, took his hand, and we turned and walked away into the light. I awoke from that dream feeling calm and somehow reassured, but not understanding until many years later what meaning it would have in my life.

I couldn't wait to graduate from high school, mostly because I knew that college was my opportunity to finally get away from home. I wanted to be someplace, anyplace else, especially some place with tall buildings and mountains. I fantasized a lot about Los Angeles, but as it turned out I only went about a hundred miles from home. All of the guys I used to hang out with in high school went to Indiana State, in Terre Haute, which is where I went, too. It was an easy school to get into, so we all got in.

I didn't wait until fall to leave home, because as soon as I finished high school I joined the Marine Reserves. I strongly identified with anything military, so the idea of spending the summer in boot camp on Parris Island was very appealing. I also joined because I wanted to prove I was a man.

My father, who had been in the Marines, thought I was an idiot for signing up. He was drafted just after the Korean War, so he couldn't understand why anyone would go voluntarily, especially when I could have enjoyed my last summer before college.

Going to Parris Island was like going to prison. I went to Indianapolis with just the shirt on my back, got on a plane, flew to Savannah, Georgia, got on a Greyhound bus, and went through the gates of hell. We pulled into the gate in the middle of the night, which is intentional. They want to intimidate you from the first moment.

We got off the bus, and they had us line up. We were standing at attention and people were yelling at us, telling us where to go and what to do. It reminded me of what I'd read about concentration camps, because they were herding us like animals and there was no escape. I thought, *What the hell have I gotten myself into here?*

Over the next couple of days they do everything to begin the process of subtracting your humanity so that you can operate in a cohesive unit. They assign you to a barracks, give you your uniform, give you the notorious haircut, and then the next thirteen or fourteen weeks they put you through extreme physical conditioning—lots of marching around, being screamed at, lots of control. We had absolute zero freedom. Your only free time is spent cleaning things. It was extraordinary. They kept telling us we were nothing, worse than nothing, that we were lower than whale shit and that whale shit is on the bottom of the ocean.

The experience was shocking, but I thrived on the regimentation and discipline. I already had a strong sense of discipline from working out, so it wasn't completely unfamiliar. I was made squad leader and guide, which is the head of an entire platoon, and I was good at it.

A week before I arrived at Parris Island, I was playing hard-nosed tackle football without any pads, and I heard my collarbone break. I knew that once I was in boot camp, if I told anyone about the injury, they'd send me home. The pain was overwhelming but irrelevant, because I wanted to be there. That experience just reinforced what I was learning at boot camp, which was that I could do anything.

Boot camp was one of the worst, most degrading experiences that a human being could put himself through voluntarily, so hiding a broken collarbone was nothing.

I'd hoped that somehow my experience in boot camp would change me, that I wouldn't be gay anymore. I thought it would make me more of a man. I'd already been through the extreme rigors of being a football player, and mountain climbing, and white-water canoeing. None of that had changed me. Not even putting a gun to my head. Still, I was good at being a Marine, although it would be years before I understood that I could be gay and a real man at the same time.

During this time I kept the knowledge that I was gay compartmentalized. I stuck it away in a little cabinet in my mind and pretended that it didn't exist. I purposely refused to think in sexual terms about anything.

I arrived at college three days after I finished boot camp, in the fall of 1978. It was culture shock for me because I was still into the mind-set of being in charge of a platoon. Most of the guys who came with me from high school were still into getting high and partying. At first I stayed away from them, but pretty quickly I let myself go and during the first half of the semester I concentrated on partying, getting high, and eating. I really let loose from the rigors of boot camp, although I still had the military haircut and had to go to reserve meetings once a month for the rest of the year.

In the middle of the semester I discovered the gym at the university and really threw myself wholeheartedly into training. I stopped smoking cigarettes. I stopped smoking pot, and I stopped drinking. I was starting to realize that I wanted to compete, and I knew I had to be disciplined if I was going to succeed in the way I imagined I would. It was the first time I really had access to a full gym, and I began meeting people who knew something about bodybuilding and had actually competed in small contests.

I worked out every day, for a couple of hours at a time. It held my interest in a way that my classes didn't. They were boring, and I didn't feel challenged.

Like most schools at that time, Indiana State had a gay and lesbian organization. There were regular meetings, and many people went secretly because you didn't want anyone to know you were gay, and for good reason. For example, I went to dinner at the dining hall one night with some of the guys I was friendly with at school. One of the guys, who was a friend from high school, started making fun of the guy who was serving mashed potatoes, who was also a student. They lived in the same dorm, and my friend found out that this guy had gone to a meeting of the gay group. He was calling him a faggot and taunted him about how he'd gone to "a faggot meeting." This guy just stood there and took it, he just took it. I let Kurt go on calling him names, and then when he walked away I said, "I'm really sorry for the way he acted. He's just stupid." But he wouldn't look up. He was frozen, and I walked away.

That experience made me wonder how people would treat me when they found out that I was gay. It was one of the reasons I began drifting away from these guys, most of whom were my old high school friends. The more I got into training and cleaned up my act, the less I had in common with them. They were into fraternities and the whole decadent college scene. I knew I wanted more out of life, so the next semester I transferred to Indiana University in Bloomington, which was about forty miles from home. It was a huge school with 60,000 students, which I thought I'd like better than Indiana State.

I went to classes for about three days and then stopped. I recognized that what I really wanted to be was a professional bodybuilder, and formal education wasn't that important. I wanted adventure. I wanted to be out in the world, and I figured there was plenty to learn beyond a college campus. In the back of my mind was the reality that I was going to have to deal with being gay, and the last place I wanted to do that was at Indiana University. So I quit school and continued working full-time at a gym, where I sold memberships and helped clients with their workout routines. My real reason for being there was to have a free place to work out.

The whole time I worked at the gym I was plotting my escape to southern California, which was the place to become a professional bodybuilder and an actor. I'd idealized guys like Arnold Schwarzenegger and some other pro-bodybuilders, and I knew that that scene was in Venice and Santa Monica. I wanted to get there and be the next Boy Wonder. And because I thought I was born to be an actor, I had to go to Hollywood.

All of this was a fantasy, because I'd never been to California.

I'd romanticized the place in my mind. It was going to be the easy life, living at the beach, far from the Indiana farm town where I grew up. I thought that Joe Weider was going to be standing at the California state line, with a big check in one hand and his other hand ready to shake mine, welcoming me to my mecca. (Joe Weider is the self-proclaimed founder of modern bodybuilding. He's been a publisher, nutritional supplements manufacturer, and "trainer of champions" since the middle 1930s.) It was going to be the red-carpet treatment because obviously my potential was enormous, or at least it was in my mind.

However, after I left Indiana I wound up even farther away from California, because I decided to move to Florida. I got fired from my job at the gym. The owner accused me of stealing supplements, which I hadn't done, but he didn't believe me. I thought about fighting it, but it was time for me to move on anyway. So I packed up my car and went to Florida, which is where my Mam-ma and Pap-pa Clark lived. I didn't know what I was doing. I was nineteen. I didn't have a job. I wasn't in school. I didn't have my own place to live. I was panicked and somehow thought that going to Florida was going to be a step toward getting to California. I wanted to start competing and figured I could try doing it in Florida.

Florida was dismal. When most people think of Florida, they think of Miami Beach or Fort Lauderdale or Palm Beach—lots of glitz and glamour. Not where my grandparents lived. They lived in Lakeland, which is in the middle of the state. To get there I drove through scrubby farm country, with shacks and half-starved cows. I was thinking Florida and what I got was the rural South. I couldn't believe what I'd gotten myself into, and I didn't know what to do.

My grandparents were very good to me. They helped me find a place to live—a converted garage behind someone's house—and I got a job as a bouncer at a nightclub. I earned minimum wage and was working only part-time, so I was always on the edge of poverty. The only thing I looked forward to was training during the day.

This was a terrible time for me, because the last thing I wanted to do was live in poverty and obscurity. I had a very big ego and grand designs for my life. I was going to be a big bodybuilding star. I saw in my own mind how I was going to get to the top of the sport. Working part-time as a bouncer, not being able to afford enough food to eat, and living in rural Florida was not how I had imagined things would turn out.

In Florida I trained at a gym where there was another body-builder whose dream it was to become a pro. He competed in the Mr. Florida competition and placed very low, but the guy who owned the gym built him up like he was the next superstar of the world. I didn't know any better and thought he was.

I was incredibly naive about the bodybuilding sport. I thought I was going to be able to make a lot of money, get a product endorsement contract from Weider, and be paid to train and live in an apartment at the beach and have a good life. I learned very quickly that that was utter nonsense because I was still a nobody. I hadn't earned anything. Who was I? It turned out that I was only this kid with a big ego who hadn't put in the work to accomplish anything.

I stayed in Florida for about three months and then went back to Indiana. My grandparents bought me new tires for my car and saw me off. I know they were wondering what was going to become of me because I seemed so lost. I didn't know what the hell to do, so when I got back to Indiana I moved back to my dad's house. I could have driven anywhere in the country as fast as I wanted, but I could never outrun the fact that I was gay.

At home I had goals, but I had no idea how I was going to get from here to there. So I did a lot of partying with old friends and took a break from training.

About a month after I got home I was at a party and got into a conversation with one of the guys I'd grown up with. Bruce and I started talking about moving to California, and he said, "Okay, let's go." I thought he was kidding at first, but he was serious. He had an uncle in Anaheim, so we made that our destination.

Bruce sold his car to get the money we needed to make the trip. Our agreement was that we'd use my car to drive and the money from the sale of his car to pay our expenses. That way it would be even.

We took Route 70 through St. Louis and across Kansas, and then drove through Colorado and south into Arizona. We made one side trip to the Grand Canyon and then took the southern route the rest of the way to California. As we drove across the desert from Arizona into southern California, I knew I was headed into my destiny. I didn't know what my destiny was, but I knew I'd find it in California.

Before we got to Orange County, where Bruce's uncle lived, he phoned ahead to let his uncle know we were almost there. His uncle let us use his Yellow Pages to look up motels with kitchenettes. So we found a motel, which was a real dive, right next to the Buena Park airport, which is just for private planes.

At the motel, we went through the want ads and both got jobs as printer's apprentices at a business-form factory. I only stayed for a short time because it was very physical work and it took away from my training. So I got a job at a gym in Anaheim called the Muscle Factory, where I'd already been working out. I did everything from sweeping up to selling memberships. I got a second job at night working on the door at a place called Ichabod's. It was a straight singles spot right across from Cal State–Fullerton. I was still only nineteen, so I had to lie to the manager and told him that I was twenty-one. Between the two jobs I was barely able to put food in my mouth.

This was not a happy time in my life. I was extremely lonely and angry all the time. I lost my temper very easily; it just came out of nowhere. I was so lost and alone. I had to become an adult very fast, but it wasn't easy going. I was on my own, paying my own way, walking a tightrope with absolutely no net to catch me if I fell. As a matter of fact, I had spikes underneath me, so that if I fell I was not only going to die, I was going to die a torturous death. It's not as if I could call home for help. I'd cut all my ties and was completely on my own. There was no turning back.

Two things kept me going during this time. One was the letters I got from a guy I had a crush on whom I'd met at the university gym back in Indiana. When I first met him, I did everything I could to get his attention. I felt so stupid, especially because by the end of high school I'd become this cool kind of kid who didn't care about anybody. Now here I was worried about how I could get this guy's attention. He was extraordinarily popular with women and good-looking, but I mentally manipulated myself into believing that I wasn't even thinking in sexual terms. I just wanted to spend time with him, so I invited him to my dorm room for silly reasons.

It was so frustrating because there was no way I could tell this guy how I felt about him, and what the hell was I doing anyway? I thought I was trying to create a friendship with this guy, but I knew I was lying to myself, making excuses for what I was feeling.

At one point we'd talked about moving out to California and training together to become pros, so his letters to me helped me keep that fantasy alive. I felt incredible whenever I heard from him. It was like a third-grade crush.

The other thing that sustained me, even more than the letters, was bodybuilding. It helped give me a focus and saved my life when things started to get really bad—and they got really bad, especially when we suddenly ran out of money. That happened several weeks after we got to Anaheim. Bruce and I were both working, but we didn't have enough money to pay for the next week at the motel, so we had to leave. Bruce had made friends with a guy at his job who had a cabin in Big Bear, up in the mountains, so I drove him up there, and

I stayed for a couple of wonderful days before I went back to Anaheim.

I had no place to go, so I parked my car in back of the gym where I worked. I lived in my car for a couple of weeks and showered at the gym. One night an Anaheim cop pulled up at three in the morning and shined a flashlight in my eyes and told me to get out of the car. I told him an elaborate story about how I lived in Big Bear and had just come down to visit someone and was waiting for the gym to open. I had all my clothes and things in the back of the car, so it was obvious that I was living in it and making up a story. He told me I couldn't stay there, so I drove around for a while and came back and went to sleep.

Another night, when I was really freezing, I went inside the gym before it closed and took my sleeping bag in and curled up in one of the changing rooms. I was a pretty low-level employee, so I didn't have a key and had to sneak in before closing.

The next morning one of the owners, a good born-again Christian, found me sleeping there and kicked me out. I told him I didn't have anywhere else to go, but that didn't make any difference to him. By then they weren't all that happy with me anyway because I'd had my ear pierced, which they thought projected a bad image for a Christian establishment. (Ironically, I had just finished going through a heavy born-again Christian phase myself. I misguidedly thought that turning to fundamentalism could "save" me from being gay. Of course it didn't, and I quickly outgrew placing such strict limits on my spirituality.) When I had my ear pierced it hadn't occurred to me that it would be a problem; it was just the thing to do. A short time later they fired me and never paid me my last month's salary.

I got a new job pretty fast, managing a gym that was being opened by a local bodybuilder named Rory. I did everything from getting people set up with their workout programs to balancing the books.

Besides giving me a job, Rory also helped me put together my first posing routine for the stage. Then right after my twenty-first birthday, two years after I first arrived in California, and about six months after I started working at Rory's gym, I won the Mr. Los Angeles competition. It was only my second time competing, so it was really thrilling. Standing on the stage in front of a couple thousand people after winning that contest, I knew that all my dreams were going to come true. Finally I was on the fast track.

My sexual experience was limited, but from my one experience with a woman in high school I knew that heterosexual sex didn't feel natural to me. This was the beginning of my understanding that my homosexuality was as much a part of me as my skin. Given the crush I'd already experienced with the guy I met at the university gym, there was really no question that I was gay. But I was still confused about how to integrate this fact into my life.

Although part of me still believed that gay people were somehow identifiably odd, I knew that the kid serving in the school cafeteria was gay and that he lived in Indiana and was just an average kid. It's sort of like when one mother comforts another who has just found out that her son is gay. She says, "It's okay. He's still your son. Love him anyway." But then she finds out that *her* son is gay, and everything isn't okay. So I didn't have a problem with other people being gay, but I couldn't deal with being gay myself.

Whenever I was attracted to a man, instead of recognizing the attraction for what it was I turned it around and convinced myself that I was envious of a person's looks or the fact that another person was very popular. I couldn't admit to myself what I was really feeling.

Learning to accept what I was took a long time and a lot of internal struggle. At least now I was beginning to allow myself to fantasize about what it would be like to hold a man I loved in my arms and to be held by him.

A year after I moved to Anaheim I learned about a gay bar from one of the waitresses at a coffee shop I went to often. I thought it was about time I came to grips with this, so I asked her if she'd take me along sometime just for laughs. She said I wouldn't like it, so I found out from someone else where it was and went on my own.

I never went into the bar. I just sat outside in the company truck I was driving at the time, and I watched people going in and out. Some people were strange-looking but most were normal-looking. It was a mixed bag. But I wasn't ready yet to go in. For one thing I was underage, so I was afraid that if they carded me I'd get caught at the door; maybe somebody I knew would drive by and see me at the door, and then I'd be exposed for what I was and have a lot of explaining to do. So I never went in, and I never parked outside for long because I was afraid of being discovered.

Then one day, friends of mine, Dick and Mary, took me to brunch in Laguna Beach. Before we got there, Dick explained to me that a lot of gay people lived in Laguna. A light bulb went off in my head, and I knew that Laguna was going to be my gay mecca. For the entire next week, I plotted out a return trip to Laguna Beach. This was my chance. I was turning twenty-one that weekend and I was going to go out and celebrate.

On the day of my trip to Laguna Beach, I got all dressed up in black pants and a loose-knit sweater over a polo shirt. I had a really big pompadour rock-a-billy hairdo. And I wore black cowboy boots.

When I got to Laguna Beach I drove around for a while and looked for a place where I saw people going in who I thought looked gay. I spotted this one place, parked the truck, and went to a drugstore across the street and started looking at magazines. While I was trying to get up my courage to go into the bar, four or five men came by and tried to strike up conversations with me, but I was being real shy so they all gave up on me pretty quickly.

Finally I got up my courage and walked across the street to the bar. The guy at the door carded me, wished me a happy birthday, and let me in for free. I don't know what I expected, but except for the fact that it was almost all men, it looked like any other bar. It was dark and very crowded. There were a lot of clean-cut men standing around talking. I went up to the bar, and the bartender gave me a free drink. I just hung out and watched. I watched two men kiss. It was a very long, sexual kiss, something I'd never seen two men do before. I didn't know whether I felt repelled or found it appealing. It made me wonder what I would actually do if I had a man in my arms.

At one point a woman walked up to me and grabbed my crotch. I pulled back and knocked her hand away, and she said, "How gay are you?" It was so odd. I went to a gay bar to meet other men and a woman was hitting on me.

I tried my best to blend into the walls, and for most of the evening I didn't talk to anyone. As I was on my way out, this guy I'd been watching for most of the evening said hello to me and we struck up a conversation. I'd worked at a singles bar, so I saw straight people do this every night of the week. One of us—I can't remember if it was him or me—asked, "Do you want to get out of here?"

We headed back to his place, and I tried to act like I knew what I was doing. I didn't let on that this was my first night in a bar and that I had no experience with men. I tried to act like I was some sort of expert. It wasn't that I said anything that would have made him think that. It was just that I acted as if there was nothing new about this at all. But underneath I was really nervous.

Kissing that man was completely different from kissing a girl. It felt very right for me. It felt normal. And we went from there. Right in the middle I remember thinking, *What would my mother think?* Afterward, we slept for a while, and then I got dressed and left in the middle of the night. He was a perfectly nice guy, but I knew he wasn't anyone I was going to go steady with or set up housekeeping with.

That night confirmed what I'd known for years. It was a tremendous relief to finally know for sure, but I also began immediately to think about how I was going to deal with the people who were in my life and whether they were going to accept or reject me.

The next day, when some friends at the gym gave me a birthday party, I felt extraordinarily elated. I wanted to leap up and down because I was so happy about finally putting the puzzle together. But at the same time I was disappointed because here I had discovered the very kernel of my nature and I couldn't share it with anyone. No question that it was a positive experience, but it left me with a sense of longing, because what I wanted far more than anything else was someone I could love and spend my life with.

Every weekend after that I made the trip to Laguna. I wouldn't necessarily go into the bars or go home with anyone, but I just liked being in the area. I liked to go out on the beach and watch the huge waves come crashing in.

The fact that I was gay was no secret in bodybuilding circles. So when I went to talk to Joe Weider for the first time and told him I was gay, it was no surprise to him because he had already heard about it through the rumor mill. Nonetheless, I wasn't truly comfortable with everyone knowing. I tried to rationalize this in my mind by saying that I had a right to my privacy.

Joe wasn't happy about the fact that I was gay, and over the next several years he encouraged me repeatedly to stay in the closet. He saw me as his new rising star, and the fact that I was a fairly open homo could definitely complicate that. He was afraid that product sales would suffer if he had a known gay athlete endorsing his products or even representing the sport in his magazines. But because of my genetic talents, the meteoric rise in the sport, my ability to communicate, and my looks, I was allowed to stay in the sport as long as my gayness wasn't made public.

The fact I was gay was kept absolutely quiet in the bodybuilding media. Journalists knew I was gay and they tried to protect me by keeping away from personal subjects. In articles about me from that time there's never any mention of a home life, family, or anything. There was even the subtle suggestion in some articles that I was straight.

There were plenty of people in the sport who tried to use the fact I was gay against me. For example, after I won the N.P.C. National Championships (formerly Mr. America) in 1983, this guy who was an old closet case went through the hallway of this huge auditorium yelling, "We have two Ms. Americas this year." The women's Nationals were held on the same weekend. But by and large I had a good relationship with other people in the sport. At least no one ever said anything derogatory to me about being gay. Three weeks later I won the Mr. Universe title and earned the right to turn professional.

I stopped competing after the Mr. Olympia championship in 1985, which I did not win. I convinced myself that I was bored, that I'd gone about as far as I could in the sport. I figured I probably wasn't going to win Mr. Olympia, and I wanted to begin pursuing a career as an actor. But that wasn't the whole story, because I was really wrestling during this time over what to do about staying in the closet or coming out publicly. I was having trouble living my life as a closeted, self-hating faggot. It felt degrading, and I started talking with my friends about what I should do.

The advice just about everyone had for me was that I should stay in the closet. These were people who were pretty much accepting of the fact I was gay, but they didn't think it was a good idea for me to come out publicly, given the likelihood that it would ruin any career opportunities I might have.

At the time, there were people telling me that I was going to be Tyrone Power with muscles, that I was on the fast track to a major Hollywood career. For example, I had a manager for a short time who was a gay man. He was very "old Hollywood," and his thinking reflected that. He said things like,

"We'll pair you up with someone to show up with at charity events and parties. We won't go out of our way to say that she's your girlfriend, but we'll pretend she is. If you want to be a star, you just have to make sure to lead a nice, quiet, discreet life so we don't get any questions." He had me linked with Linda Blair. We did American Diabetes Association fundraisers together, and while it wasn't explicitly stated that we were boyfriend and girlfriend, the implication was exactly that.

One time I had a meeting with Arnold Schwarzenegger in his office. I had just started studying acting and was about to stop competing, and I asked him if he had any advice for me. Basically he said that I should find a really attractive woman and go to all of the Hollywood parties and have our pictures taken together and get them in the newspapers.

I didn't like what I was hearing, but it wasn't that hard for me to go along with Arnold's advice and what my manager said because I wanted to be a star, and I knew that I lived in a world that would see me as a piece of garbage if I revealed who I really was. The conflict for me was that I felt I had a responsibility to be up-front and honest about the fact I was gay, to show the world that you could be successful and also be gay. It would have made such a difference in my life to know there was someone like that out there. But I wasn't yet willing to take the risk to live up to that responsibility because coming out meant losing my career and giving up on the idea that I was going to be Tyrone Power with muscles.

It all became too much for me, and I left Los Angeles for a few months. I walked away from all of it, including my manager. But that wasn't the end of the issue, because even at the acting conservatory where I was studying full-time, I spoke to people about being an openly gay actor, which I wasn't ready to do yet either. And, again, almost everyone I talked to discouraged me from coming out.

Before I retired from bodybuilding to study acting, I decided it was time to come out to my family. I did it primarily because it had become a terrible burden for me to hide the truth from them.

The first person in my family I told was my younger brother, Jim. He came out to California when I was in the National Championships. After I won, he came back with me to L.A. and stayed with me for a week. He had just graduated from high school and was getting ready to go into the Air Force. I knew I had to talk to Jim about it because I wanted him to know me for who I was, and I wanted to be honest with him. He was coming back to my home. I lived adjacent to West Hollywood, which is very gay. It was going to come up at some point, even if I never brought it up.

I told Jim the first morning we were in L.A. together. I wanted to get it out of the way first thing. I was living in a tiny little apartment then, and we were sitting in the kitchen eating breakfast. Just before I told him, my stomach seized up a little bit and my heart started beating faster. I wasn't frightened, but I was a little nervous that he might reject me. I had no reason to think he would reject me; he's a very open-minded guy. But when you're raised in a world that teaches you that the essence of who you are is something vile or despicable, naturally you're going to be fearful that your family and friends may think that you are, in fact, something vile or despicable, even if you know you're not any of those things. It's also difficult after you've kept a secret for so long to finally let it go. I'm not saying the secret wasn't a burden, but at least when no one knew, I had control of it. But as I started telling people, I was losing that control, and it was frightening.

I said to Jim, "You know, I'm gay." He said, "Yeah, I know." He said that he'd talked it over with our older sister, Lisa, and our mom. And that was pretty much it. There wasn't really much to discuss because he'd already integrated that aspect of me into who he knew me to be.

After Jim, I told my older sister and my brother-in-law. This was six months later on a trip to Columbus, Indiana, where I was doing a bodybuilding seminar to benefit the American Diabetes Association.

I was out driving with my brother-in-law, goofing off, doing nothing in particular, and we pulled into McDonald's to get something to drink. I said, "Doug, I have something I want to talk to you about." I was really nervous at this point and couldn't get my mouth to work. He said, "Bob, whatever you have to say, just say it. You can always talk to Lisa and me." Of course, he already knew and was just trying to get me to relax enough to talk. But I couldn't do it and waited until that evening and went over to their house.

We sat down in the living room. I was on one couch. My sister was on a couch opposite me, and my brother-in-law was sitting in his chair. They'd already put their two sons to bed. They said, "Feel free to tell us whatever it is, and whatever it is, Bob, just know we love you and always will." I said, "I'm gay." And they said, "We'll always love you. It doesn't make a bit of difference to us." It was such a relief. Once again I'd opened myself up and nothing bad happened.

The next day, I came out to my mother. I didn't think she'd handle it very well, given what she'd said over the years about gay people. One occasion was when Anita Bryant began her anti-gay crusade. There was a small article in the newspaper about how she was leading the campaign to overturn the Dade County anti-discrimination law that had just been passed in Florida to protect the rights of gay people. I said to my mother, "What's the problem? Why can't they leave these people alone?" My mother flipped. She said, "Don't talk about those people. It says in the Bible that they're horrible people. They're homo perverts. They deserve what they're getting." That statement had a lot to do with why I pulled away from my mother. I was beginning to realize that I was different, and even if I wasn't willing to admit to myself that I was gay, there was a part of me that knew. So I decided that if she didn't want to know about that aspect of me, she wasn't going to know *any-thing* about me. I didn't want any emotional connection to her.

But it was still important for me to tell my mother. She was taking so much pride in my accomplishments, and I wanted her to know who she was proud of, the true person behind who she thought I was. I didn't want her to base her pride on something she'd created in her mind, an image that wasn't real. She thought I was one person when I was in fact someone entirely different.

I wasn't really nervous. For one thing, I'd already gone off on my own and was self-sufficient. Also, because I wasn't close to my mother, I didn't feel I had a lot to risk.

I went over to her house and told her I wanted to talk. We sat down in her bedroom, and I said, "Mom, I think it's important for you to know who I am. It's a big part of me, and I think you already know that I'm gay." She said she knew and started crying. After a while she stopped crying and asked me why I was gay, and she then asked, "How do you have sex?" I don't know why she asked that question, but I told her that that wasn't important to what we were discussing right then, and that we should take it one step at a time. We talked for a little while, and then she started crying again, "Oh, what did I do?" She was blaming herself, and there was nothing I could say that would make any difference.

My siblings told me that after I left, my mother went into a deep, deep depression. It was more than that. It was blues, loss, grieving, and especially denial. What made it particularly hard for her was that she couldn't show me what she was going through because I was a family hero.

Even though the news didn't come as a complete shock, my mother had a very hard time understanding how one person could intimately love someone of his or her own gender. It was beyond her realm. And, besides me, she had never talked to anyone she knew was gay.

I gave my mother a book called *Coming out to Parents* and a couple of other books, but she didn't want to see any of them. A year later, when *Consenting Adults* was on television—it was a movie about a gay son and his mother—my sister asked

Bob with family (*left to right*): Dad, Lisa, Leslie, me, Jim, Mom.
This was taken just days before meeting Rod.

her to come over and watch the movie with her. She couldn't
bring herself to watch it. She was still blaming herself for the
fact that I was gay; she thought it was because she was divorced
or that my father wasn't around, all of that silliness that so
many parents believe. I didn't blame her for thinking that way
because that's what she had learned from society.

I came out to Dad about six months after I told my mom. I'd
intended to come out to him just after I told my mother, when
I was in Indiana, but my dad got disgustingly drunk the evening
I spent with him, so I wound up not doing it. Six months later,
Dad and his third wife, Ellen, came to watch me compete at
Madison Square Garden in the 1984 Mr. Olympia competition.
I did well, but not as well as I had hoped.

The day after the competition, the three of us walked all over New York. We ended the day at the bar at a hotel across from Penn Station and had a couple of drinks and some snacks. By this time I knew that Ellen had talked to my dad about me and had tried to help him deal with it. She was a very sensitive and understanding person. So I said to Dad, "You know I'm gay." He said that he knew, but then he didn't say anything else. Then Ellen said, "Bob, don't shut down. Talk to him."

I didn't really care how my dad felt about the fact I was gay. We'd had very little contact for the five years before this visit, so I didn't have a lot riding on this. Dad got very emotional, but he managed to tell me that he loved me and he'd try to understand. Then he cried a little bit and went to the bathroom to compose himself. That was about the extent of the discussion.

I was very lonely at this time. What I wanted most was to fall in love and have a relationship that was both romantic and pragmatic. Before I met Rod, I'd had two short-lived relationships that didn't meet that criteria. Unfortunately, even though I recognized that those relationships weren't what I wanted, I stayed in them long past the time when they were over.

I learned a couple of important lessons from these two relationships. For one thing, I learned that I didn't want to be involved with a closeted, self-hating person. One of the two men still tries to tell people he's straight, which I find ridiculous. Even though at this point in my life I wasn't being open about my sexuality at all times, I was working toward that. I also had issues with both of these men over what I perceived of as their racism. Those were just some of the big issues, but in both cases these men were so different from me that it was impossible to have a deep relationship with either of them. I really wondered if I would ever find someone with whom I had a lot in common, with whom I could fall in love. I was afraid I would never find true love.

What I hoped to find, my romantic ideal, was someone who

was as concerned as I was about political and social injustices in the world, who had a high level of compassion, who could keep up intellectually, and who was athletic and physically attractive to me. Basically I wanted to find someone whom I could stand with side by side.

Just before I met Rod I was very down and somewhat suicidal. I was spending all my time on the road, doing seminars and appearances all over the United States and Europe. The whole time I was running from my life, from the fact that I wasn't in love, and from my fear that there was no one out there for me. I was in a dead-end relationship, which made me feel acutely lonely. And I didn't have many real friends. I'm basically a loner, and most of the friends I had when I was competing were completely uninterested in what was going on in my life when I stopped.

All of this was compounded by the fact I was abusing marijuana pretty badly. I didn't smoke heavily, but I was high throughout the entire day, every day. I knew how to smoke so I could be high all day and still function. I could go in and work out or go to a business meeting and still be present. My excuse to myself and others was that I was just a quiet person, which was a stupid excuse, because I'm not quiet. I was so down that I thought a lot about taking my own life. And that's about the time I walked into the gym in Denver and saw Rod behind the counter.

8

Those first few months together were an incredible time for us. The whole experience was so innocent. It was young love.

We could hardly sleep, which was something I was completely unaccustomed to, being a professional athlete. I was used to getting nine or ten hours of sleep a night.

At least eight or nine hours. Bob's a big sleeper. But we just talked and made love all night. We would look at each other and get lost.

Or find ourselves in each other's eyes.

We shared all our thoughts about life and spirituality. We differed in our beliefs. My spirituality is much more grounded in life. I'm very pragmatic, so I see life as being about helping people and seeking out role models. Bob's spirituality is more out of this world. He's always trying to figure out the meaning of things. We balance each other.

During these first months, we also started having the same dreams, which was really bizarre. There were several nights when one of us would wake the other and ask, "What are you dreaming?" I'd say, "I'm dreaming I'm in a Dutch Colonial house and the walls are yellow and I'm walking down the stairs . . ." and he'd be having the same dream. We also had this bizarre vision one time when we were making love.

We were Anastazi Indians, and Rod was a young warrior. It was almost like we were watching a movie of ourselves in a different time and place.

In that time and place, Bob was a young maiden. As I said, it was bizarre.

They wouldn't let us marry because somehow we were blood relatives. We held hands and jumped into a gorge.

9

Even though we would rather remember things as being perfect during the first months of our relationship, they weren't. The realities of life inevitably intrude, no matter how much in love you are. For one thing, we didn't see eye to eye over moving in together, which was our first major conflict, and we had to deal with visits from my mother and Bob's father.

From that first weekend we spent together, we were together every night, so within a few weeks I gave notice on my apartment, although I neglected to tell Rod at first. I wasn't spending any time at my apartment; it didn't make sense to keep it. I'd been planning to move into something smaller anyway because my money was starting to run out. I'd spent it all on taking acting classes and hadn't worked for quite a while.

Very early on I asked Bob if he wanted to move in because I knew he had no place else to go. Given the circumstances, I didn't feel like there were options.

The whole thing left me feeling conflicted, because on the one hand I wanted him to move in; but on the other, I was scared, and Bob didn't seem to think it was any big deal to move in together. I saw it as a humongous deal. It wasn't that I didn't love Bob. That was the problem. I really loved him, so I knew that if it didn't work out it was going to be a mess. But he had nowhere to go and I was in love.

Oh, I would have found somewhere to go.

Bob didn't try very hard.

That's because Rod wanted me to move in.

Bob has never understood this, but part of me didn't want him to move in.

Oh, I understand it perfectly.

No, Bob never, ever understood it. It was a big sacrifice for me to live with him, and it was a major problem for a long time. Living with someone means that you can't just do what you want when you want to. It's not like dropping your date off at midnight and going home. It was a big deal giving up my freedom and my privacy, and giving up that time I'd had for myself. I'm not saying that I didn't want to be with Bob, but I was afraid of how my life would change once we started living together.

For me it was a natural step. For six months before we even got together, I'd already pictured us living in a house with a white picket fence. I just took it for granted that we were going to live together happily ever after. It was hard for me that Rod didn't feel as strongly about this as I did.

Deep down, I didn't trust Bob yet, so I couldn't share his enthusiasm or his confidence that this was forever. Part of me was still afraid that he might be trying to take advantage of me. I thought he was fickle, in part because he'd lived briefly with two other men before, so I didn't think he took living together seriously enough. I know he didn't love these people; he told me that, and in my heart I knew this was true. Unfortunately, my practical mind was trying very hard to take over and not believe that our situation was any different from Bob's past relationships.

I told Rod that this wasn't even remotely similar to these two other situations. The two other involvements had just been serious dating relationships, and very shortly after moving in together they had evolved into our being roommates. I'd lived a gypsy's life since I left Indiana, so the four walls I dwelled in weren't a home, they were just someplace to sleep.

Well, to me the four walls represented where I was going to be trapped with Bob, even when things got bad. I didn't want that. This turned out to be our first big conflict.

It was so frustrating for me because it was almost impossible to convince Rod that I was in love for the first time in my life. I told him, "Now I know what the poets write about. I've never felt this before, and there's no comparison to what I've experienced before." Finally, once I was able to acknowledge what a big deal it was to move in together, Rod gave in.

After Bob moved in, on a practical level there were no disputes. We never argued about leaving the toothpaste cap on the sink or doing the dishes or cleaning up after ourselves. We have the same level of obsession with neatness and piggishness, so it all fell into place. Bob usually picks up around the house, and he does most of the cooking. I do the dishes more often, clean the toilet, and do the laundry. Fortunately, gender roles were never an issue for us. I know that for some, cooking or cleaning isn't something a real man does. But neither of us felt at all emasculated putting on an apron and doing the dishes. You could say that we both wear the pants in this family.

We merged our finances immediately and opened joint bank accounts at Rod's bank. It was actually pretty easy to change over my accounts because I had no money to transfer.

I love it when I hear people say that when I picked up Bob he had millions in his pockets. I had to pay the rent for a long time, but it was never, ever an issue. And how much we each bring in has never been an issue. Whatever we make goes in the pot, and it all gets spent the same way.

10

Rod's mother came to visit not long after Rod and I first got together, and just before I moved in with him.

The trip was planned before Bob and I got together, and this was also the time I planned to tell my mother that I was gay. So she arrived, and the first night she was there I took her out to dinner, which was when I planned to break the news. There was no question in my mind that I had to do it. I'd made the decision long before Bob was in my life that I was obligated to myself and to my mother to do this. The fact that I was in love made me want to do it even more.

By this time, my mother was the only person close to me with whom I wasn't honest, yet she was the person I loved and respected more than anyone in the world. Having to deceive her made me feel terrible. My mother raised me to be an honest and moral person, so the natural thing to do was tell her who I was and the life I was living. But I was afraid because I knew that this was one thing she didn't want me to be honest about. I figured that once I told her she'd give me the cold shoulder the rest of my life. And I was also afraid that she'd reject me, which was especially tough to consider because here was the person I'd spent my whole life trying to please. This was not going to please her at all.

But I knew I had to do it, no matter how scared I was. If my mother and I were going to have any kind of relationship it had to be two-sided, and that meant she had to know the truth. By hiding the truth, I was keeping things superficial and easy, but our relationship wasn't real. I knew my mother loved me, but she loved who I *wasn't*, and I didn't know if she would still love me and stand by me once we had talked about my being gay. I decided that I didn't want her support unless she could stand by me as I really was.

We went to dinner at the Angel City Grill, which I'd been to several times before. I had friends who worked there, so when we walked in every gay waiter said hello. I'm sure my mother was wondering how I knew all these people.

We were having a very nice dinner, and midway through I told her that we needed to talk. I said, "I think there's something you've known for a long time and just haven't been willing to face." She said very flatly, "I don't know what you're talking about." Of course, the way she said it told me that she knew exactly what I was talking about. I knew she'd react that way because she just didn't want to believe it.

I didn't want to draw this out, so I said, "Mom, I'm gay. It's something you've had to know for a long time, and we need to talk about it." She said, "I didn't know. Maybe I worried at some point that you were, but I didn't dwell on it. I couldn't have known. How could I have known?" I said, "Mom, I was always different." And she said, "You weren't that different." I told her that I was very different. "How many little boys did you know who were as sensitive as I was. I always felt like an apple in a bin of oranges. Give me a break." I don't mean to suggest that all little boys who are very sensitive and different are gay, but I know that my mother had indications that I was "different" from most boys.

At this point in the conversation my mother was looking very perplexed, and I guess I should have known what was coming next. She asked, "What about Debbie? I thought she was very nice, and I thought you liked her." My mother never liked Debbie, and now that I told her I was gay, she was ready to embrace Debbie. It was very hard to explain, but I tried to convey to my mother that while we had an intense relationship, it was never right, that it never felt right to me. She's still working on trying to understand that one.

Next my mother asked me why I was gay. I told her that I'd finally reached a point in my life where I didn't care why. Then she asked, "What did I do wrong?" I said, "You didn't do anything wrong, and what you did do wrong are just the same things that every normal parent does wrong. You didn't make me gay. But there's definitely right and wrong ways of handling what we're discussing tonight, and how you handle it is up to you." If she wanted to talk about how she contributed to my being gay, we could talk about genetics, in which case it was her genes as much as my dad's genes that might have made the difference. But I emphasized that it had nothing to do with her parenting. I said, "I have gay friends who grew up in households of all kinds, including many who had very traditional parents and families."

Then she said, "I'm worried about the life you'll lead." I explained to her that I had dated people and cared about people, and that I was in love, that I'd found somebody I wanted to spend the rest of my life with. She said, "It doesn't work like that." And I said, "Not very often, no matter what your sexual orientation, but sometimes two people who love each other can make it work. Bob loves me and I love him. We're going to get married." That freaked her out even more because coming out is one thing, but then hearing your son say that he'd met a man he intends to marry is another. She asked me why I didn't wait to tell her about Bob, and I explained that when she met him the next day, which was when I planned for them to meet, I didn't want her to think he was someone other than the man I loved.

For a long while she was quiet, so finally I said, "Look, this is just how it is and it's not going to change." Then she asked me, "Have you tried?" I said, "There's no changing. I tried for years not to be me, and all it did was make me want to kill myself. This is me and either you love me for who I am or you don't. If you love me enough, you'll try to understand. If you don't, then you need to let me know. I'll always love you, but you've got a lot to learn about this. I'll be patient with you, but this can't take forever." My mother said, "Well, I'll always love you. Nothing could ever affect how I love you."

Watching my mother across the table was so painful. Looking into her eyes made me so sad because I knew that she felt she was watching the death of the son she wanted and thought she had. And now a stranger was sitting in his place. Not that her love for me ever left her eyes, but what I saw was the shame she felt. What it said to me was, "I failed miserably and now I have to live with this. I've ruined his life and it will ruin mine, too." I felt terrible and very hurt, yet I was so relieved to just have it out there on the table. I didn't want my mother to walk out of my life, but if that's what she chose to do, well, there wasn't much I could do about it except to tell her that I loved her. At least I could now live my life honestly across the board. No more hiding. Keeping that secret from my mother was the last vestige of self-hate, and now I'd let it go.

I don't want to give the impression that my mother reacted any differently from other parents. Like everyone, my mother had learned terrible things about homosexuality and gay people. She had learned all too well the role society gave her as an oppressor of gay people, including her own son. So it was no wonder that she was upset to have it confirmed that her son was one of those bad people.

The next morning we went to pick her up to go to this big country music festival. Rod had spent the night at my place, and she stayed in his apartment.

I knew in part that I was asking my mother to deal with a lot all at once. She was still in shock from our conversation at the restaurant, and now I was asking her to meet the man I told her that I loved. That's why part of me didn't really want Bob to be there in the first place, but Bob wanted to come. I didn't think it was a great idea, because that was a lot to put on my mother at one time. But Bob wanted to meet her, and he wanted to be there to be supportive of me. I should have said no, but I was so in love that I wasn't thinking clearly, and I naively assumed that my mother would be happy for me. Not surprisingly, she wasn't.

When my mother first saw Bob, I could see she was doing mental somersaults because Bob was not what she expected. I don't know what she expected, but she didn't expect Bob. Here was this extremely handsome and very big man. I think she was really thrown by his old, beat-up, shit-kicker cowboy boots, because she just never imagined that queers dressed like that.

It was not a fun day. My mother was very cold to Bob, and eventually I took her aside and told her that I thought she was treating Bob badly. I said, "If you have a problem with this, it's with me, not him." She said, "I don't have a problem. He's a nice person." So I told her she should treat him accordingly, but at that point I was feeling like a referee at a tennis match, not knowing which way to turn. I was worried about her feelings and I was worried about Bob's feelings, and I couldn't keep track of the ball.

I wasn't hurt. Rod's mom was a nice person, although she was very cold toward me, which was no surprise, given the circumstances. But I could see she was torn; on the one hand she wanted to hate me, but on the other I could tell she liked me because I was another boy like Rod. We came from the same place.

My mother tried to hate Bob because she wanted to believe he'd perverted me, that he'd enticed me into being gay. Given what she was taught about gay people and homosexuality, that made perfect sense in her mind. Like the majority of people at that time, she thought that being gay was a choice. But you have to wonder, if it's a choice, why would anyone choose it? Why would I choose to be something that I knew would deeply disappoint my mother, that is hated by my religion and condemned by society? Not to mention having to deal with the violence gay and lesbian people face every day simply for being who they are. Why would anyone want to be gay in a society where the cards are so stacked against them? That's been a tough one to explain to my mother, but eventually she understood that it's as much a part of me as my eye color and the fact that I'm left-handed.

After spending the day at the music festival, we went to dinner at a Japanese restaurant with Rod's friends Jill and Jerry.

My mother had met Jill many, many times, so I thought that would make things a little more comfortable. There was so much tension at the table, and Jill tried to break the ice by being funny, but it didn't come across that way.

There was a song playing in the background, and it was Judy Collins singing "Send in the Clowns." When it came to the line, "Isn't it quaint, isn't it queer?" Jill chimed in and sang the line along with Judy Collins.

My mother disappeared into her chair. Jill felt terrible, because she was just trying to lighten things up. It didn't work, but somehow we all got through dinner. The whole thing was sad, because if Bob had been a woman, she would have been thrilled that I'd found someone that wonderful, especially someone who had a similar background.

She would have been picking out dish patterns. But instead, it was as if someone had died.

11

Not long after Rod's mother came to visit, and shortly after we moved in together, my father came to see me. The visit wasn't all that significant, except that Rod and I wound up getting into a conflict over whether he was going to come along with my father and me on a day trip to Joshua Tree.

Bob hadn't seen his dad in a long time, and I knew they had a lot of issues to deal with. Obviously, they had a lot to talk about and I thought they needed to be alone.

But I didn't want to be apart from Rod.

I didn't want to get in the way. It wasn't that I didn't want to be with Bob, but I didn't want to be with them when I thought they had things to talk about. I knew his dad wouldn't be comfortable talking if I came along, and I didn't feel right getting in the middle of this family thing. After all, I had just been through some painful family issues myself, where Bob's presence unintentionally made things more complicated. I was determined to stay out of their way so they could work things out.

But Rod was my family now, and I just wanted him to meet my father and get to know him. So I thought Rod was being stubborn. But the thing that really upset me was that instead of going along with us, Rod was going to tan at the Athletic Club. The club, which was really a fitness center, was mostly gay, and I couldn't stand the thought of him being out there in a bathing suit in front of these other gay men.

I was going with one of my best friends. I wasn't going there to flirt. Besides, I was so head over heels in love with Bob that nobody in the world could have gotten my attention.

By the time I dropped Rod off at the gym, we were both pissed at each other. I couldn't bear when Rod was upset with me, so the whole time driving down to Joshua Tree with my father I was on pins and needles. I would have been uncomfortable being alone with my father anyway, given how distant our relationship had been for so long.

My goal for this day had been to make my family whole again. That would have meant sharing the day with my father and Rod, just like a normal family outing. But nothing was going right, so I wanted to turn around and come back home, which is just about what we did. We walked around for twenty minutes and drove right back. I hardly talked to my father. All I could think about was that I wanted to bridge the chasm between Rod and me.

What he really wanted was to get me out of the Athletic Club.

After tanning, my friend Michael and I went to a Mexican restaurant and had a couple of margueritas, and then I called home to see if Bob was there. He was still upset when I called. It made me angry that Bob didn't trust me.

I didn't trust Rod out of my own insecurity.

Bob really thought another man might catch my eye. We were so fresh in our relationship that, despite the fact we were deeply in love, the concrete had not yet set.

That wasn't what was bothering me. I didn't want people looking at Rod with his clothes off.

And I didn't want to be locked in a cage all my life. I also didn't like having to deal with Bob's jealousy. Looking back now, it was kind of funny that he was so worried, but at the time it wasn't funny at all. I was hurt because I thought he didn't trust me.

I drove over to the restaurant and met Rod, and then we headed back to the apartment. On the way home, I said something that made him very angry. I said something playful.

Bob was not playful. He was being mean and said, "Did you enjoy all the attention you got at the Athletic Club?"

I never said anything like that.

I freaked because I'd been talking to Michael the whole time. If Bob's dad hadn't been there we would have had a major fight, but because his dad was there I just left. I called Michael and we spent the evening together.

I was so worried all evening, but then Michael called to let me know that they were fine. He said, "You know Rod loves you very much. He doesn't even look at anyone else. Just relax and let him get it out of his system. I'll keep him out of trouble and make sure he gets home okay."

I asked Michael to call for me because I couldn't do it. My ego wouldn't let me.

12

What we're about to talk about is something we debated sharing. It certainly would have been easier for us to leave it out, but it is something we both feel strongly about and know that we have to talk about. We've decided to let the chips fall where they may.

Although I can't believe it now, Rod and I didn't discuss how HIV and AIDS applied personally in our lives until several months *after* we first started making love. Here we were in the midst of this major health crisis and all rationality had gone out the window. It had entered my mind, but I had never been tested and was afraid of the possible results. I had pushed it to the back of my mind, even though I had watched the virus destroy countless lives. I understand how selfish it was of me to not try to protect Rod. After all the years of waiting for the true love of my life, I very irresponsibly refused to allow reality to come crashing through the front door of this fairy tale.

Worrying about whether or not we were HIV-positive would have made me feel that our relationship wasn't permanent. As far as I was concerned, I was spending the rest of my life with the man I loved, no matter what, and that included the good and the bad, till death do us part.

Objectively, we know this is not the way to do things. And, despite what we did, we both knew better. I can't let Bob take all the responsibility, because it does take two to tango. Before I moved to California, I'd helped the Colorado AIDS Project, a social services group in Denver, set up a telephone crisis line, and I trained phone volunteers for about two years. And I helped care for a couple of people with AIDS one on one. So I had personally watched as AIDS stole the lives of two different men. Here I'd already been a part of the battle with a virus that I knew could kill, and now I was acting as if the enemy were benign.

I participated in some of the early celebrity fund-raisers for the American Foundation for AIDS Research and AIDS Project Los Angeles. I also attended marches and rallies.

But at the time I didn't care. I'd already been tested twice, and based on those tests, I was pretty sure that I was negative, but I didn't know about Bob's HIV status. My feeling was that if Bob was positive and I got infected, we would deal with it together. The really stupid thing that is that, given my experience as an HIV and AIDS worker, I knew exactly how the disease was transmitted and I knew how horrible HIV and AIDS were. But I just didn't care. My thinking was that, if I have five years with this person and then die, at least I will have had the five years. I never thought I'd care about anybody this much in my entire life, and my life wasn't as important as having this experience. That's completely irrational, and no one should do what we did, but that's the way I felt. Looking back now, I also believe that self-hate and a highly romanticized gothic notion about love had a lot to do with it. (The gothic notion included letting nothing come between us, including a condom.) I had immaturely decided that the experience was more important than my life. As I have grown more comfortable with myself, I realize that safe sex would not have destroyed the romanticism, but that's in hindsight.

We weren't completely irrational. I knew my sexual history, and I had been very careful about not contracting HIV. So even though I'd never been tested, I was pretty certain I was HIV-negative. The irrational part is that I assumed the same of Rod. I was in love and nothing else mattered. I didn't want to have to protect myself from anything with this person. I wanted everything to be unguarded.

That was really it for me. I knew I loved Bob and would probably never love anybody like that again, so to me it was a suspension of my normal rationality. This was the person I wanted to live and die with. I didn't want to go on if this person wasn't going to live. So I thought that if I got HIV from Bob, this was something I wanted to share. That was the irrational side of me. The rational side wondered if I was going to have to pay the price for taking the risk. But it was a choice I made, and I knew I would live or die with the consequences. It was a game of Russian roulette.

That's how I felt, too. I knew I could be putting myself at risk, just as he could have been putting himself at risk. But I knew that this was no one-night stand, and that even if this body died, our love would go on.

You have to understand that Rod and I are just trying to be honest here, and this is where we were at the time.

When the subject finally came up, I said, "You know, I tested negative before we got together." Bob said he hadn't been tested, so we didn't know where we stood. We'd been making love all the time for about a year and not practicing safe sex, so if Bob had been infected, there was a very good chance that I was now infected, too. I said to Bob, "Will you take care of me if I get sick?" He said, "Of course, honey. I'll take care of you through anything." And then he asked, "Will you take care of me?" I said, "Of course," and that was enough for both of us.

We wanted to share this part of our relationship with you, because we know for a fact that there are millions of people, gay and non-gay, who are going through or will go through making the decisions we had to make. We hope that you will be more mature and wise. The decisions we made may sound romantic, but they were stupid.

13

Four months after Rod and I got together, I decided that I wanted to go back to professional bodybuilding. I'd had vivid dreams several nights in a row about being on stage again, competing. I told Rod about it and how I thought I wanted to compete again. As soon as I said it, I could see the disappointment in his eyes.

I hated the whole freaky culture of bodybuilding. I thought it was a silly sport full of a bunch of goons supported by a lot of freaky people. My thinking has changed some over the years, but I have to admit I still feel that way about a lot of it.

When I first started bodybuilding, it was very much a cult sport, but you also have tennis nuts and golf fanatics. The difference, of course, is that bodybuilding is all about the physical body.

But these other sports don't have this underground, low-life quality that bodybuilding does, especially the 400-pound gorillas who think everybody actually wants to look like them. Ugh! Golf and tennis aren't freak shows. But I knew Bob really wanted to do it, so I told him to go for it if that's what he wanted. But I reminded Bob that his decision would have a big impact on me, because I was going to have to deal with these freaky people in his profession. And I pointed out that he'd walked out of the sport once before, and who was to say he wasn't going to do that again. I tried to be supportive, but I had to be honest and I told Bob I would never see the sport the way he did.

By the time I had stopped competing, I hated bodybuilding and the direction it was headed in. And, in fact, I *still* disagree with the direction the sport was and is taking. I saw bodybuilding as a road toward the "perfect" physical specimen. The dominant culture of the sport for the last ten years has been grotesque freakiness for the sake of freakiness.

Bodybuilding seemed like a ridiculous way to make a living. (Why I decided to go into acting, which was even more frivolous, I'm not sure.) But this was two years later, after studying acting and spending all my money, and still not really knowing what I was going to do. It was a very complex and confusing time for me. I was finishing up at acting school, and I was going to have to make some decisions, because I was very fearful that it might be years before I'd be able to get any work. Added to that was an unfulfilled dream I'd had for a long time to win Mr. Olympia.

Bob really didn't know anything else other than bodybuilding. He wasn't working and didn't have any money coming in, except for doing some personal training. We were living on that and on what I was making from working part-time at a law firm and from modeling. I think Bob felt awkward because he wasn't bringing much money in, and he was used to making a great living.

I felt very awkward, and I knew that if I started back with bodybuilding, I could earn a very good living again, more than I could possibly earn starting out as an actor. I know Rod didn't have a problem with me not bringing in much money, but I felt like a bum. I felt useless. Rod would go off during the day, and I would train one or two clients and hang out around the apartment. Well, I guess I didn't just hang out because I made Rod lunch and brought it to him at work.

Every day. And sometimes he brought flowers. I loved it.

I also took him to work every day, and I wrote a lot. In some ways it was a very carefree and wonderful time. But I felt like I wasn't contributing my share.

After having that same dream four nights in a row about being on stage and competing at the Mr. Olympia competition, I knew I wanted to start training and competing again. I had a lot of work to do because I'd dropped at least forty pounds and looked untrained. My Mr. Universe body was long gone. I knew Rod was unenthusiastic about it, but I asked him if he'd train with me.

I told him that I would. I don't think either of us could have stood the thought of one of us training with someone else. It wasn't a jealousy issue. It's just that we wanted to be together all the time. And I knew it was important to Bob that I be supportive, so I told him that I would support him and train with him as long as it was something he was committed to. I didn't want to start something and then have him bail out halfway through.

So we threw ourselves into working out three hours at a time. I would pick Rod up at work, and we'd drive down from Hollywood to Venice to World Gym. For me it was very exciting because here I was sharing with Rod something I loved doing, and I was helping Rod learn more about bodybuilding.

Fortunately we saw bodybuilding in the same way. We didn't think it was all about creating the biggest, bulkiest, ugliest, grotesque monster possible. The goal was to build the most beautiful body that you could. And that was our goal for Bob and for me to work toward, to have the most beautiful, perfectly proportioned bodies in the world.

Three months later, an old-timer at the gym came up to us and looked at Bob and then me, and said "Are you guys part of a cloning project? Where can I sign up?" Our training obviously was paying off.

14

While Bob and I were spending three hours a day training, I got a call to do some test shots for *Playgirl*. As we got into the training, I'd been neglecting my career, especially because I hated it. But I knew that I needed to update my portfolio with more body shots, so I thought the test would be a good opportunity to get it done.

I was a little nervous about how Bob would react to the call from *Playgirl*, so I didn't tell him about it until after I came home from the shoot. When I told him about it, he said he was sure I'd get the job, and he didn't seem upset. But it was another story after I actually got the job.

Rod told me that there wasn't going to be anything overtly sexual about the photographs, and he wasn't going to show everything, but I was upset. When I took my clothes off for my work, I was doing it to compete. It wasn't just for the sake of taking off my clothes. And here Rod was going to do nude photographs that lots of other people were going to see. I didn't want to share him.

Of course, when Bob shared himself with the world, I was just supposed to deal with it. But when he had to turn around and deal with me doing something as public as *Playgirl*, he couldn't cope. Also, Bob was used to being in the spotlight, and accustomed to people knowing who he was. In the world of bodybuilding he was very famous. So he was already "somebody" when we met. When we got together I wasn't well known, which was just fine with Bob. But when my career started picking up, he didn't like it.

That was part of it, but I just wished there had been a way we didn't have to make our livings off our bodies, because when Rod did that kind of work, I got very jealous. So I wanted to go with Rod to the shoot. I asked very insistently for him to let me go. I thought I'd feel better about it if I were there.

I couldn't have worked if Bob had been there, so I told him I didn't want him there and I left the apartment.

He was pretty mad when he left, and in those days whenever Rod left the house mad, I would get upset. I couldn't do anything else for the entire day. Beyond that, we had only one car, so I felt trapped and wound up climbing the walls.

I was mad because I was supportive of what Bob was doing, even though I wasn't thrilled with his profession, and yet he had a hard time supporting me. Part of the dynamic had to do with a sexist attitude.

Both of us had the attitude, "I'm a man and I'll decide what I want to do with my career, and I expect you to be supportive of whatever that is." But at the same time, we both felt we had the right to comment and try to influence each other's career choices.

That's true, but there was also a whole other dimension to the objections we each had about the other's profession. I felt Bob was misleading people by pretending in his profession that he was straight, and I felt hurt because I was completely omitted from his life. On the one hand he'd tell me he loved me and how important our relationship was, but then when it came to his profession, I didn't exist.

I thought Rod was confusing the sin of *omission* on my part with the sin of *commission* on his part—doing the *Playgirl* shoot and doing an interview with the magazine in which the implication was that he was straight. It was a lie.

To me that was a double standard, because I didn't see any difference between how we were handling the fact we were gay. However we did it, both of us kept that information separate from our work. And besides, I didn't lie about anything in the *Playgirl* interview. When they asked me what I would do with a special person in my life, I answered without ever saying the word "girl." I talked about the "person" I was involved with. They knew a lot of the models were gay, so they had no problem wording it so I never had to say girl or woman. I didn't bastardize myself, but I had to do some sidestepping, otherwise I wouldn't have gotten the job.

After *Playgirl* published the photos, you wouldn't believe the weird phone calls and letters we started getting. Bob had warned me that people would start coming out of the woodwork, so we'd already changed our phone to an unlisted number, but that didn't stop anyone. I got calls from both men and women, like the one from Tanya in Tennessee, who called to say, "I just want to see you lift your leg and see that big . . ." Finally we had to disconnect the line and get a new number.

For me this was extraordinarily upsetting. I guess I saw Rod as my come-to-life Ken doll. I wanted him all for myself, and I wanted to protect him from going through all the degrading things I'd experienced as a bodybuilder. I didn't want to have

Rod as a *Playgirl* centerfold. (*Michael Morgan*)

to think about Tanya in Tennessee fantasizing over naked pictures of the man I loved.

But this was something I already had to contend with because of Bob's profession, although I'll admit that since he hadn't yet gone back to competing it was somewhat easier for me to deal with.

In retrospect, I should have been more understanding, because this was a time when Bob was feeling pretty insecure and vulnerable. He was between careers, and he thought that I was going to hit big, that I was going to dump him and run away.

A publicity photo of Bob and Rod. (*Blake Little*)

You can imagine then how thrilled Bob was when *Playgirl* called me several months later to tell me that readers had voted me Man of the Year. That meant a guaranteed guest spot on "The Tonight Show" and having another photo spread in *Playgirl*. By this time, *Playgirl* had changed its format to full frontal nudity. Frankly, that didn't bother me, and I would have done it if the money were right and Bob could have dealt with it.

The bigger problem was that being Man of the Year meant

having to make appearances at a couple of hundred nightclubs around the nation. The appearance fees would have been great, but it meant pretending I was this straight stud. On top of that there was a Spend a Night with the Man of the Year contest. Someone wins a drawing, and you go to dinner and stay at a hotel overnight. How's that for degrading someone by turning him into an object? And they say gay people think about sex too much!

Bob asked me what I wanted to do. I told him that it was a great move for my career, that the nudity didn't bother me, that if I wanted to get into films, this was one way in. And I told him that the money was appealing and I could make lots of it, and that there would likely be career spin-offs from it. Bob hit the roof.

The frontal nudity was a problem for me. And while Rod compared what he was doing to what I did in bodybuilding, I didn't see it as the same thing at all. Bodybuilding was a sport. I wasn't doing it to turn people on sexually, which was the primary purpose of *Playgirl*.

I'd read Bob's fan mail, so I knew better. A lot of these people weren't just there for "the sport." There's a sexual element to it, and that's what attracts a lot of people. I understood that this was just a part of any public profession.

The bigger issue was that Bob didn't want to share me with anyone. He told me that my first appearance in *Playgirl* was hard for him, and it wasn't full frontal nudity. He said, "I don't want anyone seeing your penis. I'm the only one who should see it."

Rod was also going to have to pretend even more that he was a straight single stud. This went well beyond that short interview he did the first time around. I knew Rod wasn't going to flat-out lie, but it would be implied that he was heterosexual. Of course, that would have meant, as far as the world was concerned, that I didn't exist.

This was exactly the kind of thing that the bodybuilding magazines were doing about Bob. They might not have said he was heterosexual, but they never talked about his personal life.

I told Rod that if he accepted the Man of the Year it would hurt me so badly that I'd never get over it. If he did it, I knew that every person we encountered would be looking at his crotch.

I think Bob would have gotten over it, but he was adamant, so I turned it down. I still think it was no big deal, that I could have done it, but I didn't because my love for Bob was far more important to me than anything that could have come from being *Playgirl* Man of the Year.

15

I know I got more upset about *Playgirl* than I needed to, but there was another offer that came soon after the Man of the Year deal that really sent me over the edge.

It started with a call Bob got from a talent agent about a producer who was casting a new television show. He asked if Bob wanted to meet with him.

I checked it all out to make sure the guy was legitimate because I'd been through all the bullshit before. It turned out that he was legitimate and I went to see him. This was after I'd started working out and had made plans to compete again, so I was really ambivalent about pursuing acting at this point. In the end my enthusiasm, or lack of it, didn't matter, because I clearly wasn't what he was looking for.

Before the end of the interview, this producer asked if I knew any other leading-man types, blond hair, very square-jawed, who would be more appropriate for the part. When I think about it now, it occurs to me that this whole thing might have been a setup to get to Rod. Anyway, it didn't occur to me at the time, and, of course, Rod came to mind instantly. I said,

"As a matter of fact I do. I think he's exactly what you're looking for." I gave him Rod's agent's number and left. The warning alarms should have already been ringing. I don't know what I was thinking.

I know what Bob was thinking. I'd already called him on the fact that he was less than supportive of me in my career, and so he thought he'd show me that he was being supportive. Well, he picked the wrong opportunity to prove himself.

So the producer called. I'll call him Dave, but I don't know why I'm bothering to protect the identity of a certified creep. Dave asked me if I wanted to join him for lunch, and I said yes. I met him at his office at the Tri-Star building in Beverly Hills. I sat down, and he said, "You have a fantastic look, and it's just what I'm looking for." I asked him what he wanted me for, and he said we should just go to lunch and talk. So we had lunch, and he told me that I had a great presence and he thought we could work together. He asked me to meet him again for lunch. I guess I wasn't suspicious at this point because Dave was straight-forward and businesslike.

At the second lunch, Dave didn't waste any time getting down to discussing what he wanted. He said, "Are you involved with anybody?" I said that I was, and he said, "You'll have to get rid of him or her." Then he went on to tell me, "I'll put you up in a penthouse. I'll give you a Mercedes. I'm going to groom you for leading roles. All you have to do is play the game. You have to be seen and we'll put a beautiful woman on your arm." And, of course, implicit in the whole deal was that I'd have to sleep with him. I was a little shocked, but this was Los Angeles, so it wasn't that surprising.

I went home and told Bob that he'd really shot me right from the cannon into the flames. I told him everything that happened.

I felt like an idiot and I was furious. I wanted to strangle the guy, but Rod didn't want me meddling and told me to mind my own business.

He got me into this, so I told him to back off and let me handle it. I decided I'd meet with Dave one more time to see if there was any possibility of getting the work without having to play by his rules. I explained to him that I was in love with Bob. Dave said, "Just dump him. He can't do anything for you, and besides, he won't mean anything to you in a couple of years. I can give you everything. I can put money in the bank for you." I tried explaining that I was in love and that I didn't want to live my life the way he wanted. I said, "I have to have some dignity. It's one thing to act straight in a film. That's acting, and it has nothing to do with my real life, but I'm not going to go around with a woman on my arm pretending to be something I'm not. I can't live my life like that. That kind of pretense is repulsive to me." He wasn't even fazed by this, and he just kept going on about what he could offer me. And then the owner of the restaurant came up to us and said, "Oh, this is your next star." Finally Dave gave me his final pitch: "What's it going to be? You really can't pass this up." Then he told me about all these models and up-and-coming stars who were begging him to make them the same kind of offer. I said, "All I know is that people who screw to get where they want to go usually end up getting screwed, period." I told him I'd be interested in looking at his projects but not on the terms he was offering. He warned me that I was ruining my career, but at that point I wasn't sure I even wanted a career in film.

It felt great to say no. This was yet another point in my life where I had to decide what my real priorities were. I had enough dignity to know that I couldn't be a prostitute and live a lie. I told Bob that even if I never did anything with my life, I'd feel better about myself than if I'd done something like what that producer was offering me. My work has to be honest and it has to be done with integrity or I can't live with myself.

I felt very threatened. I began wondering if I was ugly and unimportant. It wasn't a role I was accustomed to after having so much success so young in bodybuilding.

This is around the time we started talking about doing work together. We knew that our relationship couldn't survive the two of us competing with each other, being closeted, and acting straight by omission. And there was no way we could handle some of the compromises we were going to have to make if we were to pursue traditional careers in Hollywood.

Whether it was a slight caused by the sin of omission or a requirement that we show up with female escorts, whatever, we couldn't do it, because even though we weren't trying to hurt each other, we couldn't help but be hurt. Being made invisible, even if it was necessary, was hurtful to both of us. So our hope was to develop projects together. Maybe one day, when things changed, we could still have careers in Hollywood and be completely open about who we were and maybe be part of a process of positive change. But that day would be a long way off, and not just because Hollywood couldn't—and still can't—deal with openly gay actors. I couldn't yet deal with being openly gay in my professional life, and even in my personal life it sometimes wasn't so easy. Coming out, for me, as for almost everyone I know, was a long and tentative process.

16

That summer, just after Rod appeared in *Playgirl*, we went to Europe for five months to work. Rod was going to be modeling in several of the major cities, and I was going to be doing fitness and bodybuilding seminars and guest appearances at bodybuilding contests. I intended this tour to jump-start my return to the sport because there were far more opportunities for this kind of work in Europe than in the U.S. I convinced Rod to go with me.

It wasn't as easy as that sounds, but before I get started with another story about us arguing over something, I should explain that the fact that we argued—and continue to argue—doesn't mean we don't love each other. But we're two very different people, with different needs, expectations, and styles of resolving conflict. We've never held back, so especially during the first years of our relationship, when we were getting to know each other, we argued with great intensity. We're both very passionate people, and we express that in many different ways.

The argument over whether or not I was going to go to Europe with Bob was the only one that ever got physically confrontational, maybe even somewhat violent.

It wasn't violent.

Well, anybody looking would have thought it was violent.

Okay, it was like football practice in the middle of our apartment. There was all this tension because Rod said he didn't want to go. And I was saying, "Please come. We'll have your agent find you work." I thought that if he didn't come with me, he'd find somebody else. I didn't think we could have survived three or four months apart right then.

I don't agree with that at all. I was in love, and a few months apart would be hard, but we could work it out. It wasn't as if I wanted to be apart, but if that's how it had to be, that's how it had to be. My career was hopping, and I didn't want to leave right then. I didn't think it was a good idea for me to be that far from the phone.

What I really resented was that Bob was thinking mostly about what was good for his career. Sure, I could get work in Europe, but that was work that would just pay the bills. If I stayed home, I would be building my career. I didn't think it was fair that he wanted me to drop everything, because I certainly never asked him to do that.

By the same token, I couldn't kick-start my career in the U.S. I had to go back to Europe and go on the road.

I didn't have a problem with that, and I knew Bob was right about that, but I didn't see why I had to go with him. Of course I didn't want to be apart. I knew it would be hard. But I had my own life, too. I never said, "Don't go." But because I never said, "Don't go," Bob thought I was saying that I didn't want him or love him enough to tell him to stay. It turns out that what he really wanted me to say was, "Don't go."

That's true. I was feeling unwanted.

There's no question that I wanted Bob, but it would have been wrong to tell him not to go. I couldn't have done that to him. The funny thing is that we're opposites in this way. Bob has no problem telling me not to do something, and I don't want him to limit me. I don't see it as a sign of love. I just feel suffocated.

Rod finally agreed to go with me, and I got the tickets for the two of us. That was about a month before we were scheduled to leave. Unfortunately, that wasn't the end of the argument, because every time we had the smallest disagreement, it would escalate into, "Well, I'm not going now." It was exhausting.

It's not fair to say that the smallest thing would start it. I didn't want to go in the first place, and I felt Bob was twisting my arm to get me to go. This was the same dynamic as when we were talking about moving in together. For Bob it was no big deal then, and he didn't think it was any big sacrifice for me to take off and work and travel with him through Europe. He didn't acknowledge what a hard decision this was for me.

The other problem we have when we disagree about something is that Bob thinks that if we hold each other and talk it out, everything will be okay. I'm just the opposite. First, when I'm upset about something, I don't necessarily like to talk about it right away. I like to let things settle down a bit so I can talk things out more diplomatically. I also need my space, so I don't want to touch or cuddle when we're talking about something difficult. Bob wants to try to make everything okay right away, and he thinks it will be all better if we just hold each other. So Bob insists on getting close, and I insist on keeping my distance. He winds up chasing, I wind up running. Sometimes it's like a rabbit and a greyhound at the race track. It's not a good dynamic.

It was terrible, because whenever Rod tried to keep his distance, I felt rejected. The other dynamic was that every time we had a major disagreement, Rod threatened to leave me, or at least that's how it felt to me. He had no better weapon because that pushed all my abandonment buttons. And that's exactly what happened over the decision to go to Europe. Ten days before we were supposed to leave, Rod began threatening that he was going to end the relationship.

I felt like Bob was twisting my arm about going and I didn't appreciate it. There was nothing worse for me than feeling cornered. This time I'd had it.

We'd reached a breaking point. Rod tried to leave the apartment, and I blocked his way. I didn't know what he was going to do so I couldn't let him go.

I feel like a trapped grizzly when somebody blocks my way and tells me what I can or cannot do. I told him to get out of my way, but he backed me into a corner. He kept saying, "Can't we resolve this?" but instead of stepping back, he kept coming closer.

I knew that if I moved he'd leave and wouldn't come back. I would have been destroyed, so I had to do something to keep him from leaving.

I freaked. I couldn't stand it and took a football stance and knocked him over. Then I stood up, but before I could move, he knocked me over a chair. It was like high school football practice. We were like two rams and kept knocking each other over, hitting each other as hard as we could with our bodies. We never used our hands to punch or anything like that, just body blocks.

That went on for fifteen minutes, and then we locked arms and fell on the floor, and we both started crying. Then we both started laughing, and Rod said, "I'll go with you, but you have to understand how hard this is for me." I told him that I understood what a sacrifice he was making for me and promised to make it up to him.

We were both pretty bruised by the time we left for Amsterdam two days later.

We've learned a lot about each other since that time, and we've learned a lot about communication, especially Bob, because he was a terrible communicator one on one. Over and over again I'd have to say, "What are you thinking? What's going on?" I got tired of pulling information out of him. He wouldn't tell me what was going on in his head, especially if he thought it would upset me. And I'm quick to get mad, so that worked against Bob feeling like he could open up.

This wasn't exactly the end of the arguments. In Holland we fought about all kinds of things, and more than once Rod threatened to go back home to California. One argument played out for everyone to see in the streets of Middleharnis, this wonderful small Dutch coastal fishing village.

I don't even remember what the argument was about anymore, but we faced all kinds of challenges on that trip, and there was plenty to argue about.

We were having a screaming argument in our hotel room and I was begging Rod to stay, that we'd work it out.

I just couldn't take it anymore. The day-to-day scrutiny of the people around Bob and the fact they insisted on treating us as if we were two single men with no intimate connection and Bob's occasional difficulty in confronting their bigotry got to be too much for me.

I blocked the door for an hour. Rod's bags were already packed, and I knew if I got out of the way he'd go back to L.A., and I might never see him again.

But I told him that I had to make my own decisions, and that if he didn't move out of the way I'd hate his guts forever.

I don't remember it that way.

Well, that's how I remember it. Bob finally realized I was serious, that I'd never forgive him if he didn't let me go, and he got out of the way.

As soon as I moved away from the door, Rod left to get a bus to Amsterdam. I looked around the room and thought, *How does this feel? He's gone. Can I live without him?* because I knew that once he went back to California, that would be it. I was surprised that I also experienced a sense of relief. I was feeling a lot of pressure, too, so with Rod gone I thought that maybe it would be an easier trip.

In the five minutes I stood there thinking, I went through a whole range of emotions from anger to terror. I thought, *Well, if he wants to leave, fine, screw him, let him go.* It was a macho kind of thing, but then I started crying.

Suddenly it occurred to me that I couldn't let this happen. I burst out of the hotel and ran down the cobblestoned streets of the village. As I rounded the corner where I knew the bus stop was, a bus was just pulling away. I ran alongside the bus as it pulled away, looking in every window to see if Rod was on it, but he wasn't. I was going to hop on the next bus to Amsterdam, even though I had run out of the hotel room leaving my passport, my billfold, and my belongings behind. But all I could do was sag to my knees. I said to myself, "Oh, I've missed him," and I felt completely dejected.

Something told me to look up, and there was Rod at a bus stop across the road, sitting there with his head in his hands, his bags between his feet. I thought Rod was still waiting for the right bus, although he told me later that he'd let the bus go and was waiting for the next one. So I sat on a wall catercorner from where Rod was sitting and just watched and waited for him to see me.

I couldn't get on that first bus, because I couldn't figure out what

I really wanted to do. I was debating in my head, "Do I get on? Do I not get on?" Because I loved Bob, but I knew that if I got on the bus, that would be it. That's the kind of person I am. Even if I loved him that would have been the end. So I let the bus go so I could think about my decision. Then I looked up and saw Bob sitting on the wall staring at me.

I'd been sitting there for about an hour.

I knew the next bus was about to arrive, and now I was really torn. I thought, *If he comes and gets me, maybe he really loves me enough so we work through our problems.* I needed Bob to make the first move. By this time I realized that I didn't want to go. I would have been miserable without him, but if he didn't come across the street, I was going to get on that bus. I couldn't bring myself to back down.

I walked across the street.

I'd never seen Bob look so innocent in all the time I had known him. He asked me if I wanted to come back to the room. I said, "Yes" and picked up my bags, and we headed back to the hotel. As we crossed the street, the bus pulled up.

We walked back through the cobblestoned streets. I told Rod that I loved him and that we could work through anything, but it was going to be hard. I said, "I don't want to live without you. I can't picture my life without you."

It's funny. There was one time we argued on this tour of Europe when I know people heard us, although I don't think they heard the details. And actually the argument itself isn't important, but I want to make a point about arguing.

The reason I know people heard us is that the next morning, the wife of one of the other bodybuilders said to me, "Are you guys okay? Someone heard you fighting last night." I said that we were fine and asked her, "Don't you and Julian ever communicate?" She said, "Julian and I never fight." This was someone who had a very traditional marriage, with strict separation between husband and wife roles. People were always comparing us to them because they appeared to be the picture-perfect heterosexual couple, and we apparently were not perfect because we argued *and* we were a gay couple.

A couple of years later, we heard that this woman had left her husband, emptied their sizable bank account, and taken everything they had.

Left him high and dry.

We're not saying that every couple that doesn't argue is destined to break up. It's just that you've got to communicate if you're going to share your life with someone. You can't be afraid to argue. A relationship is difficult even when you have good communication. If you really love each other you'll be able to survive the arguments. But if you don't let each other know how you're feeling and discuss it, you're in trouble. For us, discussion sometimes leads to passionate arguments. That's just how we talk things through.

We don't see eye to eye on everything, no two people do. We're just very loud and passionate about it, but at least we both know where we stand. It makes me laugh when people say, "Well, they can't be in love because they fight" or, "Even if they love each other, because of the arguing it'll never work out." Hey, people who love each other fight. That's just life.

We've had to make a lot of adjustments and give things up, and we've worked things out.

17

A lot of the tension between us during our first extended trip to Europe and, in fact, most of our arguments had to do with being a gay couple. Actually, we had no problem with being gay when it was just the two of us.

In Amsterdam we didn't think twice about walking down the street arm in arm or holding hands. This was really the first time it felt comfortable for us. In Los Angeles, we worried about what people were thinking when we walked through our neighborhood holding hands. We still both had to get over our self-hate and some of our self-consciousness. But once we left L.A. and were removed from our everyday environment, it was easy for us not to care what people thought of us. And that turned out to be a good thing, because people didn't think twice about calling us faggots.

I don't know what we expected in Holland in terms of how they were going to treat us, but we'd heard that Dutch people were very tolerant. Well, there were people who were accepting, but there were plenty who weren't. It was trial by fire.

One time we were walking by a trendy hair salon as a couple

of women were on their way out and they tried to hit on us, and we just grabbed each other's hand and kept walking. Sure enough, they yelled "faggots" after us.

Another time, we were in Amsterdam at an Argentine steakhouse. We were sitting at a table talking, and two attractive women came over. One sat next to Rod and the other sat next to me. I said, "Can I help you?" They introduced themselves, and I said, "Can we have a little bit of privacy, please?" And one of them said, "Maybe you and your friend would like to have a party with us."

I thanked them and told them that we were a couple.

And they called us faggots.

No, they didn't call us faggots. They called us *fucking* faggots." And then they left. As we said, the Dutch love to tell people they are very accepting.

This sort of thing happened when we were home, as well. Bob and I were eating dinner at Hamburger Hamlet on Wilshire Boulevard in L.A., and our waitress was openly flirting with me.

I started getting really mad.

As dinner went on, her flirting increased, but I wasn't paying attention. All of a sudden Bob said, "Excuse me, ma'am, that's my husband you've been flirting with," and she kind of jumped up and said, "Oh, I had no idea. I'm so sorry." We had wonderful service the rest of the evening *and* free desserts.

Heterosexual men often say they don't have anything against gays, they just can't handle it when a gay man hits on them. We have to deal with that sort of thing every day, and we generally take it as a compliment. Heterosexual men should be flattered, because there will come a day when nobody of either sex will look their way.

I don't know what it is about restaurants, but we've had all kinds of things happen when we've been out to eat. We had a problem with a waitress in a coffee shop in Olympia.

Actually, she had a problem with us. She was very rude. About halfway through our meal, a woman we knew came into the restaurant and sat down two tables over. She worked at the local Safeway. She had seen us on television and had told us that she had gay friends and that the work we were doing was very important. Before she sat down, she waved to us.

The waitress, who didn't know that this woman knew us, said to her, "I've seen them on TV. They're faggots, and it makes me sick to my stomach to have to wait on those kind of people."

Our friend was angry and disgusted, and asked her why she would say something so terrible. And the waitress said, "Because they're sick people and that's what I was raised to believe." Our friend said. "Well, in that case, I was raised in the South, so why don't you get me a white waitress, because if I believed what I was raised with, I'd be disgusted having you handle my food." The waitress was shocked.

We didn't know that any of this happened until our friend came to our table after our meal and told us.

We left a very good tip and went out of our way to tell the waitress how wonderful the service was and that we looked forward to having her as our waitress many times.

It's ironic that any member of an oppressed minority would ever turn around and try to use their ignorance against other people based solely on their status. There's no place in our society for "nigger" jokes or "faggot" jokes. We should all be able to relate to discrimination and treat each other as human beings.

The worst and best incident happened at the end of the European tour, when we were back in Holland.

I was set to do a guest appearance at a big contest in Rotterdam. There was a promoter whom I'd had a knock-down, drag-out argument with earlier in the trip, and he was determined that there was going to be trouble at this event.

Before we got there, people were warning us that there would be trouble because this promoter had bought a few hundred tickets and was going to fill the place with his thugs, who didn't exactly like gay people. They warned us that maybe we didn't want to go because "We don't want to see anybody hurt you guys."

We knew we had to go, but we talked about what we could do to defuse the whole thing. So we decided that the best thing to do was for Bob to donate his entire fee to the local children's hospital. I told Bob, "You're going to be hated no matter how good you look up there, and I'm going to be hated with you. So let's just do what we'll feel good about and let it go."

The place was packed with a few thousand people, and as soon as I went out to do my routine lots of people started booing and calling me faggot. People were really angry.

This was a really tense situation for us because this was the first time we were facing a big, public event where we had to worry. I was standing on the side watching, and people were looking at me with daggers. It was hard to listen to what they were doing to Bob, yelling faggot and other names in Dutch and English, but he didn't pay any attention. He went through his whole routine and did it with dignity, and as he went on with his routine, ignoring the jeering, people quieted down.

At the end of the evening, when they gave Bob his check on stage, he went to the microphone to explain that he was donating his check to the children's hospital. Before he started talking, there were a few people still booing and calling him faggot. So he told them about the donation and then thanked the people of Holland for their wonderful hospitality. I was cracking up, laughing.

They were on their feet applauding me. And then I said, "Most of all I'd like to thank Rod for his love and support throughout this entire time. I don't know if he can ever know how much he means to me." That brought the house down and really touched the tolerance of the Dutch heart.

That was Bob's first really public statement. It was incredible. This was a couple of years before Bob came out publicly in a magazine interview. But I was actually kind of mad because I didn't want to be the focus of the attention. I felt awkward because I hadn't done anything. Bob had done it. He stood up there and took back his dignity and taught a lot of people important lessons in the process. It was wonderful and heroic.

I knew Rod wasn't really angry, but he let me know that he wasn't thrilled that I put the spotlight on him. I knew he was just feeling uncomfortable about it.

I was so proud that I couldn't stay angry, and I told Bob how moved I was, but I told him never to do that to me in public again, that it wasn't appropriate. In retrospect, it was perfectly appropriate, and deep down I was overjoyed that he had the courage to do it.

But it wasn't just other people giving us trouble that made this a difficult trip. We were also part of the problem because we still weren't completely comfortable being up-front about being gay and being a couple.

One of the early big hurdles we faced was introducing each other to friends and people we did business with.

Bob and Rod's first trip to Europe together,
in the Swiss Alps, 1986.

Shortly before we left for Europe, I laid down the law about how
we were going to handle it. We had this discussion while we
were on the way to Colorado to visit some of Rod's friends. I
told him, "We need to set some rules in our relationship or we're
going to lose each other. We have to treat each other with respect
all the time, which means we can't introduce each other as 'roommates' or 'friends' because that's not what we are."

I warned Bob that this was going to be really hard, and that I
didn't think we were ready, but I told him I'd try. Well, when
we got to Denver we went to meet my friend Tina, whom I went
to high school with. She was taking us out to lunch. When she
showed up she introduced herself, and I said, "This is my friend
Bob." I looked at Bob, and I could see the anger and hurt in
his face. I felt so terrible. I'd just turned the most important
relationship in my life into something mundane.

Lunch went very slowly. When we left, we got into a huge
fight. Bob said, "I don't know how you can do that to me. Am
I that worthless to you? Am I that unimportant?" All I could say
was that I was sorry. It wasn't as if I hadn't warned him it would
be hard.

Bob and Rod in Bavaria, outside Munich, 1988.

Friend? I wasn't just angry at Rod. I was angry at the world for putting us in this awkward situation every time we turned around. This kind of thing happened all the time at the gym. People would come up to me and say, "I don't know what your friend's name is . . ." and I was always saying, "He isn't my friend . . ." He wasn't. He was the most important person in my life. He was my boyfriend, the love of my life, not "my friend." Having to deal with that over and over again just wears you down over time.

Bob didn't understand how I could let him down like that. He told me it was very weak on my part, and I agreed with him, but he was very harsh about it. I don't think he really understood how difficult it was to be that honest until he was in the exact same position I'd been in. That happened a few weeks later when we had arrived in Holland, and Bob was doing an appearance at a competition in Amsterdam, and we were sitting in the front row watching. Erika Mes, a Dutch female professional bodybuilder, who's a great person, came up to Bob and said hello. Then she went to shake my hand and said, "Hi, I'm Erika." I looked at Bob and he said, "This is um, um . . ." and I could see in his face that he was going through everything I'd gone through with Tina. And he told me *I* had no courage. Finally he got the words out, "This is my friend Rod." Well, he really let me have it when I couldn't live up to our agreement, and I wasn't about to let him off the hook. I was furious.

It was worse than furious. He shut down and wouldn't talk. We had a three-hour trip that evening to a fishing village where we were going to live for the next month. And all he would say was yes or no.

Bob could have gotten me to talk if he'd have just said that he screwed up and was sorry. But he couldn't do that because he felt ashamed and his pride got in the way. All he could manage to say was, "What's the matter? I haven't done anything. What's going on with you? I don't understand."

I knew what I'd done was wrong, and I was angry at myself, but I turned my anger on Rod because he was so upset with me. When we got to our hotel, Rod said, "I'm leaving. I'm going back to America tomorrow." I begged him not to go. I told him I was sorry. I told him that I wouldn't do it again.

I may have been guilty of not realizing how difficult it was for Rod to be completely up-front, but I also don't think Rod realized how hard it was for *me* to introduce him as my boyfriend. Yes, I was head over heels in love with him, so on the one hand I couldn't care less what people thought of me. But on the other hand I was very nervous about how people would react once they knew I was gay. I'd come back to Europe to resurrect my career, and people were incredibly receptive. What if that all fell apart?

In retrospect, we were both holding each other to such impossible standards that it was miraculous that we made it through that time.

Bob and Rod's first photo together in a Laundromat in Lucerne, Switzerland.

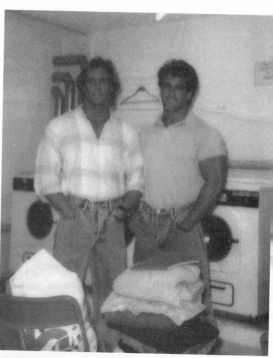

Bob and Rod in England, 1989.
Bob getting ready to compete in the English Grand Prix.
Rod took time off from work to come watch.

Later in the trip we had a revelation about how people perceived Bob and me as a couple. Bob was doing another guest appearance; this time there were 10,000 people in the audience. There were hundreds of people pressing in around Bob and me. We turned around and there was Erika Mes. She said hello and then told us, "I just wanted to tell you both that you make the most beautiful couple." That's when we realized that Erika and a lot of the people we knew didn't care. But *we* did. It wasn't people like Erika who were homophobic; *we* were homophobic. She didn't hate us. *We* hated ourselves. It was incredible when we realized that we had to stop assuming that everybody else had a problem with us.

We could see that we needed to take the attitude that we didn't care what other people thought. With that kind of attitude people generally are afraid to express their bigotry. And if they're not bigoted, then they're happy that you're being so forthright.

It amazes me when I think that Erika wouldn't have seen anything strange about me introducing Rod as my boyfriend. I was the one who thought it strange, who choked on the word and settled for one far more ambiguous.

After we ran into Erika, Bob signed photographs.

This was following my appearance. Rod and I were standing behind a table in the auditorium lobby and I was selling autographed 8 × 10s to a mob of fans. After I had signed and personalized a photo for a female fan, she said, "Can you sign this with love." I looked her in the eye and said, "Sorry, all my love is taken."

She looked over at me, and I smiled. She smiled back, shrugged her shoulders, and left.

This became a standard response all over the world as people asked for a photo signed, "Love . . ."

18

This first trip to Europe really transformed us. We went more from talking the talk to walking the walk. Every day we had to deal with the fact we were a gay couple, and by the end of the five months we were doing pretty well dealing one on one with people, whether it was checking into hotels and asking for one large bed or dealing with introductions.

One experience in particular planted the seed in our minds that one day we would need to take some responsibility for the next generation of gay young people.

What happened was that we had taken a couple of days off in Paris to do some sightseeing, which included a visit to the Eiffel Tower. We were on our way down from the top in the elevator, and there was a sixteen-year-old young man standing across from us, with his parents standing behind him. We could tell right away that he was gay. His eyes were like mirrors, and we both recognized the pain.

There were just the five of us in the elevator. Bob and I were holding hands, and we could see the young man looking at our hands, and a faint smile came over his face. He was clearly taking delight in seeing two men who were holding hands. I'm sure that deep down he was saying to himself, "Oh, there's hope. There's a possibility that I can have a life." When I was that age I didn't know there was any possibility for me to grow up and find someone to love in the way I love Bob.

It was obvious to anyone who saw us together that we were in love, including this kid. We were in the first blush of love. We couldn't keep our hands off each other, so we held hands everywhere, including in that elevator.

That day we also had on similar coats. When we were first together, when one of us bought an article of clothing, the other wanted the same thing. We have very similar taste. So we found these two checkered coats. They were different colors but otherwise identical. We liked being tied together in that way. I think it was part of our delayed adolescence. It was deep, sincere love and puppy love at the same time. We couldn't pass little folded notes to each other across a classroom or wear each other's "goin' steady" bracelets, but we could hold hands and wear matching or similar clothes.

So everyone in that elevator knew we were a couple. The sad thing was that the teenager who was looking at us smiled for only a few seconds. Then you could see a look of terror spread across his face because he was afraid that his parents might have noticed that he was looking at us. His parents saw us holding hands, but they pretended not to notice.

To me this kid looked like a scared rabbit in the middle of a freeway with a semi bearing down on top of him. It made me so sad because I could remember those feelings of fear when I was young.

You could see the sadness on his face. It was just one emotion after another across his face as we descended to the bottom of the tower. We got off the elevator and went toward the

Metro, and the young man and his parents went in another direction.

As we walked to the subway, I said to Bob, "Do you remember being that age, and can you imagine how different your life would have been if you could have seen a visible gay couple holding hands like any other couple in love?" Bob told me that he couldn't imagine, and that it would have changed his life.

I think that for both of us, seeing something as simple as a gay couple holding hands would have saved us from doing a lot of crazy things. And we both agreed that we wanted to do something that could reach young people, but at the time we didn't know what that would be.

What really hit us was that we saw ourselves in that young man and couldn't help wondering what it would have been like for us to be in his shoes, with our parents behind us, looking at two men holding hands. Just to have seen that would have been monumental.

So this trip to Europe had a big impact on us. And although it would be another couple of years before we came out in the media, we discovered that we were strong enough to survive the constant, day-to-day challenges, and that we could use some of that strength to help other people, particularly young people, come through it.

Despite all of the difficulties we faced in Europe, and probably because of them, we came back a much stronger couple. Our relationship had weathered a lot. The infatuation was behind us, and we loved each other more than ever.

19

We got back from Europe in time to spend our first Christmas together at home in Los Angeles, and it was wonderful.

Well, it was wonderful until two days before Christmas when Rod told me he was going to dinner with his friend Jill. I said, "Please don't. I want to spend time with you." But he insisted on going out, and we started arguing.

He wouldn't let me out the door. I told him he had to give me my freedom, that I needed my space. I said, "Why don't you go live with your father for a year and you'll come back begging." And he told me to go live with my mother for a year.

Something wasn't right about this argument. I was used to Rod getting mad over things that I thought were irrelevant, but this wasn't like our other fights, so I got suspicious.

We'd been talking about getting a dog for a while, and I thought he was probably going out to pick up the puppy, so I let him go, but I didn't say anything. I thought it was curious, though, that he wore my coat to go out.

I wanted the puppy to smell Bob before he actually met him.

A few hours passed, and I saw our Jeep pull up. Rod got out of the car, and I could see there was something under his coat. So I ran out to the elevator and went down to meet him. We lived on the fifth floor of the Trianon, a wonderful gothic apartment house, complete with turrets, that Mary Pickford had built for many of her retired actor friends.

When the elevator door opened, Bob jumped out and said, "Give her to me. Where is she? Where is she?" I was playing dumb, but it was a little hard to pretend that there was nothing moving under my coat. Sam was right underneath my neck. So I let her out and handed her to Bob. He was so proud of himself for figuring it out, but I was pissed that he ruined the surprise.

It was a great Christmas. We had a little tree and bought each other all kinds of presents. Rod's mom even sent some gifts for me.

We'd made it through nearly a year together and were very much in love. After months on the road, we were finally home.

20

After we came home from Europe we settled into a regular life, paying the rent, planning the future, and facing the reality of our life together. Things became more realistic at that point. We were past our first year, which was, on balance, magical. For a while we just lived a commonplace life. Bob continued to train and compete and do exhibitions in the U.S. and Europe. And I continued modeling.

Everybody wants to believe that real love is going to be the birds and the bees and singing all the time, that life will be perfect. And during those first years we both discovered that neither of us was perfect, and that was a letdown.

I found that Rod was very stubborn. When he held an opinion, even if I knew he was wrong, I sometimes wouldn't state mine because I didn't want to start a fight.

And that caused fights, because I wanted Bob to stand up for what he believed in. But Bob didn't want to disagree. He wanted us to see eye to eye on everything and that was impossible. I'm very opinionated and willing to fight for what I believe in, and I want Bob to fight for what he believes in.

But I didn't want to fight all the time.

It was hard for Bob to accept that we could agree to disagree, but the fact is that we didn't agree on some things. But he hated conflict and wanted agreement on everything.

Not on everything.

On most things. It was very rare when Bob would actually stand up to me, except when we had five-hour-long, intense political discussions.

In every other realm, I'm very accustomed to standing up to people. I couldn't do it with Rod, because I felt vulnerable with him. I was afraid that if I disagreed with him I'd lose him. Fortunately we really do see the world in the same way, so there isn't a lot to disagree about. If there had been, I would have lost my mind because I'm a very opinionated person also. I couldn't have suppressed my differing opinion all the time and kept my sanity.

At first, it used to drive me nuts. I'd ask Bob what he thought about something, and he'd give his opinion. Then I'd state my opinion, which was occasionally different from his, and he'd say, "Okay, I agree with you." I'd get really mad and say, "What do you really believe? Do you believe what I said or do you believe what you said?" He thought he was keeping the peace by agreeing, but instead he made things more difficult.

Granted, I may have gone overboard trying to keep the peace. But I felt that Rod drove every disagreement over the top. He was always threatening to leave and I would have to beg him to stay. But if I was ever justifiably mad and said I was leaving, he would say, "Okay, there's the door." It made me feel that he had no commitment to me.

Fortunately our fights are more calm now. They don't have

the same life-and-death tone to them. And when Rod threatens to leave now, I know it's a part of the intense love we have for each other.

Now that we have a history, there's more predictability. We spend so much time together that it's perfectly natural for us to want to get away for the day or for a two-hour drive. I don't think either of us is threatened by that anymore.

One of the things we continued to argue about over the next couple of years was when I was going to come out publicly. Rod was pressing me to do it, but I was afraid of what would happen. Even though I wasn't happy being closeted, I had the comet by its tail at this point. Professionally I was having my best year.

But I was tired of being Bob's dirty little secret. It was no secret in his profession that he was gay and that I was his lover, but whenever Bob was interviewed, I was completely invisible.

We were together about three years when I was finally getting close to doing a coming-out interview with one of the body-building magazines. I wasn't exactly eager to do it, especially when my colleagues were urging me not to. They thought I should just be quiet about it, and said, "It's nobody's business. Besides, you can't change the world."

I was conflicted because I was miserable keeping secrets, and deep down I thought I had a responsibility to change the world and maybe could use my position as a successful professional athlete to make a positive difference. And I couldn't lie anymore because I was hurting myself and the love of my life.

But before I could make up my own mind on this, we got a call from a friend that *Body Power*, a top bodybuilding maga-zine in England, had published an article in which I was identi-fied as gay. We shouldn't have been surprised because Rod and I had traveled on three different tours of Europe for our work. So we wound up being seen as a couple everywhere.

Diane Bennett, the editor of *Body Power*, met Rod on one of these trips. We'd known each other for years, and after meeting Rod she told me how nice it was to see that I was happy.

As soon as I heard about the article I called Diane and asked her what was up. She said it was a very simple article about courageous people in sports, people who had overcome adversity. It had a photograph of the first black Mr. America, and there was a photo of me. She said that the caption identified me and said that I had openly acknowledged my homosexuality and was still thriving in the sport. That was the first time it had ever been printed that I was gay.

I freaked. First of all, I felt she had no right to do it without at least asking Bob if it was okay or making him aware, because publishing that information could potentially have such a big impact on his career. Second, it was now out of our control when Bob came out in the U.S., because if he didn't do it soon, someone else would publish something about it.

I was so upset. I felt violated. Even though I'd been planning to come out, I wasn't ready. I wanted this to be my decision, and instead it was made for me. I was also hurt on a personal level because Diane knew what the stakes were for me, and she should have talked to me first. But she and her husband, Wag, had seen how comfortable I had become with my sexuality since I had been with Rod, and they just assumed it was okay.

An additional concern was that I didn't want this information to dribble out. I wanted to make a clear statement about the two of us, and I was afraid the article in *Body Power* would lessen the impact of whatever I said in the U.S. press.

I had to make the best of things because I couldn't change anything. I had an interview coming up with *Ironman* maga-

Bob and Rod on the first cover *ever* of an openly gay couple on a sports magazine—published in England. Our first magazine cover together, too.

zine, and I decided that I would use that interview as my opportunity to come out. It was a chance to speak for myself before somebody got hold of the information and beat me to the punch.

Ironman is a no-nonsense bodybuilding magazine—no fluff, a real trainer's publication. I was interviewed by Lonnie Teper on a bench outside World Gym, where Rod and I worked out. It was a typical, sunny L.A. day. Lonnie asked me questions about my training, how I thought I was going to do in the Arnold Classic, those sorts of things.

At the end of the interview, Lonnie turned off his tape recorder, and I said, "I want to do a coming-out interview." He said, "Great, great. Let me just turn on my tape recorder." I said, "No, wait. I'm scared, and I've got to talk to Rod to make sure that it's okay because it affects both of us." That wasn't quite the truth, because Rod and I had talked endlessly about me doing a coming-out interview, but I needed more time to think. So I told Lonnie that I'd let him know when I was ready.

I waited at the front desk of the gym for Rod to finish working out, and then we went to our Jeep. Rod asked me what the interview was about, and I told him it was just a standard bodybuilding interview. He was silent, dead quiet, all the way home. I kept looking over at him trying to start a conversation, but he wouldn't talk to me. I knew what was going on. We had talked so many times about me being honest and up-front about our relationship, and here was my opportunity to do that and I didn't. He didn't know that I'd talked with Lonnie about doing it in the future. But that wouldn't have mattered, because Rod felt that I'd already waited too long, and with the news already out in England, I was out of time.

We'd been talking about this forever, and I had run out of patience. I knew it had to be Bob's decision and that he had to do it when he was ready, but this affected both of us. It's not that Bob was actively lying in that interview or all the others he did, but it was the sin of omission. He just happened not to

mention anything about his personal life, including the relationship that he had told me was the most important thing in his
life. I was his lover. He told me he couldn't live without me, yet
he pretended that I was no more important than a roommate,
which made me feel less than worthless.

I told Bob, "I love you, but I can't live like this anymore. I'm
leaving. I love you too much for you to pretend that I don't exist.
If we're going to put success, fame, and money above our love
for each other, then this love obviously isn't that important."
Then I started to cry and told Bob that I loved myself too much
to let him hurt me the way he had, that he couldn't say, "You're
the most important thing in the world to me" and then pretend
I didn't exist. I couldn't stand it anymore. The whole thing made
me feel that our relationship was something sick, something to
hide. What was so terrible that he couldn't talk about it?

There was no question that Rod was—and is—the most important person in my life, and if I'd been heterosexual I
wouldn't have hesitated to talk about my lover or spouse,
especially because I was so in love. But I was afraid. I'd just
come back to competing professionally, and I knew that it was
going to be a very hard road once I came out. Also, I'd hidden
my "private life" for so long that talking in an interview about
Rod was a huge line for me to cross. Up until this time, the
people who wrote about me played right into it. Everyone in
the press knew what my "private life" was, but they were happy
to ignore it. No one ever even asked me about it.

This wasn't something I got upset about overnight. This had
been building for a long time, and we'd talked about it endlessly.
So when Bob passed up this opportunity, I'd just had it. It was
the last straw. I loved this man, but I didn't want to live a lie
any longer. I told Bob that I couldn't allow us to keep doing this
to each other, playing this game of pretending we weren't a
couple and criticizing other gay couples for doing the same thing
we were doing. I couldn't handle the hypocrisy anymore.

Bob and Rod on the cover of *The Advocate*.

I started crying and asked Rod to please forgive me, to please stay. I tried to explain to him that I was scared, that I was afraid of jeopardizing my comeback and my entire future. At this point I was reaching the height of my professional career.

I told Bob that he needed to make a decision, and that I was making the decision that was right for me. I said, "I can't live like this. I'm not telling you what you have to do. I just know that I'm miserable and the shame is destroying me."

I didn't exactly like it either. I was miserable having to lie by omission about my life and about my love for Rod. So now I had the opportunity to remedy it all the way around.

I told Bob that I'd give him some time, and I also warned him about what could happen, that there was a 90 percent chance that if we went through with coming out we'd both be pumping gas next week in Montana. I said, "Can you live with that?"

Of course I could live with that. No matter what the outcome, I knew I had to do it. So I called Lonnie and told him I wanted to set up an appointment. During the conversation I also explained to him that I didn't want the article to focus on politics, that this had to be a piece about us as human beings.

We went over to Lonnie's house the next day, and he did the interview. I talked about our lives, how I'd been taught to hate myself because I'm gay, and why I hadn't come forward before. I talked about my life with Rod and our love for one another.

When we saw the final draft, it was exactly what we wanted it to be.

Then we sat back and waited for it to be published.

Two weeks later, when I competed in the Arnold Classic, word had already begun to spread among insiders that the interview had taken place.

One of the judges said to us, "So I hear you guys have a surprise coming." I said, "If you know about it, I guess it's not all that surprising, especially since you've known me for several years."

He said that a lot of people didn't think what we were doing was very smart, so I told him to worry about his life and we'd worry about ours.

Within a week of the article's publication, we went to our post office box and there was a notice to pick up a package. It was two mailbags full of letters, and that was only the beginning. Within a month we got 10,000 letters. We tried to play it down because we didn't think anyone would believe us.

Almost all the letters were positive, with people writing that they thought what we did was wonderful and courageous. We didn't get letters from anti-gay religious people, although we did get a few of their little booklets. Some of the letters we got from gay people were odd. They'd start by saying what a wonderful thing we did and end by saying that we were going to have to pay for being so public. A few of them were even negative. They said, "If you keep telling the world that there are gay people, you're going to make things terrible for us. If you wind up on the street, starving to death, you deserve it because you should have been quiet, and what did you expect?"

I really wonder where that sentiment comes from. I think part of it has to do with self-hate. Or because these people aren't in a position to do it, then why should we be able to do it? And if we do it, of course we'll be punished for "breaking the rules." I know that some of these people were very upset at us for making waves.

At first we thought we could answer all the mail, but we could barely keep up with reading each letter. When we moved to Washington a while later, we took 40,000 letters with us, and I had in my mind that I was going to answer each and every one of them. There was a follow-up article with Bob in *Ironman* a year later; with the publicity that followed, we got another 40,000 letters.

We eventually wrote a letter to the editor of *Ironman* thanking the people who wrote, explaining that we couldn't answer each individual letter personally.

We did answer some of the letters, especially the ones from young people. But it would have been a full-time job to answer all the letters, and we had to pay the mortgage.

The letters were the fun part. But then we had a *National Enquirer* photographer sneaking around, the phone never stopped ringing, and we found people peeking in our windows. Most of that happened after we got married. That's when all hell broke loose. Apparently it wasn't as big a deal when a bodybuilder came out of the closet, but two guys getting married, especially a professional athlete and model, that really got people going.

Once Bob and I had been interviewed for *Ironman*, we felt free to go ahead with getting married. For a long time I'd said that I wouldn't get married if we had to be at all secret about it. This was supposed to be a celebration of our love, not something to be ashamed about. Neither of us wanted to worry about a photographer or a reporter showing up uninvited. Now that we had nothing to lose, we quickly went ahead with plans. The way it worked out, the magazine article came out a couple of months before the wedding, which we set for July 22, 1989.

21

Rod and I wanted to be married because in our culture that's the highest level of public and private commitment we could make to one another. We wanted to get married in a church and before God—whatever God is—because we both have deep spiritual beliefs. And we wanted to be married in front of our friends because we wanted them there to witness us making an important statement of commitment.

I was raised a mainline Christian with Southern Baptist overtones and Rod was raised a Lutheran. Neither of us had been active in organized religion for some time because of all the bigotry against gay people. So we knew we wanted to find a minister from a denomination other than the ones we grew up in. We had read about the Unitarian Church in a book called *In Search of Gay America* and learned that the Unitarians have been generally welcoming to gay and lesbian people.

Bob was in England on a seminar tour when I first started calling around to find a Unitarian minister who would perform our wedding. The first one I talked to made absolutely clear that he would be doing a "union" ceremony, not a marriage, and that two men couldn't get married. He said, "It's not the same thing.

LET THIS BE OUR DESTINY
TO LOVE, TO LIVE
TO BEGIN EACH NEW DAY TOGETHER
TO SHARE OUR LIVES FOREVER

RODNEY LYNN JACKSON
AND
ROBERT CLARK PARIS
WILL BE JOINED IN MARRIAGE
ON SATURDAY, THE TWENTY-SECOND OF JULY
NINETEEN HUNDRED AND EIGHTY-NINE
AT ELEVEN O'CLOCK IN THE MORNING
UNITARIAN COMMUNITY CHURCH
1260 EIGHTEENTH STREET
SANTA MONICA, CALIFORNIA
REVEREND ERNEST D. PIPES, JR.

RECEPTION TO FOLLOW

Wedding invitation.

A marriage is for procreating children." Even though I know a church can't legally marry gay people, I felt he was treating me like a second-class citizen, so I told him he sounded like a bigot. He said that he had many gay people in his ministry, but to me that didn't mean anything because he was still setting up a relationship hierarchy in which my relationship to Bob was second-class. So I kept looking.

At the next church I called the secretary said they had many gay members. Then I asked if they were treated like everyone else, and she said, "Of course." She was really open with me and suggested I speak with the minister, Ernie Pipes.

I called the minister and told him our situation, and he said that he wanted to meet with us. He explained that he didn't marry anybody until he had a chance to sit down and talk with them.

I got back a week later, and we went in to meet with Reverend Pipes. He had all kinds of awards on the wall of his office for his civil rights work, so we knew we'd come to the right place. We also had the same sense of humor, so we really hit it off with him.

Reverend Pipes told us that he wanted to meet with us three or four times for about an hour each time to talk about why we wanted to get married and how we envisioned our relationship. We explained to him that we wanted to get married because we loved each other and wanted to spend our lives together. And that while we weren't a traditional heterosexual couple, we still wanted to participate in some of the traditions we'd both grown up with.

He also asked us about our spiritual beliefs. We told him that while neither of us felt welcome in our denominations because we're gay, we were very spiritual people. We also explained that one of the biggest problems we had with our spirituality was that we couldn't find people who shared our concept of what God is. Reverend Pipes explained to us that the Unitarian Church, a mainline Christian denomination, is humanistically oriented, and they let people form their own beliefs.

Reverend Pipes made a point of asking us if we understood that we would invariably face some hard challenges in life. We'd already been together for over three years, so we knew that everything wasn't going to be perfect.

So many young couples don't understand that there will inevitably be illness and eventually death to deal with. He said to us, "You can be in love with somebody, but if you don't want to tow the long road, don't bother getting married."

One of the things he asked us was how we resolved our differences. We told him that we fought like cats and dogs, but that we always come to a resolution. He told us that many people say it's best to resolve things before you go to bed, not to let the sun set on your problems. And then he asked if we did that. I said, "No," and explained that there are some problems that are too big for the sun, and that we wait for the sun to go back up again. He laughed and said, "Okay, as long as you both understand that and find that it works for you."

Reverend Pipes really emphasized how difficult it was going to be, that being married meant taking care of each other through the good times and the bad. I don't think he was trying to discourage us, but he wanted to be sure that we knew what we were committing to, that marriage wasn't to be taken lightly. We explained to him that this was a very serious decision for us, that we weren't just another number in each other's long list of men, that there was not going to be another true love for either of us. This was it.

By the end of our third meeting, when Reverend Pipes was convinced that this was what we wanted and that we understood what we were doing, we began to discuss the ceremony itself. The Reverend explained that the wedding ceremony was basically a piece of theater and that our role was to create a wonderful event for ourselves and the invited guests. The more wonderful the event, the more memorable it would be.

We talked about the standard Unitarian wedding ceremony, and then the Reverend asked us if we wanted a traditional ceremony or if we wanted to create something on our own. We told him that we wanted a traditional ceremony, including the vows and the part where you say, "You can kiss each other now." We also told him that we wanted to write something to each other that we would read during the wedding, and we told him that we wanted to exchange rings, and that we'd already bought our rings three years earlier, knowing that we would want to get married one day.

We were in Lucerne, Switzerland, and stopped to look in the window of a jeweler. These wedding bands caught our eye, so we went in to look at them. They were kind of rough, different from the usual wedding band. They were solid platinum, and one had a band of gold overlay three quarters of the way around, and the other had a gold overlay one quarter of the way around. Together they made two complete circles with two precious metals.

At first the young clerk was kind of confused. I spoke enough German to keep us out of trouble, and she spoke enough English to get herself *in* trouble.

She tried to explain to us that these were wedding rings.

And I said, "Yes, these are wedding rings, and we want to be fitted for them." At this point, an older woman who was very prim, and very Swiss, came out from the back to see what the problem was. We explained what we wanted, and she said that there was no problem at all and proceeded to take our ring measurements.

On the inside of my ring we had inscribed, "Forever, Bob." And on the inside of Bob's ring it says, "Forever, Rod." The young clerk just wrote it all down and never really seemed to understand what was going on and what our relationship was to each other.

I think she figured that she had just sold an extraordinary set of friendship rings. So we picked up the rings a few weeks later and put them in a box to save them for our wedding day.

With the ceremony arranged, we chose our wedding day, July 22, 1989, and started planning the reception and working on the invitations.

We went to the PIP printer on Sunset Boulevard, just above West Hollywood, and we talked to the guy we'd done a lot of business with in the past. He was gay, and when we said that we wanted to look at the books of wedding invitations, he was charmed. We asked to see something that wasn't gaudy, with clean lines, and in the colors of our wedding, which were salmon, silver, and ivory.

We picked out off-ivory stationery, with salmon and silver-lined envelopes. It was pretty standard, with the date and time.

We ordered 300 invitations because we decided that we would send them to our entire families, from our grandparents on down to second cousins. I wanted every single person in my family to know I was gay so that the next time they told a faggot joke they'd have to own part of it.

Both of our parents had begged us for years not to come out to our grandparents. But we told them that they were going to find out whether or not we sent them invitations to the wedding. We wanted to do it clean, so we sent them invitations.

We also sent invitations to everyone we knew from business, including people like Arnold Schwarzenneger, Maria Shriver, Lou Ferrigno and his wife, Carla, and Joe Weider. We also sent several invitations to people we knew and worked with in the press. This event was for us; we had no idea it would become so political. This wedding invitation left no doubt what our relationship was. And that's how we wanted it, totally up-front.

We included with the invitation the usual things, like the RSVP card and return envelope. We also sent our family photo, which had been published in the *Ironman* article in which I came out. It's the one with Rod sitting in a chair and me standing behind him with Barney, our bird, on my arm. Sam, one of our dogs, was also in the photo. We sent it all out and waited for the returns to come in.

Two days after we mailed the invitations, we walked into the gym and there was a buzz. People couldn't believe we were crazy enough or had the courage to do this.

I overheard a couple of the old-timers at the gym kind of jokingly nudge each other and say, "Yeah, will you marry me?" We heard all kinds of things, but the one that I think was perfect came from a guy I know who's a bodybuilding writer. He was on the telephone with Joe Weider and asked him what he thought of the "Bob and Rod situation." And Weider said, "They're either very smart or very stupid."

Over the next couple of weeks, people got really strange about the whole thing, even some of our friends. People were afraid to show up because they were worried about what people would think if they came to the wedding of two men. We got so fed up that we told several people that we didn't care if they came. We said, "You got an invitation. You're a part of our life. You're welcome to come, but if you have a problem with it, please stay away."

We couldn't believe some of the things people said. One of the bodybuilding judges we invited told us he didn't know what to expect at a gay wedding since he hadn't ever attended one. That was perfectly reasonable, but then he asked if somebody was going to wear a dress. I looked at him and said, "Sure, Art, you can wear a dress. We won't mind."

Mostly we didn't hear things directly. People usually sent emissaries to convey their concern. Or friends would tell us that someone who had been invited said blah, blah, blah, and that they told them they were being stupid.

There were some people we knew wouldn't attend, but we sent them invitations anyway, like Arnold and Maria. We never heard anything from them. Given his political affiliations, he couldn't have come even if he wanted to. From what I heard, a few people from the gym who couldn't make up their minds called Arnold to ask him what he thought they should do. I was told he said, "Look, grow up. Do you like these guys? If you do, go."

It amazes me that these adults couldn't even make a decision on their own. They had to call Arnold to make sure he wouldn't be mad at them before they made their own decision. It shows me how paralyzed society is when it comes to homosexual issues.

Joe Gold, the guy who owned the gym where we worked out, who has been very good to me over the years, gave his invitation to one of the assistants at the gym. He told her to deal with it, somehow. She called me and didn't know what to do. I told her that I really didn't care what Joe did, that if he didn't want to be there, he shouldn't come. I told her that she might point out to him that if I was marrying a woman, he'd be there with bells on. Then she asked if *she* could come with him and I told her she could come with or without him.

This started to happen a lot—people who hadn't been invited to the wedding letting us know that they wanted to come. They wanted to show their support or they were just curious.

For example, we got a call from a friend who said, "So and so wants a ticket for himself and his girlfriend." They told him that they wanted to show their support for us by coming to the wedding, but at the same time we knew they wanted to be part of what was quickly becoming the hottest event in town that summer.

They wanted "tickets" as if this were a prizefight at the Garden.

I heard the conversation Bob was having on the phone with our friend and I went over the top. I was yelling in the background that our wedding wasn't some kind of spectacle. Our friend could hear everything I was saying, so Bob didn't have to do a lot of explaining. Bob just said that we weren't giving out tickets to the event because there were no tickets, just invitations, and we only invited people we knew. It's not that we didn't appreciate their support, but we didn't know these people. The phone rang and rang and rang.

Really, it was hilarious that this turned into an event that people felt they had to be a part of.

Unfortunately, for the most part our families didn't feel the same way. No one from either side of the family attended. We didn't even get the RSVP cards back from everyone. It was heartbreaking.

In defense of my brother, he did want to come but couldn't afford the trip. He also got caught in the middle of a family quarrel over whether or not to go, so even if he'd had the money, I'm not sure he would have made it. And both my sisters wanted to come, but they also couldn't afford the trip. They returned the RSVP cards and wrote, "We can't come, but we're with you. Love . . ." So they were trying.

I heard from my Aunt Kate and Uncle Larry, who sent the card back. My grandparents also returned the RSVP card. One of the hardest things for me was that my mother didn't call until two weeks after she got the invitation, and then I had to bring it up. I said, "Don't you have anything to say about it?" She said, "Oh, I don't know what you're talking about." Then we got into it and I asked her if she was coming, and she said that she was really busy at work and money was tight, so she couldn't come. That was one of the worst things she ever did to me. It made me feel awful and worthless.

I confronted my mother with the fact that she had recently gone to my brother's wedding and never mentioned that she had money problems. Finally, she said she'd try to be there. But by then I was so angry and so hurt that I told her I didn't want her there if she couldn't come and celebrate our wedding for what it was. I said, "It's a wedding, not a funeral. If you feel that ambivalent about it, you don't need to come." I hung up on her and didn't talk to her for several months.

This was such a happy time in my life, and I wasn't going to let my mother spoil it because she couldn't get past her homophobia. She's come a long way since that time, but I can't say that it was easy to forgive her for not being there.

When I first talked to my mother about the wedding, she said she'd try to make it. But then her brother must have gotten hold of her because she wrote me a letter that sounded very similar in tone to the one I received from him a day later.

My mother said she wasn't going to attend and then referred to the *Ironman* interview, which had come out a few weeks before. She said it was full of shit, and how dare I hurt my parents and cut down my grandparents after everything they'd done for me. I didn't even mention my grandparents in the interview. She ended by writing, "Neither I nor any member of this family will be attending your 'wedding.' "

I sent my mother's letter back to her along with a letter that wasn't extraordinarily nice, but it wasn't as mean as I wanted it to be because Rod convinced me to tone it down. So I said, "I feel sorry for you that you would do this to your own child, and I pray that someday you'll discover what it means to be compassionate."

The next day I got my uncle's letter. He'd been married and divorced three times, and I knew he had been a terrible parent, given how frequent a topic of conversation this was in our family. He's a born-again Christian and a total hypocrite. He wrote a fire-and-brimstone letter, saying that I was going to kill his parents, that I didn't deserve all the tears that his mother was shedding over me, that I was perverting my nephews' morals, that Rod had obviously twisted my mind, and that I should burn in hell. And, oh, "P.S. We love you. We just hate your sin."

My uncle just about blamed me for the destruction of the entire Western world. It was a horrible, horrible letter. It made me furious. I wrote across it in dark-yellow marker, "Screw you, bigot. Who the hell are you, anyway?" And I folded up the letter, put it in an envelope, and sent it back to him. It felt good to send the letter back, but it still haunts me to this day. I could never imagine being as evil as he was to me in that letter.

One of the ironies here is that this is a man who, if not for the changes in his church in the past thirty years, would have been condemned to rot in hell because he divorced and remarried. But at least he could take comfort in the fact he wasn't queer like his nephew.

My Aunt Sharon came through for me even though she couldn't come to the wedding. She called and said, "I just wanted to tell you that we love you. We can't make it out, but I want you to know that we'll be there in spirit. I hope it's a beautiful day." We talked for a while and I told her that I loved her. She said, "I've always known you were different, even though I didn't know how. But I love and respect you. If this is who you are and you want to get married, I think that's fantastic." She was there for me from the beginning, and she never disappointed me.

You would think everyone in our families would have been as happy as Rod's aunt that we wanted to include them in our lives.

It's ironic that I was raised by my family to be honest, especially by my Mam-mas and Pap-pas, who espoused strong religious and moral beliefs. To them, honesty was everything. When I finally had the courage to be honest with my family, their attitude was, "Why couldn't you just continue to lie? We don't want to know the truth." The truth was simply that Rod and I had found each other, fallen in love, and wanted to spend the rest of our lives together. What was so horrible about that?

Some of our family members did such hurtful things to us. One person who disappointed me was my Aunt Margaret, who's a year younger than I am. We'd been very close. I even sang at her wedding. After she got the invitation, she called and said, "I love you, and I'm glad you're back in my life." Before she got the invitation, she didn't know that I was gay, so she said that the invitation solved a mystery for her. She said, "I couldn't figure out why you left here so abruptly and why you've been so distant. Now I understand. I'm really going to try to make it out to the wedding. I'll give you a call."

My Aunt Margaret never called back, and she didn't come to the wedding. I suspect my mother and my grandparents played a part in her decision. It really hurt me that she wasn't strong enough to decide on her own. It made me sad because I thought I'd been there for her when she needed me. I never judged her on the things she did, or on who she was, and there were times I certainly could have. I loved her no matter what, but I was disappointed. She could at least have called back. But I guess she was getting a lot of pressure and didn't know which way to spit.

With my Mam-ma Paris, it would have been better if I hadn't heard anything from her. She returned the entire invitation to us, stuffed crudely into an envelope. Across the envelope was scrawled in her handwriting, "We don't know why you've chosen to hurt us, but you're going to burn in hell. May God help you." These were the grandparents who turned against me when I left home for California as a young man. At that time, my father and I parted on very bad terms, and he was bad-mouthing me to them. They took his side and made me a nonentity and family pariah. Then when I started winning world championships and wound up on the covers of magazines, I was suddenly a hero. Now all of a sudden I'm going to burn in hell. I haven't even got a quarter of an ounce of feeling for them anymore.

I was going to keep the letter for evidence later to show the rest of the family what they'd written, but Rod convinced me not to keep it. He didn't want me going over it again and again and getting upset. So I threw it in the garbage.

After the wedding, my Mam-ma Clark wrote a card and said, "Obviously you've made this choice and if I could have changed you I would have. We can't be there for you physically or emotionally. But we love you and pray for you." It wasn't evil, but it was still filled with the limitations of their religious bigotry.

Despite how hurtful this all was, by the time our wedding day came nobody was missed. There was no sadness about somebody not being there, because we realized at that point that they had missed something, but we hadn't missed anything. But I'm getting ahead of things, because before we could have the wedding, we had to finish planning the event.

A friend of ours offered to help us put together the reception. Michele worked for the City of Santa Monica promoting the city as a business and tourist destination. One afternoon she came up to us in the gym and asked, "Are you guys going to be doing your reception around here?"

We said yes, although we didn't yet have definite plans. And she said, "I think it's great that you are doing it. We've all noticed how in love you've been for years, and I'd love to help you with your plans, because God knows, two men don't know how to plan a wedding." We started laughing, because she was right about that. We were having a really hard time figuring out what to do.

So Michele did some research and put together a list of restaurants for us to choose from. She tested food, talked to caterers, and then looked for a hotel for the wedding night.

Michele asked us to come look at the restaurant she liked the best. It was a place on the water in Marina Del Ray called Shanghai Reds. It had a nice function room with a view of the water. We met with the manager, who was very, very nice. We talked about the menu and the wine, and made all the arrangements. They dealt with us as they would any other couple.

Rod found a Hungarian baker with a small shop in Pacific Palisades to do the wedding cake. We ordered a very simple white cake with raspberry inlay, and a complete white-chocolate wrap around the cake. It had three layers held up by solid white-chocolate columns. And it was topped with roses, surrounded by white chocolate leaves.

We joked about putting two grooms on top of the cake, but that was taking tradition a little too far. The roses were just fine.

Grooms on top of the cake seemed a bit too Capra-esque to both of us. It was silly enough that we were both going to be in monkey suits for the day.

We went to a tux rental place to get the clothes for the wedding. We wanted something formal but summery.

If it had been up to me I probably would have chosen black tie.

I didn't want to do that, so Michele, who came with us, suggested we go with black pants and white dinner jackets, which was both formal and informal. So in the end we settled on white jackets, black pants, salmon cummerbunds, bow ties . . .

. . . and black cowboy boots.

The ceremony was set to take place at Reverend Pipe's church. It's a California bungalow-style building in Santa Monica just off Wilshire Boulevard.

One of the things we had to figure out was where we would come into the church. We didn't want to come down the aisle for a couple of reasons. First we didn't want people to be confused that if one or the other of us came down the aisle that the one who came down the aisle was the bride and the one at the altar was the husband. Or even if we both came down the aisle it still might have confused people. Besides, there was nobody at the wedding, such as our parents, to escort us down the aisle.

I joked that we could hook up a trapeze to the ceiling on either side of the room and swing in. Reverend Pipes thought that was a pretty jolly idea, but we decided to walk in simultaneously through doors on either side of the altar.

22

The days before the wedding were just a blur, with friends arriving from all over the place. Our apartment was full of people for days. We loved it, but we wished we'd had more time to visit with everybody. The night before the wedding, we had a "bachelor shower." Our friend Jill came up with the idea in place of having a bachelor party, which we weren't interested in. For one thing, we weren't interested in all the typical macho stuff. Second, we had two grooms, not a bride and a groom. So Jill said, "Let's do something that's non-gender specific and call it a 'bachelor shower.'"

In the end we decided to call it a "bash" for short—that's a combination of *bach*elor and *sh*ower.

Instead of invitations, since Jill was a paralegal she decided to be clever and print up subpoenas.

A few of our friends got a little scared and sent them back without opening them, because they were afraid they were real.

Jill invited a lot of our friends who lived in town and friends

Bob and Rod at their bachelor shower ("Bash").

who had already arrived from out of town for the wedding. About sixty people were there.

Jill's sister and brother-in-law hosted the party at their home, which was just down the street from the Playboy Mansion.

People brought all kinds of gifts, including some dirty little gifts that you'd expect people to give at a shower. Someone gave us matching brassieres. Another friend gave us Playboy garters. And there was a money tree.

This was also three days after my birthday, so Jill surprised me with a beautiful birthday cake. No one had ever surprised me on my birthday before. It was so much fun.

Ideally we would have gone home to sleep right after the bachelor bash, but we had one more thing to do before going to bed.

When Bob and I first planned the wedding, we decided that we wanted to write a poem for each other as part of the ceremony. We'd discussed this with Reverend Pipes, so every time we met with him he asked us how the poems were coming along.

Every time he asked, we said, "Coming right along."

Nothing like two people who'll lie to a minister.

We hadn't written a word.

We put it off until the absolute last possible minute. The night before the wedding, with our apartment packed with friends who were staying with us from all over, I got out of the house and went to Zucky's, an all-night deli in Santa Monica. We had to be in the church at seven in the morning, so I didn't have a lot of time.

While Rod was gone, I sat in our bedroom and wrote my poem. I knew what I wanted to say, but I wanted to do it in the same meter as "Wood and Stream," the first poem I wrote for Rod, because it was really a continuation of that poem. It turned out to be very complicated to do.

I also knew what I wanted to write, but I'm not someone who's organized about it. When I feel it, I sit down and I do it, although I'm not sure what I was feeling at three in the morning, but I had to do it. So I let my heart write for me and finished it in about half an hour.

While I was working on the poem, the waitress who was pouring me cup after cup of coffee asked me what I was doing. She'd seen the two of us there all the time. I'm sure she'd seen us there holding hands. I told her I was writing a poem, and she asked what it was for. I said, "I'm getting married tomorrow at nine." She said, "Oh, I think that's so romantic. It's so nice to hear about couples getting started in their life together." And then she just stood there leaning against the counter caught up in her own thoughts. You could see her thinking back to when she got married. Marriage and love are such universal experiences.

I got home at five in the morning and Bob was still up. He said, "Let me hear it." I said, "Nope, you'll hear it later today." Then he asked if I wanted to hear his, and I said that I'd hear it at the wedding. I wanted to hear it in that moment when we were there together taking our vows.

23

The morning of the wedding I should have been exhausted, but I was more exhilarated than anything else. I was also scared, because I was afraid to get married. I was really afraid of a lifetime commitment and the responsibilities that come with it.

We were both scared. Until we took our vows in front of 200 people and God, we could have walked away at any time, no harm, no foul. Of course, there would have been the emotional trauma and it would have been complicated because our lives were so intertwined, but once we were married, we couldn't walk away that easily. We took these vows very seriously.

The morning of the wedding was very, very hot, and the church was packed.

We came in from the sides and met at the altar. The room was completely silent.

The ceremony opened with a prayer from Reverend Pipes, and then our friend Tom sang a beautiful song by Kathy Mattea, "As

Bob
putting on
Rod's bowtie.

Bob and Rod with Tina and Mike, just before the wedding
service.

Rod reading his poem to Bob. *Left to right*: Jill, Tom, Bob,
Reverend Pipes, Rod, Tina.

Long as I Have a Heart": "As long as I have a heart, you have a
safe place to dream in, a tree to carve your name in, as long as I
have a heart." Right away I was crying. Then our friend Kelliey,
from Arizona, read a poem called "What Love Is." After that, I
read the poem I wrote for Bob.

I was such a mess while I was reading the poem. I was sweating
because of the heat, crying, and the whole time I was trying to
keep my hair out of my face.

His hair was really long then, and he looked like Cousin It.

I heard one of my friends say, "If he doesn't stop playing with
his hair, I'm going to cut it all off." I was trying to keep it out
of my face so I could read, but I guess I was also nervous.

The whole event was so emotional. There had been all this
buildup and the personal turmoil and my fear of, "Oh my God,
what if this isn't right?" But it felt right while it was happening,
and I couldn't stop crying. I was so happy, and it was such a

release. I don't know how anybody understood a word I said because I was snorting and sniffling.

Before I read the poem, I took Bob's hand and held it the whole time. This is what I read to Bob:

If I could promise you
the moon and stars
in all their azure blues
and shooting light
I would
But all that's mine to promise you
is a heart of flesh and blood

If I could promise you
that I could protect you
from all of life's harm
I would
But all that's mine to promise you
is that I will stand proudly next to you
through the days
as they number and cultivate into years
never keeping you from experiencing life
as God has intended in his plans

If I could promise you
the peace of spirit to be
the most honest and compassionate person
you are *and were meant to be*
I would
But all I have to promise you
is a shelter to foster sense of self
a shield of pride
and a space with enough room to grow
to rest when you are weary and to lick your wounds

If I could promise you
that I could teach you how

to live life deeply and full
yet lightly and lithe
I would
But all that's mine to promise you
are guiding thoughts
from my sometimes scared and confused heart
for I am much more a pupil
than a teacher
and the journey will be equally shared

If I could promise you
that I know and would share
the secret to live life true
I would
But all that's mine to promise you
is honesty and valor
to search for a sometimes elusive truth

I could promise you
all the things through time
that all the poets chime
But all that's mine to promise you
when the morning sun casts its first
tendrils of shy, yet persevering light
is the fusion of a maturing heart and mind
only me

As soon as Rod started reading the poem I started crying, and as I reached for my handkerchief I looked out at the congregation, and with all the handkerchiefs going back and forth it looked like everyone was surrendering.

When Rod finished, I wanted to savor the moment because it was so overwhelming. No one had ever written anything like that to me before. It captured the essence of everything I always felt he couldn't really ever say to me. Yet he said it. But there was no time to pause and savor that moment with Rod because we had to go on with the ceremony. So now it was my turn to read, and I took Rod's hand in mine and said:

> *Oh my word*
> *I can't believe it.*
> *Here at last*
> *I finally stand.*
> *All dressed up in my tuxedo,*
> *Holding onto Rodney's hand.*

With that, everybody burst into laughter. It was such a relief, because there was so much pent-up tension. We both laughed, too, and then I continued:

> *Look at him.*
> *I see how lucky*
> *I have been*
> *to find the one.*
> *In his eyes*
> *I see the ocean,*
> *stars, the moon*
> *and rising sun.*
>
> *He's the one*
> *pulled my heart strings*
> *sent me tumbling*
> *head o'er heels.*
> *Picked me up*
> *and through the distance*
> *gave me strength*
> *to drop my shields.*
>
> *We were walking*
> *through the desert*
> *moonlight bright*
> *nightshadows dance*

holding hands
whisper secrets.
God's wondrous gift
this sweet romance.

I want to tell him
I do love him
that I'll never
leave his side.
That he has
to hold forever
my bursting heart
so filled with pride.

Over the miles
we had journeyed
reaching, growing
face to face.
We must remember
oh my darling
it was love that brought us
to this place.

Now it's time
to tell each other
that we'll be
true for life.
The dance
is only just beginning
hold on
through whirlwinds,
strength, and strife.

Oh, my word
can you believe it?
Here at last
we finally stand.

All dressed up
in our tuxedos
holding life
right in our hands.

I thought it was wonderful. He wrote from the heart. He wasn't trying to be someone else. He was being his own person, my person. It had his sense of humor, his timing. It was wonderful.

After Bob read his poem, we did the "I do" part of the ceremony, and then the minister said, "I now pronounce you spouses for life." He looked at Bob and said, "You may kiss him now." Then he looked at me and said, "You may kiss him now."

So we kissed, and everyone burst into applause.

We went out of the church first and then everybody followed us in cars to the restaurant for the reception.

Our friends told us to rent a limo for the day, but we just had our old beat-up Jeep. During the wedding, some of them decorated the whole thing with crepe paper and put a "Just Married" sign on the spare tire. We had about a ten-mile drive to the restaurant, so people were driving by us and honking and cheering. I don't think everyone who honked at us figured out exactly what was going on, because we could just as easily have been mistaken for the groom and best man.

The reception was a blast, but the problem was we never had more than a minute or two to visit with anyone, and we had people who had come from far away to be there. So it was also frustrating.

We had the reception in the waterfront room of the restaurant. It was beautiful, and we had a very nice buffet. We hired a twelve-string guitarist and, just to have something quirky, a numerologist. She had a line waiting for her the entire day.

Bob and Rod in front of their decorated "limousine." ("Just Married" sign and tin cans were added later.)

The wedding party (*left to right*): Tom, Michael, Jill, Rod, Bob, Michael, Tina, and Darren.

Bob and Rod with the wedding cake.

Bob and Rod cutting the wedding cake.

Bob feeding Rod some cake.

During the reception people told us that they'd never been to such an emotional wedding ceremony before. I think some people were surprised by its emotion and dignity. It was clear to everyone that we got married because we were in love with each other, not as a publicity stunt.

I have only one regret from that entire day: I wish I hadn't had so much to drink.

But it was hard to say no to people who had come from so far who wanted to buy us drinks.

If there's one way to work me, it's to make me feel guilty, so I couldn't say no, even though I normally didn't drink hard liquor. We both knew we'd had too much to drink, but we still had a very romantic evening after the reception.

We got taken to the hotel in the back of a limousine that some of the wedding guests had rented. There was no way on earth we could have driven to our hotel. For a wedding gift, several of our friends got together and got us the honeymoon suite at the Sheraton on the beach in Santa Monica.

We walked into the hotel barefoot, arm in arm, not too steady on our feet. Our friends had gone ahead of us and gotten our key, so we headed right up to our room and didn't come out until the next morning. We had breakfast in bed, the whole nine yards.

24

After the wedding, the press really hounded us. The phone was ringing constantly, especially with calls from the television talk shows.

We didn't have a problem being public, but we didn't see what we were doing as sensational, and that's how we were being treated. So for the first few months, we decided that we weren't going to cooperate with anyone, but then people wrote things anyway which were not very flattering.

We finally decided that people weren't going to leave us alone and that we would be better off if we cooperated. And we naively thought that if we did a few things, after a while it would quiet down. So when the *Oprah Winfrey* show called, we decided that we would go on, but only if they agreed to do what we wanted.

We didn't want to be presented like a freak show, so we asked that we have enough time with Oprah alone to present ourselves as human beings.

When we actually got on stage, we were pretty nervous.

It's one thing to talk about civil rights, and it's another thing entirely when your personal life is the focus of that discussion. It made us very uncomfortable. People are surprised when we tell them that we're really private people and that we detest the spotlight.

We just happen to be good at being in the spotlight and feel we have a responsibility to do it. Again, it goes back to that kid in the elevator in the Eiffel Tower. We knew we could make a difference in the lives of people like him and felt we wouldn't be living up to our obligations if we didn't speak out.

As soon as Oprah introduced us we got into a discussion about language.

She said, "Here's Mr. Universe, who married his lover, model Rod Jackson . . ."

I told Oprah that it wasn't the right term and she said she thought it was a nice term. I said, "I think it's a nice term, too. It's just not the right term."

I asked Oprah if when she married her fiancé she planned to call him her lover or her husband? Then she understood the point we were trying to make, which was that lover is fine before you take your vows, but it doesn't fully describe your relationship once you get married. Rod was my spouse.

It took us a long time to get to that word. We chose it because it represents our marriage and there's no gender bias.

The word "husband" didn't work too well because when people hear that word they assume there's a wife. Then there are all sorts of questions about who plays what role, in other words, who's dominant and who's passive in all aspects of our life. With spouse, there isn't any of that overlay.

We thought about using "partner," but that's vague. Do you mean business partner, workout partner, or what? So people, if they want to fool themselves, can think your relationship is something other than what it really is. In fact, given the option, many people would much prefer to think that you're business partners rather than partners in life. With "spouse," there's no confusion that this person is your married partner.

The one word that was out of the question from the very beginning was "lover." I think it's a wonderful word, but it wasn't appropriate for us anymore because we were married.

We were the only guests for the first half of the show, and it was pure interview. It was great having a chance to really explain things. For the second half of the show they had on a lesbian couple, Martha and Alix, who were fighting to get a family membership at a health club. Also on the show was famed civil rights attorney Gloria Allred. And they threw in a couple of anti-gay bigots to round out the panel.

It was a good audience, although there was a row of black fundamentalists praying the whole time. Toward the end of the show we got into the Bible, and I said, "The Bible was used to keep African-Americans in slavery not too long ago." Then things got really heated.

It was such a mishmash, and Gloria Allred was holding Bob in his seat. Looking back at it now, it was kind of funny, but not at the time. It was really infuriating dealing with people waving the Bible at us. After the show ended, we were talking to Oprah, and a fundamentalist man came up to us and said, "I can't believe you would do a show like this and let perverts get this kind of attention. I'm going to pray for you." As he walked off, Oprah looked up and said, "You do that," adding very quietly under her breath, "asshole."

We were amazed by the response we got to being on *Oprah*. After the show we weren't sure if our message had gotten out there, but people let us know. When we got home we had tons of messages on our machine from people who called from around the country.

People come up to us almost every day and let us know that they support the work we're doing. I remember one occasion when we were at a Denny's outside Sacramento. We figured that our waiter was gay. He was very nice but never said anything. We were getting ready to leave, and he brought the check and left a napkin with it. On the napkin he'd written a note, which said, "I didn't want to bother you guys or gush, but I wanted you to know that the work you're doing is so important . . ."

. . . and it's changed my life." When something like this happens, it pushes us on, because there are times when we feel overwhelmed and wonder if what we're doing is making any difference.

We've had all kinds of people in all sorts of circumstances come up to us and tell us that what we're doing has had an impact on their lives. This happens to us all the time at the airport (since we just about live there). One time a woman who worked in the baggage claim area came up to us and said, "I'm just a straight old grandma, and I want you to know how much your work means to me and my friends."

Another time, I was traveling alone, meeting Bob for work, and as I was getting off the plane, a gay man came up to me and handed me an envelope. He said, "I know how busy you are, and I didn't want to bother you, but I think you and Bob are fantastic, doing great work, and I respect the hell out of both of you." Inside the envelope was a four-page letter detailing how all the different work we'd done over the years had affected his life personally. Although, I have to point out that *we* didn't change the quality of this man's life, *he* did it himself. But it's truly rewarding to hear about how we've been a part of the process. And, of course, he then became a part of my process, inspiring me with his story.

The mail poured in again after *Oprah*, but it was different from the mail we got after the *Ironman* article. We got a lot of letters this time regarding gay civil rights, and we heard from a lot of young people.

So many of the letters stand out, but there were two in particular that overwhelmed us. The first one was from a fifteen-year-old boy who wrote to tell us that he had planned to kill himself until he saw us on *Oprah*. He'd planned to kill himself the very next day. He said that he'd always known he was different and tried to fit in but couldn't. He explained that he thought he had to be a child molester or wear dresses. He said, "I don't want to hurt anybody, and I don't want to be a woman or dress like one." He was confused and asked his high school counselor what he thought about gay people. The counselor looked him right in the eyes and said, "I think they should all kill themselves." So he wrapped up his affairs and planned his suicide. Then he saw us on *Oprah*. He wrote, "It was so nice hearing you talk about love and realizing that I didn't have to be anything anybody told me to be. And I decided not to kill myself."

The letter was devastating. We were in the car and Rod was reading the mail out loud as I drove us home. As he read this letter, he began to get very emotional, and I pulled over to the side of the road. We both sobbed, and Rod couldn't even finish the letter at that time. It was especially painful for me because here was a kid who was in the same position I had been in. He was so alone and thought his only way out was to kill himself.

Letters like that one weren't just devastating; they also gave us the resolve to go on and do this work. We knew that we had to show gay and lesbian youth that you could be anything you wanted to be, that you didn't have to fit into molds, that you could get married if you wanted to or not get married, have children or not have children. You could do whatever you wanted, but it was your choice. Being gay or lesbian was not a choice, but how you lived your life was.

A couple of days after we got the letter from the fifteen-year-old, we got a letter from an eleven-year-old boy. He'd seen us on *Oprah* and wrote to tell us, "Two months ago I told my mother that I was gay and she said, 'Why couldn't you have just killed yourself and saved me the misery?'" He told us that he was having a very hard time because his mother didn't love him anymore, but that he'd try to hang in there. It's sick that someone would do this to their child, but society encourages that kind of thinking. We wish we could say these were isolated letters, but the fact is we've received hundreds from teens across the country and they could have been carbon copies of each other.

People sometimes ask us why we care so much about kids when we don't have any of our own.

At one of our lectures a man asked us this question, and I said, "I have millions of kids, and so do you. They might not be our flesh and blood, but they're our kids, and I want to change things so they have a chance to grow up and have good lives."

25

After *Oprah*, the press attention intensified. Friends told us they'd been getting calls from reporters at the *National Enquirer* and the *Globe* who were looking for dirt on us. I asked everyone who called to please not cooperate. A couple of photographers who had taken pictures of the two of us called and said, "They want to buy photos, and they're offering a lot of money." I asked them not to and said I'd deal with it.

Finally I got a call from this guy who said he was from the *National Enquirer* and the *Globe*. Before he could say anything I started screaming into the phone. I used every dirty word I know at least twenty times. I told him he deserved to be shot, quartered, and on and on. He waited until I paused for a second and said, "You can go on if you like. It doesn't bother me. I'm used to it. We're doing a story whether you cooperate or not, so all your cursing isn't going to scare me off, but we'd rather have your cooperation." I hung up on him and went into the bathroom and threw up.

I freaked. I figured that whatever good we might have done would be ruined. I couldn't tell Bob what was going on because he was in Europe, and I couldn't reach him.

The guy called back in a few minutes and said, "Hanging up on me isn't going to work either." He said, "Look, if you can cooperate a little bit, this will be a lot easier." I told him I had no intention of cooperating, and then he asked if we could at least release a photo of the two of us together. I told him I wouldn't and he said, "Fine, then we'll use your *Playgirl* center-fold and we'll use a muscle shot of Bob. We'll put the photos side by side and let people draw their own conclusions." That would have defeated everything we were trying to do.

I gave in. I told the guy that I would work with him, but that I had a few demands. I said, "First, I want you to know what a worthless piece of crap you and your magazine are. I'm disgusted that you've blackmailed me into working with you. It's evil and sick. None of you people have any morals. I also want you to know that whatever you guys print, you have blood on your hands. You already have blood on your hands because magazines like yours make being gay seem like such a terrible, sick, circus sideshow thing. Kids walk by and see how you portray gay people and then they go home and blow their brains out." Then I asked him if he had any kids and he said, "Yes, three." And I said, "I hope you aren't responsible for putting a gun to any of your children's heads and pulling the trigger. Think about that when you try to sleep at night."

He was quiet for a minute and then said that if I gave him an interview and released a photo of Bob and me together, he'd let me have approval on the story. I said, "That really means a lot coming from a reporter with the *Globe* and the *National Enquirer.*" I really didn't have much choice but to trust him, and I did the interview. Bob was away, so I did it on my own. I talked to Bob before I did the interview, and he told me to ignore the whole thing. But I said that I couldn't because it was going to happen whether or not I helped, and maybe it would be better if I cooperated.

I called our wedding photographer Artie Zeller, who had some physique photos of us, and I told him he could sell them.

When the reporter was done with the article, he faxed me a copy. It was okay, and they even made the changes I asked for. And then we waited.

We figured it was going to be a disaster for us when the article came out. Even without the article there were people who saw us as freaky because I was a pro-bodybuilder and Rod was a professional model. It was hard enough establishing our legitimacy without being on a page opposite an article about a three-headed baby with an alien mother.

They were going to take something that was beautiful to us, our relationship and our love for each other, and turn it into something trivial and sick. I knew exactly what they were going to do, or at least I thought I did.

A couple of months passed and we forgot about the whole thing. We were in L.A. working, and one night we were in the grocery store late. I was taking groceries out of the cart and putting them on the conveyor belt. And as I was reaching into the cart, something caught my eye, something familiar. I looked up and I saw the cover of the *Globe*. The whole room starting spinning around, and it felt like the walls were moving in on me. All I managed to say was, "Rod."

Before I could even look, a woman came up to us and said, "Children, you look hot!" There we were on the cover, the two of us, with the headline, "Gay Shocker—Exclusive. Mr. Universe Marries Male Model." The photo they used was a side chest pose of the two of us on the beach.

When I looked up, there were a dozen people smiling, talking, whispering, and pointing at us. Then the man at the checkout counter said, "I suppose you're going to want a couple of these." He grabbed a couple of copies and ran them across the scanner. We got out of there as fast as we could; it felt so claustrophobic.

We had no idea that they were doing our story on the cover. That was the first surprise. Then we opened it up and we were the entire centerfold.

Some of it was stupid, but it wasn't at all negative. In fact, it was probably the most positive thing they'd ever done on anything gay. I figured that maybe I actually reached the reporter who did the story. And he probably realized that our story was sensational-sounding enough without any embellishment.

The response to the article was phenomenal because millions of people saw it all over the country, right at the checkout counter of their groceries. To this day, we have people who come up to us and say that after reading the article in the *Globe* about us, they felt good about themselves for the first time. Who would have guessed!

About a week after the *Globe* article came out I went to England to do a seminar tour.

I went along, and the promoters were billing me as a sidekick attraction, which was odd because I'm not even a competitive bodybuilder.

All the magazine write-ups about my tour seemed like they were saying, "Come and see Bob Paris and his queer sidekick, Rod."

The promoter met us at the airport, and as we were walking through the terminal he said, "You know, we've had a bit of bad publicity." It was a bit of British understatement because "a bit of bad publicity" turned out to be the cover article in the *News of the World* with the headline: "Mr. Uniperv Gets Married and His Blushing Bride Is a Bloke." They'd obviously bought the story and the photos from the *Globe* and rewritten the article to suit their purposes. They made it sound as if we'd been very closeted and had this secret ceremony that the press found out about.

They also changed one of our quotes around so it sounded like we considered our pets our children. We can laugh about it now, but it hurt at the time.

It was traumatic because after being labeled a pervert by a major English newspaper, I was going around to twenty-two cities giving seminars. I never knew from city to city what was going to happen.

In one city I was guest posing. This involves appearing at a local competition to serve as the star attraction. I started doing my routine, and a couple of loudmouths started jeering me, calling me a faggot. So there was a point in the music where I was making a transition from one pose to another and threw them a little kiss. Then I stuck my butt out and gave them a limp-wristed wave.

The audience went crazy, absolutely nuts. I was so proud that Bob actually made fun of himself; it takes a lot of courage to stand up there in posing trunks and make fun of your own stereotype. He was totally vulnerable on stage in front of a few thousand people, and you never know if they're going to clap or boo, or whether someone will pull a gun out and kill you. Besides all that worry, I was proud of Bob because he's not very good at making fun of himself. And if anyone makes fun of him, he gets very, very mad.

It felt great to do that. It was better than flipping them off because what I managed to say with that gesture was, "You're saying something that's obvious. It's no secret. What's your problem, Einstein?"

26

After the *Globe* article, the press interest intensified again. We turned almost everything down, but we said yes to Joan Rivers. One of her producers called and told us that Joan loved us and wanted us on her show. This was after she had sent us a telegram telling us she thought we were fabulous.

The producer was totally straightforward with us, which I appreciated, so I listened to what he had in mind. They were doing a show with an on-air wedding. The producer said they wanted us to give advice to the soon-to-be-married couple. I guess we were their alternative couple. He told us that it would be fun and uplifting, and nothing else. Of course, we were going to make it political even if that wasn't what they had in mind.

But we weren't going to be really heavy or anything. We just wanted to make a few points. So when the producer asked us if we'd wear tuxedos, we said that we'd be happy to. After all, it was a wedding and we were going to be guests.

It was pretty clear to us from the time we first talked to Joan that she had an agenda as well. Before and then during the show, Joan said how she had lots of gay friends in Hollywood and they

Bob and Rod with Joan Rivers, on her show on marriage.

didn't feel the need to have a wedding. And we kept saying, "But we're not those people." We tried to explain that these were people who never felt the need to be who they were. I'm not judging them, but these were very closeted people, and she was trying to compare them to us. It seemed that she was trying to tell us that we were young and these friends were older and knew how things were supposed to be, and why weren't we doing it that way? It made us angry.

It seemed to us that part of Joan's agenda was to let us know that our marriage wasn't the same as a heterosexual marriage, and we didn't let her get away with it. But after a little back and forth she turned the whole conversation into camp and we just went along with it. By then we'd made our points about the challenges faced by gay and lesbian teenagers, and how we all need to find dignity in our lives.

In the end, we had fun. Joan asked us if we had any advice for the newlyweds, and we said that they needed to talk to each other and that if they communicated they would probably make it. The whole thing was very sweet.

Everyone seemed very comfortable with us. We met both of the families, and the groom went out of his way to say, "I think you guys are great."

So in general we were pleased with how the show went, but when we saw it on TV the title under our names was "The Odd Couple." We told the producer how much we objected to the label, and he said he had no idea where it came from; despite our objections that's how it ran. That sort of thing makes us incredibly angry, but a lot of it is beyond your control, no matter what anyone promises. So I guess Joan got the last word in anyway.

27

It would have been bad enough if all we had to worry about was the *Globe* and being called "The Odd Couple" on *The Joan Rivers Show*, but we also had trouble with the gay press. We were surprised by how little support we got from them, and in fact we found that some of the gay press was pretty hostile toward us.

One gay publication implied that all bodybuilders were high-paid prostitutes, and they made fun of the fact that I referred to Rod as my husband. They couldn't distinguish between the guys who posed for men's magazines and professional body-builders.

It's a little different being Mr. Universe and being Colt model of the month, but most of the gay publications couldn't make that distinction. Bob had worked for years to rise to the top of his sport, and even if it wasn't the NFL, he was still a professional athlete.

It was a constant fight over language. In an interview we'd say "spouse," and then it would show up in print as "lover." Oth-

Bob and Rod in the New York Gay Pride Parade, 1992.

ers were writing that we did it for the money and the attention, that our careers had been going nowhere, and that this was a way for us to cash in—as if there's a fortune to be made as gay activists. It couldn't have been just that our love had inspired and demanded sincere public honesty on our part, no matter what the cost. I think they wanted to crush us.

We were talking about love, family, and marriage and children, and many of the gay people who worked in the gay press at the time didn't like what we were saying. They thought we were judgmental of people who chose to live a different way, but we weren't. We were just saying how we were trying to live. Then there were some who accused us of being "sex negative," because now that we were married we supposedly weren't into sex, and they criticized us for talking about monogamy. It really hurt us when people said these things because we were doing what we thought was right and some of the gay press was not at all supportive. They criticized us constantly. I guess I had a hard time understanding what valid criticisms they could have. We were talking about civil rights denied to gay and lesbian people simply because of our status.

I also think that envy played a role. We were living many people's dreams.

We had the love they were all looking for.

But they had to claim that they were never interested.

You know, we can take criticism, especially when we were getting so many supportive letters from people who saw us on television and read about us, but it took its toll. We were fighting a lot, and we were constantly angry. It was especially tough because we didn't have a real support system. We're each other's best friend, and we spend almost all of our time together, which we love, but that has meant we have very few friends. We're not the kind of people who have 2,000 good friends. We surround ourselves with quality, not quantity.

Even before we got together, I never had many friends. And many of my friends now are people who were Rod's friends. It's very difficult to make new friends because we've discovered there's often a hidden agenda. It's a lot like when I was in bodybuilding. People want to know you for what you can do for them.

I have trouble trusting people in the first place, even family members. Add to that the "celebrity dilemma" that we now face, and you wind up being very careful about the people you let into your life.

So we felt we were out there on our own, getting attacked in certain quarters of the gay press and also having to contend with mainstream journalists who wanted to sensationalize our story.

I'm really surprised that we survived as a couple through all this. We didn't have enough distance from the whole thing to see what was happening and what we were doing to each other. We also made the mistake of only seeing the bad things people were writing about us. Nobody sent us the many positive articles that were written. It turned out that there was plenty of support from gay publications around the country, but we didn't know about it.

Both of us went into a blue funk after the *Ironman* article and the wedding and all the press that followed. It was especially bad for Bob. He went into a major depression, and it was very hard to live with him. I felt I had lost my private life. For Bob, the depression was over the negative impact all the publicity was beginning to have on his career, and he took a lot of the bad things people were saying to heart.

I just had no idea how bad it was going to be. I knew it would be a fight, but I didn't think it would be one thing after another.

For example, I spent a week working at a fitness camp at Loyola Marymount University. Top professional bodybuilders, plus experts on kinesiology and nutrition came to give seminars to people from all over the country. This was my first year doing it, and it was just after *Ironman* published the coming-out article.

After I got home, I got a letter from a gay man who participated in the program. He said that during one of the recreational seminars they were playing a word game, which was being directed by Dave Zelon, one of the top guys in the camp. One of the questions during this game was, "Besides bodybuilding, what's Bob Paris's favorite activity?" It was asked

Bob and Rod after giving their first human rights lecture, Rollins College, 1990.

with lots of winks and nods. The answer was theater, but obviously he was trying to be funny and make a point about the fact I was gay. A question or two later, when someone got an answer about something else wrong, Dave wrote the word "fag" on the board several times in a very dramatic way, and said, "You don't want to be like Bob Paris, do you?"

Bob and I were both furious.

I called up the guys who ran the camp and told them about the letter I'd just received. I asked them what they were going to do about it, and I could tell they were upset. I was furious, especially since Dave had talked to me during the week and said that now that the article had been published, maybe I could get on with my life. I didn't think he meant anything by it, but obviously he didn't like the fact I was gay.

This whole thing made me feel second-class. I was already having a hard enough time dealing with the possibility that my career might be over, and this demonstrated that it was going to be a lot harder than I thought it was going to be. I guess I should have been prepared for the behind-the-back personal attacks, but I couldn't handle the emotional impact.

Next I called Dave Zelon himself. At first he denied he had said anything, but then after it got back to him that other people had witnessed it, he admitted that he'd done it. But he said that he didn't realize that "fag" was an offensive word.

I was on the phone with him when he said this. He said, "It didn't really mean what it sounded like." I said, "You're Jewish, aren't you, Dave?" He said, "Yes," and I told him that "kike" was just the same as "fag," and that I had a hard time believing he didn't know how offensive it was. Then I called him a bigot, and he tried to show me how enlightened he was by telling me that his father was an ACLU attorney. I said, "Really, and what did your father have to say about this incident?" After he hemmed and hawed to avoid answering me, he admitted that his father told him what a terrible thing he'd done. We argued back and forth, and finally I said, "You have two choices here. You either own up to what you did and apologize to Bob, or you keep claiming that you've done nothing wrong and I'll push it until I get your job."

I was so livid that I couldn't talk to him.

I was emotional, but I also challenged him to own up to what he did. Finally he said, "I'm sorry." I told him that I wasn't the person he should apologize to and handed the phone to Bob.

What made me so angry was that he really hurt Bob badly. And ironically, that year and every year following, Bob got the highest marks on his evaluations of anybody who worked at the camp.

On the positive side, this turned out to be an opportunity to educate people. Dave Zelon wrote a letter of apology to the man who wrote the original letter of complaint. They offered him a free week the following year. And the people who run the camp counseled all the camp counselors about having respect for their gay clientele. From then on, the camp turned out to be a very embracing environment for everyone.

That was hardly the end of the problems Bob had over coming out. A couple of months later we got a letter from someone who had attended a bodybuilding contest in New York. There was an audience of about 2,000 people, and keep in mind that more than a few of the people who attend these events are gay. The man told us that the event included a black comedian who, as part of his routine, made fun of Bob and me, inciting the audience to go out and bash gay people. We failed to see any humor in that, although some of the audience seemed to enjoy it. He said the comedian was calling Bob a faggot and claimed Bob had AIDS, and he also said that Bob had married a faggot. But even worse, the comedian got the audience to chant, "Go bash a fag. Go bash a fag." The writer explained that he was closeted, so he felt there wasn't anything he could do, but he asked us to do something about it. Scary stuff—it sounded more like a neo-Nazi rally than a bodybuilding contest.

I called one of the show's major sponsors, Bev Francis and her husband, Steve. I talked to Steve and asked him if this had happened, and he said that it had. I told him that it had to stop, that I was going to get the national Physique Committee to pull the promoters' sanctions, which gave them the right to hold the contests. It's all very regulated.

So Steve called the promoters who had arranged for this comedian to appear at two contests. He told them they'd better not hire him in the future or there was going to be trouble. When the comedian heard about this he threatened to sue *us* for discrimination.

Ad for Shanti.

He said it was bigotry. This was an African-American man inciting violence against gay people, which, of course, included African-American gay people. But what really upsets me is that our community has to bear some of the responsibility for letting this kind of thing happen. In that crowd of 2,000, you can bet there were a few hundred gay people, and only one of them wrote, and no one stood up to challenge this guy or talked to the promoters. We have to put our butts on the line if we expect things to change. African-Americans and women put their lives on the line because they knew that that was the only way things would change.

This kind of thing really pushed me over the edge into a funk. And on top of the constant little things, my work fell away. Things were canceled. Nobody would book me. I went from being booked solid to nothing, with the exception of Europe, where I continued to do some seminars and guest appearances.

I didn't think I'd ever see the end of that depression.

It got very difficult for both of us and put a tremendous strain on our relationship.

The fact that we'd just moved from L.A. to Olympia, Washington, didn't help. It made things seem even more uncertain. We were living in a small town where we didn't know anybody. My work was dwindling, and we hadn't yet started doing gay rights work.

There wasn't very much money coming in, and we had spent our savings putting a down payment on a home. We were broke, and this whole time we were having to tell people that we were doing fine because we were proud. Plenty of them warned us that if we came out we'd pay for it, and we didn't want to give them the satisfaction of knowing they were right. We were just trying to ride it out, hoping things would turn around, but that meant we couldn't tell anyone what was happening. The only person I shared any of this with was my mother, who helped out financially through a couple of rough spots.

I loved Bob so much, but there didn't seem to be anything I could do to help. It scared me. I'm the kind of person who may have a blue funk for a couple of weeks. But with Bob it went on for two months, three months, four months, and I couldn't reach him.

I also felt an awful sense of responsibility for what happened because I'd strongly encouraged Bob to come out. I'd forced Bob to take the path I was on, but maybe it wasn't the right one for him.

I don't remember it being as consistently bleak as Rod remembers. I had highs and lows during that year.

Well, Bob was in it, but my experience of it was that it was pretty consistent. Fortunately, we had this continuous stream of supportive mail that helped sustain both of us. If not for the mail and all the support, I think we would have packed up and moved to a self-sustaining cabin in the Rockies, because with Bob's depression it was like having a storm cloud right over our house the whole time.

Finally, I told Bob that he had to start crawling out from under this depression.

I listened to Rod, but it wasn't easy. You have to understand that this crash—both emotional and financial—followed the best year financially that either of us had ever had.

And now there were times when we didn't even have enough money to buy groceries.

So you can imagine how sweet the victory was after I came out of my depression and we began to get back on our feet financially and emotionally. I decided that we couldn't let these people win. It was a very strong motivator.

Deep down I knew that if we could hang in there we could make it. But we needed to convince everyone that we were doing fine because if people knew what had really happened, we would never get back on our feet again. They'd look at us as failures and write us off. We didn't like hiding the truth, and it wasn't that we wanted to mislead people, but we knew the best way to get through it was to pretend that everything was okay.

At one point we sat down and talked about what we were going to do. I said, "Do we believe in what we're doing?" We agreed that we did. I said, "Are we going to let every negative editorial and every homophobic incident ruin our lives for a month?" which is what we'd been doing. We realized that, even though we were telling people they needed to take control of their lives, what we were doing was giving strangers power over ours.

We decided that we could take whatever people dished out. We had to do the work we knew we were destined to do.

It was a very challenging time, but on the plus side there was a real cementing that took place in our relationship. We knew we had only each other to count on and that brought us even closer together. Despite everything, we loved each other even more.

28

We knew that coming out in the media would close some of the doors that might have been open to us professionally if we'd chosen to stay in the closet. We weren't wrong, because lots of doors shut tight.

New doors opened, and to be fair, there were some doors that were open a crack, but we still had to use our ingenuity to open them up all the way.

I've had the opportunity to write two books on my sport, and I've just signed for a third. The first contract, which was with Warner Books for *Beyond Built*, was being negotiated just prior to the publication of the *Ironman* article. I'd been wanting to write this book for several years, and I'd procrastinated, so it was exciting to have it go to contract. I wanted to put into words the philosophies about nutrition and training that I'd crafted over a number of years.

Before the contract was finalized and before any money had changed hands, the *Ironman* piece ran.

Right after that, the Warner Books editor came to the Night of Champions to see me compete. We also thought he was there to gauge the reaction of the audience to me now that I was publicly out. Perhaps it was just a coincidence that the contract and the advance arrived one week later.

The book wound up being a bestseller and led to a second contract, for *Flawless*, which is also doing extremely well.

The irony for me about the success I've had with my books is that here was one of the largest corporations in the nation investing in my future, with the understanding that I still had a very large, growing, and supportive audience. Yet Weider and the International Federation of Body Builders were and are completely unsupportive. If I had been a non-gay pro-bodybuilder with my level of success outside the traditional avenues of the sport, they would have promoted me like there was no tomorrow.

We've also done one book of photographs together, and we're working on a second. I had the idea for the first art book back in 1988, before the *Ironman* interview. I thought it would be great to have a book that showed two people together who loved each other, without explanations and without regret. Growing up, this was the kind of book and positive images that could have changed our lives. We believed that we could do this book, which is called *Duo*.

I thought it was a good idea, so we began looking around for a photographer to work with us on some experimental shots. We did this while I was on tour in Europe, and we wound up working with someone in Paris.

It turned out that the chemistry between us transferred to film, so when we came back home we started working out our ideas and thinking about who we wanted to work with. I thought it would be great to work with Robert Mapplethorpe. He'd done all this beautiful but controversial work, and we thought he might be interested in making another kind of political statement. So Bob sat down and hand-wrote him a three-page letter.

Robert and I had worked together a few years before, and I told him that I was in a committed relationship and that my husband was named Rod. I told him that we wanted to do a book of images that showed the positive side of gay life, the kinds of images that could empower gay people. I explained that we had never had any role models growing up that the dominant culture allowed us to see, and that what we were trying to do was show images that might give some hope to the next generation.

We got a call from a man who worked with Robert who told us that he was very ill. He said that he'd read Bob's letter to Robert and that he cried. He also said that Robert was very, very interested, and as soon as he was well enough to work again, he'd let us know. He asked us if we could be ready at a moment's notice to come to New York.

We would have gone in a second, but Robert only got worse and died a month later. So I called Herb Ritts. I'd worked with him before and we'd kept in touch. We worked with him for a day, and it was brilliant stuff. He brought us to Twin Palms Publishers.

When we signed the contract we really hadn't thought ahead to how we were going to handle this, because at the time we weren't out publicly. We just knew that this was an important project to do. Later we thought, "Now we're going to have to deal with being public." It wasn't like we saw *Duo* as forcing our hands, although obviously subconsciously we had to have known that whether or not we made the decision to go public about being a gay couple, *Duo* would do it. It's a very revealing book.

In the end, we did the *Ironman* article first, so the timing worked out well.

Duo turned out to be a beautiful book. The first printing was sold out before it was ever printed, which was incredible.

The success of *Duo* led to a new art book contract with another brilliant photographer named Tom Bianchi, to be published in 1994. Both photographers have very distinct styles; therefore each book makes its own separate statement about love.

Besides the art books, we've also done magazine covers together. About a year after we came out, *Body Power*, the top bodybuilding magazine in England, published a cover photo of us. The exciting thing about this was that it was the first time an openly gay couple had ever been featured on the cover of a mainstream sports magazine. It was *Body Power*'s best-selling issue of the year. I had had dozens of covers on fitness magazines all over the world, but this one was both historic and meant more to me than all the others put together.

Because of the success of the *Body Power* cover, *Robert Kennedy's Muscle Mag* ran a cover of us a year later. And that was only the second sports magazine in the world to feature an openly gay couple and the first in North America.

So, despite some of the closed doors, we continued to work in the fitness industry pursuing our careers as much as possible, but now as openly gay people and as an openly gay couple. Needless to say, that led to just a few unique situations.

Rod and I were both being shot for *Muscle & Fitness* magazine and something really funny happened. I was doing the cover of the magazine, and Rod was doing a shoot a day later for a photo layout.

I went in to work and met the woman with whom I was going to be shot for the cover. She was a *Playboy* centerfold, and her dressing room was just across from mine. As she was taking off her clothes she was trying to get my attention, and it was clear that there was more going on here than an attempt to have a conversation.

We were talking, and she saw the ring on my finger and asked if I was married. I said that I was, and she asked me what my wife did. I said, "I don't have a wife. I have a husband, and he's a model." And she said, "You're kidding, right?" I said that I wasn't kidding, and she said, "Oh, you're a wildman, aren't you?"

Just because I was gay, she assumed that I was some kind of sex fiend, yet here she was standing naked in front of a total stranger. I told her, "That's not true. You couldn't find a more tame person in the world, but what does that have to do with anything, anyway?" She got kind of flustered and went back to getting ready for the shoot.

Bob came back to the hotel and told me the whole story, and I thought it was very funny. The next day I went in, and the model I was working with was crawling all over me and cooing and moaning. Between shots, she kept rubbing against me and tried her best to arouse me. It wasn't exactly the most professional shoot I'd ever done. Ordinarily models just want to do their work and go home.

So she started talking to me about my work and then asked where I lived. I told her that I lived in Washington State. She said, "Well, I worked with a guy yesterday who lives in Washington." And I thought to myself, "Dear lord, please let this be what I'm thinking." She said, "Maybe you know him. He's supposed to be a famous bodybuilder." I said, "Maybe I do. What's his name?" She said, "Bob Paris." I said, "Hmm, Bob Paris . . ." and this whole time she's rubbing me and touching my chest. I know it wasn't very nice, but I really milked this. She asked, "So do you know him?" And I said, "As a matter of fact, I'm married to him." Well, she jumped up, right in the middle of a shot, and said, "It fucking figures, two of the most gorgeous men I've ever worked with, and they're married to each other."

Even after she was finished working, I had more work to do. She waited around for her boyfriend to pick her up. When he came, they were watching me work and she kept saying to him, "Isn't he gorgeous? Isn't he gorgeous? He's married to Bob Paris, the guy I worked with yesterday." Then the photographer looked up from behind his camera and said, "Who's married to Bob Paris?" She said, "He is." And the photographer said, "Oh, cool," and we went back to work.

29

Another project Rod and I worked on together was a video specifically for gay and lesbian young people. From the letters we'd received and from conversations we had with many of the people we'd met, we were inspired to come up with some ways we could help empower gay and lesbian youth, to help them feel less isolated. As youngsters, both of us wrestled with thoughts of suicide, and I almost did it several times throughout my life, so we wanted to do something to reach out to young people who were struggling with the same issues we once did.

As young people we were not exposed to what a gay person truly was or could be. I couldn't find anything to read about homosexuality in my hometown library. And certainly I didn't learn anything positive or enlightened in school.

So when we were approached by a video production company, Twenty-First Century News, in Tucson, Arizona, to do a video-tape for gay and lesbian teens, we were interested. They said they wanted to do a video with a racially mixed group of ten gay and non-gay young men and women. We were to be there in role-model positions so they could ask us whatever questions they had about issues surrounding homophobia, making hard decisions, and learning how to live with dignity. Everyone involved in the project was eager to work together to focus on the important issues.

It was important that the video have a positive outlook, and to focus on the human aspects of being gay or lesbian, rather than on political issues. And we wanted the video to be engaging, to be something that we would have wanted to see at that age.

We also thought it was important to make distinctions between sex and sexuality. We wanted to focus on sexuality, how we see and experience the world as gay people. We didn't want to focus on sex in the physical sense.

What was most important to us was that we counteract in some small way all of the negative images and messages kids get. So many young people are either killing themselves or committing slow suicide by not living up to all of their potential.

Given who we are, and given the way we look and the way we speak, we're able to get teenagers—gay and non-gay—to watch this video and to listen to us.

To do the actual video, the people who produced it went through the Tucson school system and got a great mix of young people. We taped for a couple of hours, and by the time we finished many of the production people were crying. Some hadn't had the opportunity to see this kind of interaction before and it was very emotional. Bob and I were moved as well by the things these kids asked and how they responded to our answers.

We covered everything from teen suicide to homophobia to deciding if and when to tell your parents that you're gay. And the whole tone was positive, despite the seriousness of the subject. We wanted to give the participants, as well as those who would be watching, positive encouragement. We also want non-gay youth to understand the issues of diversity, difference, and human dignity.

We kept very careful control of the content of the video as well as the packaging. It might be frustrating for some people who want to do work with us, but it's very important to us, when we're involved in a project and our image is being used, that we have control over how we're presented. The people making this video wanted to use a photograph of the two of us in bathing suits doing a bodybuilding pose for the video cover.

They tried to tell us that the photograph would get people's attention. We said absolutely not because that kind of photo would allow people to dismiss us.

Who would listen to these bunny boys? In a lot of circumstances that kind of image will hook people in, so they listen to us, but in other circumstances, like this video for teens or other serious political work, it's inappropriate.

This was a video that we wanted to get into school systems and church groups. So a body shot would have been rejected and then the video's content wouldn't matter at all.

In the end, the producers agreed with our position, and we used a photograph of the two of us, fully clothed. And even that got some negative comments. Our tape was being previewed at a gay and lesbian health conference. One of the producers overheard a lesbian couple commenting on the cover, talking about how we were just another couple of stupid, good-looking macho men. Can you imagine what they would have said if we'd put a body shot on the cover?

In general we don't mind if people use our body shots or one of the pictures from *Duo* to promote an upcoming television show or fund-raiser. That's the nature of television and advertising. But when we do political work, we insist on a standard head shot of the two of us.

We're very proud that "Be True to Yourself" has won several national awards, and it has also aired on PBS stations around the country. What really delights us is that the video is even being used as an educational tool in schools and churches.

After we did the video, the next opportunity to do something specifically for gay and lesbian youth was a special *Donahue* show.

They called with an idea for a show about teenagers and homosexuality.

By this time we'd stopped doing television because we were so burnt out by it. But the video had just been released, and this was a perfect opportunity to promote it.

Phil and his producer explained that they thought we had great rapport with teenagers, and we could also attract a large audience. We'd been on the show once before, and they were thrilled with the results.

It turned out that Phil wanted to do exactly the kind of show we wanted to do. They told us they wanted to fill half the audience with gay youth and the other half with straight kids. The teenagers would come from a broad spectrum. Phil wasn't even going to be there. He told the producers to give us the show for the day because he knew we could do a good job. So there was no moderator, just questions from the audience and the two of us on stage.

It turned out that only a handful of the teenagers in the audience were gay and only three or four felt comfortable enough to speak up. There was so much hostility in the room that it was no wonder so few of the gay kids wanted to risk saying anything.

We taped for two hours, and by the time we finished I felt terrible about the whole thing. There was so much negativity. Some teenager went on and on about Sodom and Gomorrah. I doubted whether he could even spell those names, let alone have much knowledge and understanding of the Bible. He wanted to know if I was a Christian and if I'd read the Bible, and then a lesbian woman stood up and really let him have it. It was exciting, and she did an incredible job defending me and defending herself against this Bible-waving kid. It was obvious to everybody there that he was using the Bible for hateful reasons, and he probably had never even read a single word of Jesus' teachings. After two hours of this I was afraid to see it edited down to an hour.

The final show was very strong. We were both surprised that it was so interesting and educational. It wasn't at all sensational, and it made a strong statement for human rights. I worried that it was going to do more harm than good, and it turned out to be far better than we could have hoped for.

And once again, the mail began pouring in.

30

Speaking at colleges and universities around the country has been a wonderful, positive surprise for us.

In the beginning, Rod and I didn't pursue gay rights public-speaking engagements. We received a letter from an administrator at Rollins College, a small college in central Florida. This person wanted to bring us in to be part of their diversity week. He explained that Rollins was a very bigoted and conservative school, which made it an even more interesting idea for us. So Rod and I talked about it.

I thought we might make a difference in the lives of a few young gay people who were likely to be in the audience. All of my work had always been one on one, but Bob had done lots of public speaking, so I think I was more scared than he was.

This was different. I was used to giving motivational speeches and talking about nutrition and training. Now I'd be sharing my personal life with hundreds of people. Despite our reservations and our fear, we decided to do this one speaking engagement.

They packed the hall with more than 400 people. Before we went in, people told us they hoped nothing would happen. They were afraid someone might bring a gun or that the frat boys were going to heckle us. Frat boys we could manage, but the idea of a gun was unnerving at first, although it's since become typical, and it doesn't hold the same power over us anymore.

We took turns telling about our lives up to the point when we met. The first thing I said was that I was a Lambda Chi Alpha in college, and that shut some people up right away. We talked about our relationship and our political beliefs, and then went to a question-and-answer session. One of the first questions was from a woman who started to ask, "When two men are having sex, does the friction . . ." and I stopped her and told her to buy a book. I explained that we were there to talk about civil rights, not sex.

There were several people from the surrounding gay community in the audience, and one of them asked if we thought that being married was selling out to the heterosexual community. We both got pretty heated in answering that question because we feel so strongly about it. I explained that Rod and I no longer allowed the non-gay world to define us, so why should we allow the gay world to define us and tell us what our limitations should be. Our decision to marry was based on what we wanted to do, not on what anyone told us we should or should not do.

Most of the questions were the kind you would expect, like, "Is it a choice?" "Why are you gay?" "Are you going to adopt children?" "Isn't it against God?" and that sort of thing.

What we were able to do during this event and the speaking engagements that followed was put a face on the "monster." By sharing who we are and by speaking straight from the heart about our lives together and our love for one another, they could see that we were people, not alien creatures.

I was terrified the whole time, from the minute we went on until the last question. But then they gave us a standing ovation and I melted. It was a wonderful feeling to see them standing and applauding, because clearly we'd reached these people. Lots of them came up to talk to us afterward, and when we got home, we got a lot of letters. Many said that we'd been a catalyst in helping change the face of the campus that night. Not that there weren't still problems, but they explained that this was the first time homosexuality was made a part of the civil rights movement on campus. Some of those who wrote said that they were now openly gay and that nobody had said anything negative.

Then Miami University of Ohio and Kent State University wrote and asked us to speak. They'd heard through the grapevine about our talk at Rollins College. So once again we talked it over and discussed whether or not this was a route we wanted to go. I wasn't sure I wanted to become a "professional queer," that I wanted to define my life by the fact that I was gay and married.

That was part of it, but the bigger issue for me was giving a part of our lives—the very private part—to everybody all the time. I didn't want to give people access to all my personal feelings. I knew that someone had to do it, and although I wasn't sure I wanted to do it, we agreed to go.

Kent State was incredible. They had a couple of thousand people in the audience, and even though people warned us once again that they hoped nobody would kill us, we got a standing ovation from every single person in the room.

After that, we did another couple of college speeches, and then we signed with one of the top lecture agencies in the country. After several more dates, we were selected as a showcase act for the National Association of Campus Activities convention in Dallas, Texas. It was a coveted spot for all college speakers, because representatives from nearly every school in the country would be there. We were only one of a few featured speakers during the convention, and we were the very first gay-rights act ever selected for a NACA showcase.

At the end of our showcase, we were given a standing ovation, and we were thrilled to see Mary Wilson, who was also there to showcase (she once sang with the Supremes) in the audience. For our generation and the one before, Mary is a cultural icon whose work we deeply admired. Now she was on her feet applauding our work, and it felt great.

Since the NACA convention, we've been booked solid.

It's been incredibly rewarding to speak at schools all over the country, but it's also very draining. For one thing, we've had to deal with having our lives threatened. At almost every single school people have said, "We hope nobody stands up and shoots you, but don't worry, we have security people." Or they tell us they don't have security people.

This happened when we spoke at Marshall University in Huntington, West Virginia. This is where Kentucky, West Virginia, and southern Ohio come together.

Even before we got there, our agent for the speaking engagements said that there was a problem with the hotel. That wasn't a good sign.

It was traditional at Marshall University to put up a poster of the speakers in the lobby of the hotel where they were staying. The hotel where they booked us, the Radisson, refused to hang our posters. So they moved us to the Holiday Inn. They hung up our picture with pride.

In the meantime, the local newspaper and every major newspaper in West Virginia had done a front-page feature story about us. Consequently lots of people were calling the school, outraged and threatening violence.

When they came to pick us up before the talk, one of our hosts said, "We hope nobody hurts you guys tonight." Fortunately nothing happened, but when we got back to the hotel that night, the phone rang. I picked up and the person on the other end of the line said, "You're both dead," and hung up. Bob asked, "Who was that, Rod?" And I said, without any expression on my face, "Just another wacko."

We know there are certain risks doing what we do. But as in any battle, you can't let the fear of those risks paralyze you. And while you never grow accustomed to the risks, you learn to put them in the back of your mind. It's sad that it just becomes a normal part of your work.

We're not going to walk away from our work, and we're not going to be forced to walk away.

Plenty of times student groups have organized lectures with us only to be overruled by a dean or college president. They pull the funds, and then the students are left scrambling to find another way to pay for the event.

Sometimes the students have gone out and raised the money off campus. But even if they wind up not having us, there's inevitably a debate in the school newspaper, and it's discussed in classrooms across the campus, so at least the issue is raised and debated. This is a step forward in ending the conspiracy of silence.

The presidents of two colleges attempted to stop us from coming, but both wound up coming to hear us speak. Afterward, they apologized for what they'd done.

It's relatively easy to deal with the cancellations and the threats. It's the stories people share with us as we've traveled to campuses across the country that get to us.

In Michigan we met a young woman at lunch prior to our talk.

She was one of several students who, along with the director of student activities, took us to lunch. Throughout lunch she didn't look at us or communicate. I thought she had a problem with us being gay. It's happened to us plenty of times before.

After the talk she came up to us, and she was crying. She asked if we could talk, so we went over to the side of the room, away from everyone. She thanked us for speaking, and we told her that we were just doing our job. She said, "No, you're not. This is nobody's job. This is everybody's job." And then she said, "You probably noticed that I couldn't even look at you during lunch." And I said, "Well, everyone's got their own issues." She said, "They're not what you think they are. My brother was gay and he killed himself two years ago. My mother still thinks it was the best thing that could have happened."

It gets worse. This young woman told us that she had a gay sister who was afraid to tell their mother because of how she reacted to her brother. Then she said, "I feel so ashamed." I asked her why, and she told us that her brother came out to her but that she didn't know how to deal with him. "I loved him, but I didn't know what to do, so I pushed him out. I didn't understand that he was just another human being. Nobody told me that it was okay to love him. In fact, my family was telling me that I couldn't love him. And then it killed him." We all held each other and cried.

She believed what her family and society taught her, that her brother was evil and unworthy of love and respect. She had stood by and watched his life be destroyed by bigotry and hate.

She told us that she didn't know if she'd ever be able to forgive herself, but that we'd given her the tools to understand that while she couldn't be there for her brother, she could be there for her sister. She sent us a letter a while later and told us that her life had changed.

What is it that makes people see us as being so evil and vile? Are we scapegoats for an entire society's hatred? Do we reflect back to other men a feminine side that they don't want to see in themselves? Is it that heterosexual women see us as competition for other men? What is it?

When we do speaking engagements, we know that people sometimes come with plans to heckle us. We talk about who we are, and how painful it was growing up. And even if they're anti-gay, it disarms them because we make ourselves vulnerable and human. We feel like we're going into a war zone on most of these dates. It is certainly no walk in the park. The issues surrounding being gay and lesbian divide the country the same way racism and sexism has divided the country.

At these speaking engagements, we talk about how we never gave up on the idea of falling in love and spending our life with someone.

Everyone in that room can relate to that desire, and before you know it, no matter who they are or what their sexual orientation or political agenda, the people in the audience are identifying with us on some level.

One particular night, at a reception following our talk, a woman said to us, "I came here tonight because I thought you were both gorgeous, but I was a bigot. I didn't understand gay and lesbian rights. But now I see that you're just people, that you're two guys who really love each other. Tonight wasn't about sex, it was about love and human rights."

She told us she was ashamed of herself for how she was thinking, and she vowed that her daughter would not grow up like she did. She also shared with us that for years she had spoken out against gay and lesbian people who had children. She said, "I pray to God that you have children, because you'll be great parents."

I think that part of what disarms people is that we're just as proud, if not more proud, of the love we have for each other as any non-gay couple. People rarely get a chance to see that. At first people giggle when we talk about how we met, and how I felt the wind knocked out of me when I saw Rod. They get nervous, but they understand what I'm talking about because it's a universal experience.

But not everyone hears our message, which is something we're most likely to discover during the question-and-answer period. Every now and then we'll get some off-the-wall questions, like, "If you fell in love with your mother, would it be okay to marry her?"

"Let's say you fell in love with your horse, would it be okay to have sex with your horse?" And my response to that is, "It sounds like you need a psychiatrist."

Some people objected to that response and came up to us later and said that we could have handled it better. I explained that we're not going to take the time to dignify those kinds of questions because the people asking them know how ridiculous and insidious they are.

Often we'll get gay people in the audience who have become obsessed with fundamentalist Christianity—as well as other fundamentalist sects—and think that through some miraculous process they have become "ex-gays." They ask us if we know that we can get over being homosexual if we just do what they've done and accept Jesus as our savior.

There are hundreds of thousands of gays and lesbians who participate fully in their own religious denominations. Bob told one of them, "You can make whatever claims you want, but everyone in this room knows that in time you're going to be facing the same issues you're running so hard from now. No matter what you say, you can't run away from yourself."

I also said that there was no such things as "ex-gays," that it was all a sham and that, 99.9 percent of the time, after a short time people are right back where they started. The problem is that once they realize they can't get over being gay, they hate themselves even more than before they tried to become "ex-gays."

When these people attempt to embarrass you, you just have to embarrass them back because dealing with them compassionately doesn't work. They are brainwashed with fundamentalist dogma and there's no reaching them.

We can't worry about that one person when we have 200 gay people who want to be empowered. We're not going to reach this one person because he hates himself so deeply. Maybe he can be reached one day, but that's not going to happen in the few minutes we have to address his or her question. We can only hope that we are part of his or her process.

We also get very frustrated when someone who is well-meaning stands up in an audience and says that they're so glad that we've shown the world that two gay men can be real men.

That's just pure self-hate as far as I'm concerned. It's accepting what society tells us, which is that men who aren't masculine or aren't "masculine enough" are sissies, that they're not as good or as valued as "real men."

The reason this upsets me so much is that I understand exactly what people are saying when they try to pay us a compliment by telling us we're "real men," because at one time in my life I would have taken that as a compliment. But it's wrong to feel that way. Just because someone doesn't fit society's definition of what a man or woman should be doesn't make them any less important as human beings. There is nothing wrong with being what some people think of as a sissy.

I grew up a sissy. Effeminate gay men and masculine lesbians are no less role models than anyone else. Yet they're constantly put down by both gay and non-gay people. It isn't right.

We both grew up sissies. And it's not like I didn't try to be more masculine growing up. Vocal training lowered my speaking voice. I didn't want to sound gay, whatever that is. Now I don't care how I sound. And anyone who's seen me knows that I'm not the most masculine-sounding or -acting person in the world.

When Bob and I first started doing public gay-rights speaking and political work, we did try to project a more masculine image because we thought that would be more acceptable. But our focus now is just on being ourselves, which makes being masculine or feminine irrelevant. That's who we are and if someone has trouble dealing with that, it's not our problem. It's their problem.

People often don't understand who we are. There was the time after a lecture we gave at Penn State when a reporter from a Philadelphia gay newspaper asked us, "My readers are going to want to know if any of them stand a chance." I asked him what he meant, and he said, "You know, to go to bed with you guys." I looked at him, I looked at Rod, and I said, "I'm married to the most beautiful man in the world."

I said, "So am I."

And I asked the reporter, "What do you think?"

I really don't think it's anyone's business whether we are or aren't monogamous. How any two people handle this issue is a matter of personal choice and shouldn't be subject to anyone's approval. Unfortunately, people try to pass judgment on the legitimacy of gay relationships based on whether or not a couple is monogamous. If we applied that test to heterosexual marriages, the majority of those relationships would have to be considered invalid. So if you're going to hold gay couples up to that standard, then you better damn well hold up the entire world to it. Monogamy or non-monogamy has no bearing on the legitimacy or the quality of a relationship, as long as both partners agree to whatever arrangement they have.

It does make me angry, though, when people assume that because we're a gay couple we're not or can't be monogamous. We've made a commitment to stay true to each other, and when people assume otherwise it's hurtful. We hear stories all the time about people who claim they've slept with one or both of us, people we've never met.

There are people, especially heterosexual women, who have said to us that we're going to waste not sharing ourselves with other people. My answer to that is, "There ain't nothing going to waste."

But we can deal with all the frustrations of having to answer ridiculous and misguided questions and having to respond to the comments about our masculinity, because it's all more than counterbalanced by the positive experiences, for example, the time we inspired two people in the audience at a talk we gave at St. Lawrence University in Canton, New York, to come out of the closet.

From the first minute we walked into the auditorium, which was filled with about 600 people, probably a third of them gay or lesbian, it was like a revival meeting. Everyone was right there with us. They understood our humor; they were right there listening.

There were sparks flying, positive sparks.

You could feel it come back from the audience. It just kept building and building. It was so positive you wanted to dance on stage, and the room was spinning, and everyone's hearts were so full of love.

During the question-and-answer session, a woman stood up and said, "I agree with you that what we need are role models both in the gay and lesbian community and for the community at large. I'm on the faculty here at St. Lawrence University, and I'd like to take this opportunity to come out as an openly lesbian person. Here I am!" Everyone got up and gave her a standing ovation, including us.

It took forever for people to settle down again. And then after three or four more questions, a man stood up and said, "This all feels so good. And I would be neglecting my responsibility as a member of the faculty if I didn't take this opportunity to say that I am now an openly gay man."

Once again, there was a spontaneous standing ovation.

After we finished, people in the audience who were from a Catholic seminary school told us that they learned a lot from the evening. They said, "There's so much that needs to be changed in the Catholic church, and we're the ones who are going to do it."

We're under no illusion that the world is a perfect place after they hear us speak. People change in increments, so nobody is going to walk in the door and leave a different person. Nobody, gay or non-gay. But everybody goes away changed somehow.

Besides the satisfaction of knowing we've helped change minds and helped people feel better about themselves, the speaking engagements have helped heal our own wounds. Every gay person has them from growing up in a world that doesn't want us. So each time we go out there and talk to a college group, we feel a greater sense of pride, we feel better about ourselves, and the scars from our wounds fade a little bit more.

31

One question that comes up almost every time we speak at a college or go on a television talk show is when we're going to have kids of our own. It's something both of us have have thought about since before we met.

I knew that I would have to be with a man who wanted a family. The fact that I was gay never got in the way of that idea. When Bob and I met, one of the things he asked me was, "What's important to you?" I told him that I wanted to be a parent and that I intended to structure my life so that I could be. He said, "You're kidding." I told him that was what most people said. He said, "No, I think that's fantastic. I always wanted to be a parent, too."

The very first night that we were together, we talked about how we both loved kids. After our relationship developed, I could see that we would be very good at making a home for children. We both have a lot of love to give. In my mind I saw the two of us raising three or four kids.

We're very pro family, as long as it's a group of people who love and support and nurture each other through thick and thin. By that definition, I would say that my own birth family wasn't ideal. Even though there was love, many of the other elements I believe a family needs were missing. There was a lot of anger, violence, and divorce. Given that experience, some people might be put off by the thought of having their own children, but I think I've been able to rise above that experience for the most part. I look at my sister Lisa as a role model. She grew up in the same incredibly dysfunctional household I did, and she and her husband, Doug, have grown into incredible parents.

When we started to seriously research having kids, either through adoption or surrogacy, from the very first we decided that we wouldn't do it if we couldn't be completely honest about our relationship. We didn't want to pretend that I was a single man who wanted to adopt a child. Unfortunately, because there's still so much homophobia and the legal system hasn't adjusted to the realities of gay and lesbian families, it's much easier for a single man to adopt than for a male couple.

With a single gay man, the adoption agency can pretend that he's not gay. With a male couple, you can't pretend that they're something other than what they are. And even when male couples go to adopt a baby, most often only one of the two is the legal guardian since two people of the same sex are almost never allowed to adopt the same child. Married non-gay couples can do it, but only rarely can gay or lesbian couples do it, although that is rapidly changing.

The only way we would have children is if both of us can be the legal parents. Without that, our home would not have the dignity, integrity, and sense of pride we know we need to raise emotionally healthy children.

We've taken the step of meeting with adoption agencies and talking to people who arrange for surrogacy. We're in the exploration stages, so we really don't know what we'll wind up doing, although having a biological child is very appealing. A biological child would be a piece of us, whether it was my biological child or Rod's.

We'll do whatever we think we can handle, whether that's surrogacy or an adopted newborn or an older child with special needs or an HIV-positive child.

As far as surrogacy goes, we know there are people who think it's wrong, but we think that if a woman is willing to enter into that kind of agreement, it should be up to her, not the government, to decide. So we went to meet with a couple of different agencies that make surrogacy arrangements. We found out about these agencies, and there are only a few, through a man in New York who saw us on the *Donahue* show. He and his male spouse had just had a baby through a surrogacy clinic, and he wrote to tell us that he admired what we were doing and thought we would make good parents. He told us how he and his spouse did it and said we should call if we wanted any help. So I called him and he gave me the information he had about a couple of different places.

I called one of the agencies to make an appointment just to talk. I spoke with the head person by phone and told him that we were a gay couple. He told me that they didn't deal with gay couples. I said, "Excuse me?" And he repeated what he said. So I told him that I understood that he didn't deal with gay couples, but I would really appreciate it if he could meet with us to at least talk. I said that we'd gladly pay the consultation fee without any expectation that they'd work with us. I said, "I think the least you can do as a human being is sit down and speak with us." He said, "Let me think about it," and hung up. He called back thirty seconds later and suggested a date and time.

A couple of weeks later we went, and the counselor explained to us that he always takes a tough approach with gay couples because he wants to be sure they're absolutely serious about having a child. Because we're gay, he wanted to be sure we were tenacious enough and had enough confidence in ourselves to get past his initially discouraging approach. It's a tough road for gay couples who want to have and raise children.

Then he had us fill out some forms. One of the questions was, "Why are you here?" And I wrote in, "We want children." One of the next questions was, "Why are you infertile?" I looked at Bob and wrote down, "Because we are lacking a uterus." Bob said, "Rod!" I told him that if we couldn't laugh about this whole thing then we were in big trouble. Sure enough, when the counselor began reading the completed form, he started laughing. He said, "Hey, that's good. I've never heard that one before."

After the counselor read over our forms, he explained to us how the process worked. He told us that once we selected someone we wanted to work with from their list of potential surrogates and that surrogate agreed also, then they would arrange for more counseling and eventually insemination. He told us that we didn't even have to be there, that we could ship the semen. At this point I said, "Whip and ship?" Before you can get anywhere near the point of choosing a surrogate, you have to go through extensive screening.

Next we had to go through a psychological examination with one of the staff psychologists to make sure we were psychologically fit, and to see if they felt we had the proper skills to be parents, and on and on. She asked all kinds of questions, like "How do you plan to be a good parent? How are you going to deal with the unique situation that your family will be in? Have you thought about who will be the sperm donor? How do you deal with confrontations? When your child is grown up, what do you hope he or she will have taken from the experience of growing up in your home?"

The psychologist also asked about our family backgrounds and if we considered them good role models. That was an easy one to answer. We both said, "Absolutely not." She also wanted to know how we would raise a child properly if we couldn't go by the example of our own families. We told her that we would read a lot and that we'd look to other people who were suitable role models. In fact, we've already got a shelf full of books on children and parenting. I think we know more about the subject than non-gay couples who are about to have babies.

The psychologist's final report was that we'd make great parents. She said, "I think you're both honest, that you both understand the inherent problems, and you're making plans to deal with them. There's nothing better than active parents."

Our pregnant women friends love us because all the straight guys will be off somewhere talking about sports or whatever, and we want to talk about babies and amnio tests, the whole business. Not that we don't like sports, but we find a woman eight months pregnant far more fascinating than a ball falling through a hoop.

There are times when we've felt discouraged by how much of an effort we have to make to have children of our own. We really have to want to do it and invest the necessary time, energy, and money. Adoption and surrogacy are expensive processes. Raising a kid and putting him or her through college ain't cheap either.

We've been taking every opportunity to spend time with our friends who have babies. A couple of years ago Jill and Jerry had a baby. We went to visit when the baby was two days old. We'd been around babies before, but never one so young. I was scared because you have to be careful with a baby's head. I was afraid that I'd break his neck.

We were both so uptight, figuratively and literally. We were so tense and had our shoulders up the whole time. They were making fun of us.

Jill's mother, who was there, thought it was hilarious seeing two huge men so intimidated by this little infant. She said, "Their shoulders were so hunched up that they're going to be very sore tomorrow." She was right. We had terrible neck aches the next day.

Despite the neck pain, we called the next day and asked when we could come over again.

Jerry said, "We wondered how long it would take you to come back and conquer the little guy." We went back three days in a row.

It was wondrous. It was magical. This tiny person with little fingers and fingernails. All the parts in miniature.

Whenever we talk about having kids of our own, people often say that it's not fair to the children for two gay men or two lesbians to raise them. Well, my answer to that is that most families aren't the *Leave It to Beaver* ideal. You had plenty of child abuse, spouse abuse, alcoholism, and philandering going on in those *Leave It to Beaver* homes. What many of these homes never had enough of was love.

Our children will never, ever be screwed up for lack of love. And if someone ever attempts to harm my children because we're gay, I'll attack them without hesitation. I'll be the biggest Papa Bear you've ever seen.

Of course, any child raised by gay men or lesbians is going to face special challenges that kids raised by heterosexual parents aren't going to have to deal with. But the problems won't be in our home. The problems are with a society that still teaches children to hate people who are different, whether it's their skin color, their religion, or their sexual orientation.

We know that there are things we'll have to do to make sure our kids are treated the same as all other kids.

We'll go to the school before enrollment to make sure there's no problem with kids who have gay parents. And if an individual teacher is a problem, we'll go to the Board of Education like any other parent whose child is not receiving just treatment from an educator whose salary is being paid by our tax dollars. We'll let them know that homophobia and bigotry are not acceptable. And if we have to, we'll take them to court.

We're both tenacious pit bulls when it comes to things like this. I think it's good for kids to know that their parents will go to bat for them. I wish my parents had been strong enough to fight for me when I ran into problems at school. When a teacher at school treated me unfairly, my parents' attitude was, "It's your fault." It didn't matter how unjust the teacher was.

We've already told our parents that unless they get on the road to understanding who we are, we will not allow our children to spend any time with them. We will not allow that kind of bigotry in our home. Our children will face enough of that in life without experiencing it from their grandparents and other relatives.

No one from our families of origin will be allowed to undermine our family unit.

If we wind up having to exclude my family or Bob's family, then we'll find other grandparents for our kids, people who can love our children without judging them because of their own homophobia. Even if we don't have to exclude anyone, we plan to bring plenty of people into our lives for our children. We know it's important for them to have many different and positive role models in their lives.

It's not quite the right time yet to move ahead with our plans to have children. We're on the road an average of 200 days a year and too publicly involved to bring a child into our lives. We want to pull back from the public eye before we become parents. And we want to establish ourselves in our community where we can raise our children in an environment that's as normal as possible. But when we're ready, we now know what our options are.

32

Part of the reason we decided to leave Los Angeles for the Pacific Northwest was that we wanted to get settled some place that was ideal for raising kids.

But that wasn't the only reason. We also left because we had grown tired of L.A. It's a great place to visit, but we didn't want to live there. I couldn't stand the bullshit, the back-stabbing, people killing each other over make-believe. So many people were nice, nice, kiss, kiss, and then they'd cut your throat. People would say, "It's so good to see you. I love your work." And then they'd say to your agent or anyone else who would listen, "I don't know why they work instead of me when I'm so much better than they are." I know this isn't just people in L.A., but it is so much more intense when people's careers live and die on image. And in L.A., you are your image.

We just wanted to do our work, do it right, and then go home.

But in the industry we worked in, the most important things were the kind of car you drove, the kind of house you owned, and the clothes you wore. I'll admit that on a personal level those things matter to us, but we don't make those kinds of choices based on who we're trying to impress. And we don't judge people that way. So when we started talking about leaving L.A., we knew we wanted to find a place where people were more down to earth.

Another issue is public scrutiny. In L.A., people knew who we were and knew what we were doing. And if we weren't at a certain party we felt like we should have been there because it would have been good for our careers. It was too much.

Getting closer to nature was also important, and the Northwest offered more possibilities to get in touch with nature. Rod wanted to be near the water, I wanted to be near the mountains, and we both love the forest. We also wanted a distinct change of seasons. That was especially important for Rod, because farm families mark their lives that way. So we went down the list of what we wanted, and everyone we talked to said that we'd love Washington.

They were right. Unfortunately, Bob was away in Germany when I went house hunting, and I wound up choosing our new house, which was in Olympia, without Bob's help. It wasn't exactly the house I wanted, but I knew it was a house Bob would like. It also wasn't where we really wanted to live, but in Olympia we could afford the kind of house that would have been out of our reach in Seattle.

After we moved to Olympia, many of our friends thought we'd be back in Los Angeles within six months because they didn't think we could deal with such a quiet life.

But it was really perfect for us. We're homebodies. We don't go out to party, dance, or socialize much. Our idea of a good time is going camping alone for the weekend.

Another reason some of our friends thought we'd be back was because we were moving to a place where there weren't a lot of openly gay people, or at least visible gay people. But that didn't matter to us. We planned to just live our lives, and if anybody didn't like it, they could go to hell. We really didn't care.

One day we were shopping in a mall in Olympia, and a sixteen-year-old kid walked by with his girlfriend, and we heard him say, "That's Rod and Bob." He'd obviously seen us on television and knew we lived in Olympia. We're pretty low-key in public, so we didn't acknowledge it and just kept walking. He got about fifty yards away from us and turned around and screamed, *"Faggots!"* I turned around and yelled, *"Bigot!"* As we started walking toward them, they ran out the door into the parking lot.

There are all levels of derogatory language, and Bob and I had decided long ago that we would much prefer to be "faggots" than bigots.

Being gay is just who we are, but being a bigot is a choice.

There were a couple of times when we had to work through some things. When I looked for a realtor in Olympia, I explained that we were a gay married couple and if they had a problem with that they could either hang up or give us someone who wanted to work with a gay couple. I found a good realtor who also helped me find a banker.

When it came time to fill out the forms for the mortgage, I told the banker that I was going to fill out the application for both Bob and me even though it wasn't set up that way. He told me it wasn't legal, and I told him I didn't care. I said, "You're getting my money and I demand that respect." He said fine, so I filled out the forms as I wanted and they went through.

Another time I had a problem.

We were in the yard meeting our new gardener, Hart, and he was going on and on about how Bob and I "must have lots of chicks." This was the first time we'd met him. He said, "Man, they must fall all over you." Neither of us said anything. I purposely didn't say anything because I'm usually the one to speak up, and I wanted Bob to speak up this time.

I'm embarrassed to admit that I still have trouble being direct, and this was after we'd had hundreds of these conversations with people, after we'd done dozens of lectures together all over the country, had dozens of articles printed, and been on lots of television shows.

I find it easier to talk to a crowd of a thousand or two thousand people than to deal with someone one on one. I was afraid of a confrontation with the gardener. I know it may sound crazy, but even after we've been so public and spoken so confidently about who we are, I still sometimes fall back into my old patterns and conditioning, those feelings of shame about being gay. That makes me feel self-conscious and insecure about speaking up, as if I will yet again be judged harshly, when I just want to live my life. This was one of those times, so I pretended I didn't hear what he said.

After Hart left, Bob was being really sheepish with me. I knew why—he was ashamed that he hadn't said anything—but I wasn't going to let it drop. I said, "Look, I'm really disappointed that you didn't speak up, and I have the feeling that you're disappointed in yourself too, so let's talk about it." About an hour later, Bob finally said, "You're right. I'm ashamed that I didn't say anything."

I decided to write Hart a letter and explained that we were a gay married couple. I wrote, "We didn't want to embarrass you in front of your workmen, and it was an awkward situation for us. In the future, maybe you shouldn't make presumptions."

Hart called two days later and told me how embarrassed he was and apologized. "We just didn't want to make a big deal out of it, and sometimes we get tired having to set the record straight," I said.

Even though I'm hard on Bob about this, I also find it's hard to deal with every day. Especially after we've been so public. I've already told the world that I'm gay, why do I still have to deal with it?" But you don't just come out of the closet once.

I used to think, it's done, now everyone knows, that's it. But it never ends.

I'm not really a friendly neighbor, so it took us three years to become a part of the neighborhood, and then we left. But a couple of weeks after we moved in, Tam, who lived to the right of us, came over to tell us that she'd seen us on *Oprah* and thought we were great. She said, "My parents also thought you were great, and we think you guys have a lot of guts. We really admire you." How could I not like her after that introduction?

When we got to know Tam and her husband, Larry, better, Tam asked us if she could drop off her newborn boy some morning. She said, "You guys come by and tell me when I can drop him off." For her it would have been a break for a couple of hours, and she also wanted us to experience taking care of a baby for an extended period of time. We would have loved to have done it, but we felt weird asking for her baby for the day. Nonetheless, the neighborhood kids would often come over to our house.

Some of our city friends couldn't believe that we didn't have problems; they just assumed that our neighborhood was in some way special. But it wasn't. We didn't hand-pick it, and we didn't know anyone when we moved there. I don't know if all our neighbors liked us, but people seemed to respect us, and they treated us like human beings. And we were just ourselves. People saw us kiss good-bye at the front door. They were genuinely saddened when we moved to Seattle, and so were we.

They also heard us arguing. They saw us working in the yard together, playing with the dogs together, and being around each other twenty-four hours a day. They saw us bringing home the groceries and unloading our station wagon. When we met our neighbors for the first time, if I was doing the introduction I'd say, "Hi, I'm Bob, and this is my spouse, Rod."

What we've found is that if you let people know that you expect to be treated with dignity, that's how you'll be treated. That's not always the case, but it usually works. If you send the message that you expect to be treated like a second-class citizen, that you don't deserve to be treated well, then that's exactly how you'll be treated.

Last year, when we could finally afford to, we moved to our dream neighborhood in Seattle. Besides being breathtakingly beautiful and a city that really works, Seattle has a reputation for being one of the most gay-friendly cities in America. We realized it wasn't going to be paradise on earth, but the fact that Seattle has a gay civil rights law was a factor in our decision, as were the good schools.

We had some anxiety about how convenient Washington would be for our work, because we need to travel so much. But it hasn't been a problem, and with the move to Seattle, we're even closer to the airport. Now the challenge is to find more time to enjoy our home and spend less time on planes.

33

We spend a lot of time on planes and at airports because we're both workaholics, and we have a hard time saying no when people ask us to participate in fund-raising events for gay and lesbian causes.

We like working together, but it has drawbacks. There's no separation between our work life and our personal life. There's no such thing as leisure time, whether we're on the phone, planning, writing, traveling, lecturing, whatever.

Even though we moved to Washington so we could take time off to camp and hike more often, our lives are busier than ever.

One of the few times we did get away, I'm afraid I have to admit that I spoiled it because I couldn't put the work aside.

We had just made up after having had a fight that was primarily the result of several different projects coming to deadline at the same time. We hadn't been on a vacation in years, because whenever we travel we do it for work. So we decided at the last minute to take off to the San Juan Islands, off the coast of Washington.

We packed up the car and had a great time getting there. The first day was a lot of fun, and by that evening all the tensions started melting away and we were feeling really relaxed and romantic. Then somebody had the great idea to call in for messages.

I couldn't help myself. Bob was in the shower and I thought, *I'll call in and see if anyone's left a message.* There were twelve, and they were all urgent—from television shows, three newspapers, and so on.

When Bob got out of the shower, I said, "You're going to kill me," and he knew right away what I'd done. He said we should deal with them when we got home, but I said they were too important to wait.

We couldn't think about anything else that entire next day, so we just went home even though we had planned to stay four or five days. It didn't make any sense to stay if we couldn't enjoy it. But I couldn't blame Rod because I understand his motivation. We're always both afraid that if we miss a call or an opportunity to speak that we might be passing up the chance to advance gay and lesbian civil rights. It's hard to put that thought aside.

We can't seem to take time off because we're devoted to the work we're doing, and we get so caught up in it that we lose some of the tenderness between us. But then we'll go away for the weekend or not answer the phones for the day, and we rediscover each other.

On the plus side, the work is exhilarating and rewarding, and best of all, we get to spend time together doing something that is ultimately so rewarding.

We used to go camping every weekend when we first got together, which we don't do very often anymore. Still, it's important for us to get away and renew our love for each other.

Our eighth anniversary is coming up and I think we're going to find some time to escape and celebrate together.

34

Nowadays Bob and I are putting much less emphasis on our independent work. We're doing another art book together, we do our college lectures, the civil rights work, and many other combined projects.

I compete in my sport only about once a year at this point. For a couple of years, I competed twenty times a year, but with all of the other work Rod and I have taken on I just don't have the time. Besides, I've had to take on other work because they've made it impossible for me to make a living in the sport, and we do have a mortgage to pay. The only reason I'm continuing to compete is that I don't want to be chased away from the sport. It was important for me to stay with the sport after I came out. I didn't want to walk away.

They've tried desperately to get rid of Bob.

Even before I came out, they did everything they could to let me know that I was a second-class citizen. During a nine-city Grand Prix competition tour in Europe following the 1988 Mr. Olympia competition, the federation had set up an extensive tour with many athletes. A lot of the athletes' wives and girlfriends also came. Of course, I wanted Rod to go with me.

They didn't think Bob would have the nerve to bring me, and they didn't think I'd have the nerve to be there, but I went.

The first stop on the tour was Munich. Just before the contest began, I went out into the audience to touch base with Rod. I looked for him in the front-center section where all the wives and girlfriends were sitting, but I didn't see him. It turned out he was given a ticket for a seat way over on the side, completely behind a pillar, and he couldn't see the stage. I started walking back into the audience and I spotted him. I called to him and asked him what he was doing there.

I told Bob that that was where they put me. I had a terrible cold that night, and I didn't care where I was sitting and wasn't in the mood to fight with anyone.

I took Rod's ticket and went to the show's German promoter and said, "Look, you——, I don't know what your problem is, but this ticket had better be changed for one in the section up front, right now, or I won't be competing, but I'll go out and tell people why I'm not on stage." He tried to pretend that someone else had made a mistake and said, "I don't understand. This is wrong." But he knew exactly what had happened, only he didn't expect us to challenge him. He got Rod another seat.

It was all so hypocritical. At the same time they were saying that Bob was just a faggot, they used him in the advertisements and the promotional posters to get people to buy tickets. No matter what they thought about him, they didn't hesitate to use him to make money for themselves.

But it wasn't until after the *Ironman* article was published, when I came out publicly, that the judges decided they needed to get rid of me. The first time I got a sense of how they planned to do that was at the Night of Champions competition in New York, directly after the *Ironman* interview was published.

Bob needed to go out there and show those people that he had no shame, that he was proud of who he was and what he did.

I knew it would be a pretty rowdy crowd of a couple thousand people. If they hate you, they hate you, and if they love you, they love you.

I walked from the back of the auditorium to my seat in front. Every head turned toward me, and people stopped talking. It didn't bother me, but I was nervous for Bob. Then the guy who wrote the article about us in *Ironman* came up to me and said that the editor of another muscle magazine told him that he thought Bob's coming out and what we were doing was the worst thing that could have happened to the sport of bodybuilding. This was right after that editor had said hello to me and had been very friendly. People never said things to our faces.

Backstage everything was normal. The athletes have never, ever been anything but respectful toward me. People may have said things when I wasn't around, but not to my face. Most of them even complimented me on the article and said they hoped everything went well for me.

For the most part, the competition was uneventful. I had a lot of fans in the audience. People applauded me, and it was a warm welcome. There were a few catcalls, but nothing much.

A few people yelled, "Faggot," "I love you," "Hey, pretty girl." But that was nothing new because people had been doing that for years.

At the end of the night show, I did my routine and it brought down the house. I wound up placing fourth, and the audience booed the judges. Most people said I deserved to place much higher.

I have to make the point here that I mean absolutely no disrespect for the athletes who placed ahead of me at those times when I believed I was unfairly placed low. I'm very good at what I do, and I think I simply deserve to be placed justly. My unfair placements are not just my observation. I have received thousands of letters from fans who wonder why I'm being unfairly treated when I compete.

What happened that night was just the start of what happened in the years that followed. No matter what I did, they placed me lower and lower. There were a couple of times when I competed at less than my best and deserved to place low, but that's not what I'm referring to here.

For you to understand what I'm talking about and the prejudice I experienced, I have to explain how the sport of body-building is structured. The ruling body of amateur and professional body-building is the International Federation of Body Builders, the IFBB. Its president and founder is a man named Ben Weider, who, along with his brother, Joe Weider, owns Weider Health & Fitness. That company puts out the Weider food supplements, and they publish *Muscle & Fitness, Flex, Shape,* and *Men's Fitness.* It is a near-monopoly, because they control the entire sport and have always tried to drive out of business anyone who goes up against them, whether it's a magazine or a competitive bodybuilding organization.

When it comes to judging the contests themselves, at each show there are seven judges, who come from a very small circle of friends. They all know each other and socialize together. The person who heads the judging is also the vice president of the professional division of the IFBB. He's the person athletes are supposed to go to if they have complaints about the organization, yet he's the vice president of the organization and also a major contest promoter. To top that off, the judges' individual scores are kept secret. They're never revealed to anyone, especially the athletes or press. There's no accountability whatsoever.

I'd begun to hear that high officials within the IFBB were making extremely derogatory remarks about me, saying how I would never win a show because I'm queer. After a contest in which I was placed unjustly low, I was told that one very high-ranking official was bragging about how he had gotten me placed low enough that he was sure he'd gotten rid of "the faggot."

They were hoping Bob would get so frustrated that he'd quit.

It gets worse. Around this same time, my endorsement contract with the Weider company was coming to an end, so I went to meet with Joe Weider. During lunch I told him the story about the high-ranking official, and I asked Joe if this kind of discrimination was the policy of the Weider company. I told him how I was being screwed in the contests and how his magazines were hardly writing about me. People thought I'd retired because they rarely saw a glimpse of me in the Weider publications.

Joe reassured me that he planned to renew my contract and couldn't understand why the magazines weren't doing a better job of covering me. That was in 1992. Lo and behold, when the contract expired, it wasn't renewed, despite the fact that I'd lived up to and exceeded all the terms of the contract, and despite Joe's verbal commitment to renew. When I telephoned Joe to negotiate a new contract his exact words were, "I don't have any use for you anymore." It's also important to note that other pro athletes were having endorsement contracts renewed at this time.

So I wrote Ben Weider, Joe's brother, who's the head of the Weider companies and president of the IFBB. I told him that I was being discriminated against and outlined what I thought was going on. He wrote back and said there was absolutely no discrimination and that unless people came forward to say they had heard these things, it was nothing more than gossip. His one concession, if you can call it that, was the promise to add sexual orientation to the IFBB constitution's anti-discrimination clause. This measure will have to be voted on by the entire IFBB World Congress, whose representatives come from over 100 nations, including China, Russia, Poland, and a wide range of other countries that still openly violate gay people's civil rights on a regular basis. I'm not holding my breath for its passage, but then maybe the Weiders will finally get an idea of the adversity openly gay athletes face in their sport.

If there were another organization to go with, I would, but it's the only game in town. And they don't want me. I haven't retired, but they've retired me because I've broken the rules by coming out of the closet. I've rocked the boat, and they want to push me overboard.

If Bob wanted to, and if they judged him fairly, he could compete successfully for another ten years. After all, he's one of the most popular bodybuilders in the history of the sport.

But even if I stay with it and do well, I won't win anything because the judges have made it very clear that they will discriminate against me. At first they didn't place me any higher than third, but when it became apparent that I wasn't going to stop my civil rights work, I started placing in the twilight zone. The last time I competed, which was in Chicago, I was placed tenth, and I was probably in the best shape I'd been in for a long time.

The responsibility for the discrimination against me doesn't just rest on the Weider companies. Someone at a high level at another suplement company said that while gay dollars represented a high proportion of money spent in the fitness industry, there had never been any demands that those dollars be acknowledged, so those dollars are taken for granted. It makes me angry that so many in this industry take gay and lesbian dollars without treating us with dignity. Rod and I look forward to the day when gay and lesbian people insist that those who want our dollars treat us with respect.

What Bob really wanted, and the primary reason he went back to bodybuilding, was to win the Mr. Olympia title. That's not going to happen, because as one of the officials told me, they would never allow "a queer" to be Mr. Olympia. But I've urged Bob not to give up, not to walk away from it, to make them get rid of him.

At this point, it appears that my bodybuilding career is over, whether or not I walk away from it. But I'm not going to go quietly. I still have many unfulfilled goals as an athlete, and I look forward to the day when bodybuilding becomes a true sport with no room for bigotry. At this point, I'm not yet sure what I'll do, but I know that I've got to do something to make sure that the next gay or lesbian athlete who comes out isn't discriminated against the way that I've been.

I'm thinking about my options. It's not over yet, but that's a whole other book.

35

One of the things we've been working on together that we're really excited about is a foundation that we've just started.

Several years ago, I told Bob that I thought we should develop a foundation that had something to do with gay and lesbian youth. Because of our work and our life experiences, we understand how much need there is to deal with the problems faced by gay and lesbian young people. Why not use the spotlight we're in to focus more energy, attention, and light on issues important to gay and lesbian youth? I wanted to do something that can develop during our lifetimes and that will continue long after we're gone.

At first, a scholarship fund, which is something I could have used when I was a teenager, seemed appropriate. But as we thought about it, we decided we wanted to do something that could have broader impact.

What we've come up with is the Be True to Yourself Foundation. It's a non-profit foundation that will fund all kinds of projects across the United States specifically targeted at gay and lesbian youth. And we'll use our names and our contacts to raise the money to both fund projects and to build an endowment.

We hope to fund ongoing programs developed by places like the Gay and Lesbian Adolescent Social Services (GLASS) in Los Angeles and the Hetrick-Martin Institute for the Protection of Lesbian and Gay Youth in New York. And we want to fund education projects, like "Be True to Yourself," the video we produced with Twenty-First Century News for gay and lesbian youth.

The way it will work is that people will make grant applications and then the board will determine which are the most worthy projects.

We think it's key for us to take responsibility for raising a new generation. None of us wants yet another generation to go through the kinds of anguish we did growing up. And if we work hard enough, we can make sure that things are better for each successive generation. I truly believe that every gay and lesbian person who has been lucky enough to survive the turmoil of growing up is a survivor. Survivors always have an obligation to those who will face the same challenges.

We want gay and lesbian people to overcome their fear of having anything to do with young people. When we first started speaking out about gay and lesbian youth, we were hesitant because we knew that ignorant people would label us child molesters or recruiters. That's so much worse than just being called a faggot. But we decided not to let that fear stop us. We knew we had to stand up for what we believed in and fight for the young people who need our support.

We've been so indoctrinated in the lie that gay and lesbian people are born child molesters that we've been immobilized by the fear that we'll be accused of having ulterior motives. That's kept us as a minority from saying or doing enough about the appalling numbers of gay and lesbian young people who take their own lives every year. We can't let that happen anymore, and I don't care if people call me a pervert or a child molester because . . .

. . . We know the truth. I have first-hand experience of how self-hate can lead to drug abuse and a life's potential unfulfilled.

If we can help to save or improve the quality of one life, it will be worth the effort. These kids are important to all of us.

There are people who still think we should keep our heads down and be quiet. We've gotten letters from gay people telling us this also. They're afraid that focusing attention on gay youth issues could hurt the minority. But we don't believe that. We can't stay quiet anymore and let so many lives be ruined. Rod and I are in a position to do something, and with the help of millions of gay and lesbian people, we can make the world a better place for future generations of gay and lesbian youth.

36

Even with the work of the Be True to Yourself Foundation, we know that it may be a long time before gay and lesbian kids can have normal lives, growing up in homes where they're accepted and loved in the same way that heterosexual kids are.

What gives us some hope is how far our own families have come over the years in learning to deal with us and accept who we are. But if our families are any example, it's going to be a difficult and long road. My mother, for example, has really changed a lot in her attitudes since that first dinner when I told her I was gay, but the change didn't happen overnight, and it has been an anguished, draining process.

I remember the first time we went back to Windsor and went to Rod's mom's house. Rod and I were sitting next to each other on the couch, and his mom was very uncomfortable. She kept bringing up Rod's old girlfriend and what a wonderful and beautiful woman she was.

I had to remind my mother that she never liked her when I was going out with her.

And when we were loading some of Rod's things into our Jeep, I said to Rod, "Hand it over here, honey . . ." and Rod's mom cringed. Now when she sees us kiss it doesn't even register.

But there was a time, not too long ago, when she came to visit us for Thanksgiving in Olympia, that she walked away when something happened at the grocery store. I was hurt and furious with her. This was a couple of years after we first moved to Olympia, and by then everybody at the grocery knew us and knew that we were a gay couple. We'd already been on several TV shows by then.

I was at the checkout counter, and my mother was with me. Bob and I had just had our checks redone so that instead of two separate last names they were printed with "Bob and Rod Jackson-Paris."

We're a family unit, and it just seemed natural to join our names. We first started doing it answering the phone, "Jackson-Paris" and then changed our names legally.

The woman at the counter looked at the check, and then looked up and asked in a really smartass way, "Oh, are you guys brothers?" She knew damn well that we weren't brothers. This was just her attempt to put me in my place and remind me that I was a second-class citizen. I was furious that she was challenging me when she knew better, and that she was trying to embarrass me in front of my mother.

What made me even more mad was that I felt embarrassed, that I still hadn't been able to completely shake society's condemnation of me. So I looked her right in the eye, with anger boiling in my stomach, and I said, "No, we're spouses, and you damn well know that. So please just ring up my groceries, unless you don't want our money." She lowered her eyes and went back to work. She wasn't so brave anymore.

In the middle of all this, my mother suddenly developed an intense interest in barbecue charcoal and 100-pound bags of dog food at the front of the store. I was so hurt that my mother would not stand there with me after everything I'd been through. I knew she still wasn't completely comfortable with the fact I was gay, but I thought she had at least reached the point where she would stand by her child. If the grocery checker had been taking my money for granted and treating me like trash because of my skin color, I know my mother would have stood by me. I now knew that the shame of having a gay son was still more powerful than the love she has for me.

I should have confronted my mother right after this happened, but I didn't. In fact, I didn't say anything and was hurt and angry for the rest of her visit. After she went home, I didn't call her. She'd call me and I wouldn't take the call. If I answered, I'd tell her that I didn't have the time to talk right now and that I had to go. In retrospect, what I should have done was talk to my mother right away. But I wasn't feeling like being an adult about it because we'd been over the same ground fifty times. I know that wasn't a reasonable way of dealing with my mother, but I was tired of telling her how to be a supportive parent.

After a couple of months I called my mother and told her that I was angry. I said, "You know why, don't you?" And she said, "Well, I'm not sure, although I have a good idea." I said, "Do you know how that made me feel? You don't have to understand me, but you have to accept me. If you want my respect as your son, you have to treat me with respect and you have to stand with me. But if you can't, then I don't want you in my life." I explained to her that I was tired of having to point out when she did something that was hurtful to me. She knew what I was talking about and said, "You're right. I was wrong, but I was uncomfortable. I didn't know what to do. I still have things to work through."

For both of us, that's been the hardest thing with our mothers, getting them on the path to working through their thoughts and feelings on this issue instead of just saying they've worked it through. My mother was notorious for saying she'd worked things through and then turning around and doing something ten minutes later that demonstrated she still had problems with the fact I'm gay.

Just to give you an example of how much my mother has changed, we were at a truck stop for dinner with my mother in Wyoming, on the way back to Colorado following my grandfather's funeral. Much to my surprise, she wasn't at all self-conscious talking about gay subjects, and believe me, this was red-neck heaven. There were people all around us, and in the past if we were talking about anything gay, she'd whisper. But not this time. She didn't whisper, and she didn't stop talking when the waitress came by. I don't know what happened, but she wasn't uncomfortable talking about our relationship, and later when we were back at home, she was perfectly comfortable with us being physical, like sitting next to each other on the couch and touching.

My mother has really accepted our relationship, and I think she's proud of us. And I'm proud of her, especially because the other day she asked me what she could do when people say things that she doesn't like. She said, "I'm going to start fighting with them now. I want to get even with them." I told her that it didn't do any good to get even, but it made me feel so good that she's willing to stand up now and say, "That's my son and that's his spouse. What's it to you?" I didn't ever think we'd get to this point.

I think Rod's grandfather's funeral was a big turning point for his whole family. We were both there for it, and I got the chance to meet some of his relatives for the first time. I had wanted to go because Rod's grandfather had shown respect for me. When he was sick, Rod and I sent a few gifts, and twice he wrote back. This was a man from a generation where men never wrote letters, yet in his scrawled, shaky handwriting, he wrote to the both of us. He signed off with, "Not feeling so well, but hope you guys are doing good. Love, Grandpa."

Some of my family had met Bob, and everybody knew about him, so it was appropriate for him to be there—although I have to admit that I had some ambivalent feelings about him being there, because I hadn't had the chance to be with many of these people as an openly gay person. I had reservations about dealing with them and having Bob there at the same time.

So we flew to Denver, rented a car, and drove to my grandmother's house. When we got there I hugged her and told her that I loved her, and she told me that she loved me, too.

Then she hugged me and said that it was nice to meet me. I told her that I was sorry about her loss.

I was amazed. My grandparents were farmers all their lives. They're good people, but extremely conservative. So for my grandmother to reach out and hug anybody's spouse, let alone my gay spouse, was a big deal. My grandmother is known as being very generous, warm, and outgoing, but I don't come from a huggy-feely family. My grandmother doesn't feel the need to physically express how she feels much of the time.

We were both very conscious of the fact that this was in no way a political event. It was a funeral. So we let other people take the lead and if they were comfortable with us, fine; if they weren't, we weren't going to make an issue out of it. It's not like we didn't touch each other, but we didn't challenge anyone, like my brother, for example, who wouldn't even talk to me. In fact, we haven't talked since 1986. There were other relatives who had problems with us, and we didn't have much to do with them either.

I really can't complain about my family because half my relatives love Bob and get along with him fine. These are the people I love and respect, and they in turn love and respect me and my spouse. For example, my Aunt Sharon and Uncle Wes, Aunt Margaret and her husband, Mike, and my Uncle Moe and his wife, Jennifer, took Bob in like he was one of theirs. I can't say this happened overnight; it was years after they first learned I was gay. But in the end I think they saw that we were human, that we weren't there to prove anything to anyone, that we were there simply because we were family and we belonged.

Before we left, my grandmother talked to us about coming to visit us, which is something I never imagined I'd see happen in this lifetime. When we were getting ready to leave, I hugged my grandmother and said, "We're going to send you a ticket." She said, "I know." The whole time I was looking to see how she reacted to Bob, but before we left she grabbed him, and they hugged for as long as she hugged me. He said, "We're looking forward to having you come visit." And she said, "Send me that ticket." That was a real shock to me. It made me feel so good, because while she may not completely understand, she understands how important Bob is to me.

I think she understands that I'm taking care of the grandson she loves so much and that he's happy and we have a good life together.

37

I've had a rougher time with my family than Rod has had with his. It's not just the gay issue here, it's a lot of things. Things have gotten a lot better since the years when I didn't talk to anyone in my family.

I had a complete break with my father in 1988. That happened during a Christmas visit, when my dad came to stay with us in Los Angeles. Rod had already met my father a couple of years before.

Dad arrived three days before Christmas, and he seemed okay with us at first, but then he started getting a little funny. Rod was setting the table for Christmas dinner, and my dad said, "Oh, you guys don't need to bother making Christmas dinner for me." I explained to him that it wasn't a bother, that we were a family and we were having our family Christmas dinner.

I told him that he was more than welcome to join us or he could go out to the living room. I don't think he meant anything by it, but this was the tenth time Bob's father had made a comment like "you boys" or "you roommates."

It was like we were just these guys hanging out. He was having trouble recognizing that Rod and I were a family, not just a couple of roommates. But it wasn't just that. Dad and I had not had a chance to talk anything through since he had stopped drinking. I wanted to talk, and it became increasingly clear that if we were going to talk it would be up to me to push it. Every time I tried to bring something up, he said, "We don't have to talk all the time. You can just relax." Well, I needed to talk, so a couple of days after Christmas I suggested that we drive up the coast to Santa Barbara. I thought he'd enjoy seeing a bit of the countryside.

I started in on my father as soon as we were on the road. I said, "We've got so much to talk about. Why won't you talk to me?" We wound up getting into a huge screaming match. We were screaming and yelling the whole way to and from Santa Barbara in an open-top Jeep.

With my father there was always a history of denial and the inability to talk about anything honestly. You could never get into the heart of any subject with him. I expected my father to be as far along as I was and be willing to talk openly. When I realized that he wasn't willing to take responsibility for the things that had happened in the past, I got very angry. I didn't disagree with my father that we had to let go of these things, but I wanted to talk about them first. And then he said things like, "I understand what you're going through being gay because I've been an alcoholic, so I know what it's like to have a sickness, too." That sent me over the top.

When we got back to our apartment, Rod and I went to the gym. When we got back, my father was gone. He'd packed his things and rented a car and left. Two days later a card arrived. It said, "Please forgive me for the things that you think I've done to you, and I hope that someday you're able to forgive me." We didn't speak for years after that. Not a word was exchanged. Nothing. We sent him a wedding invitation and didn't get any response.

About a year or so ago, after a couple of years of Rod encouraging me to get in contact with my father, I decided to write him a short letter.

I encouraged Bob by telling him that his father was never going to be the person Bob wanted him to be. I said, "Just learn to live with the fact that he'll be himself."

He really is a good person and has a lot of great qualities. He's just never wanted to deal with the past. He thought we could make amends as long as he was reconciled in his own head. He wanted to do it without talking with the people he'd done bad things to.

Not long ago, we were speaking at the University of Cincinnati, and I had memories of a couple of times my dad had taken me to baseball games there as a kid. It was one of my few good memories of times with my dad, so I decided to write him a letter. I told him that we'd moved to the Northwest and were doing fine and said that I hoped he was okay. This was not an easy note to write because I felt that I hadn't done anything wrong. I didn't think I should be the one to reach out and make the first move.

As soon as Bob finished writing it, I made him mail the letter right away, because I knew if he waited until morning he wouldn't do it. We were already getting ready for bed, but I made him put his clothes back on and go down to the hotel lobby and mail it. When he got back he said, "I wish I hadn't written the letter."

I thought it was going to be one more well-intentioned but failed effort. A couple of days later, Dad called and it's just gone from there. He still doesn't want to talk about the past, but I'm hoping he will one day.

I think Bob and his father were both wrong and both right. It's just a matter of different perspectives. Bob's dad's attitude is,

"Grow up and move on with life," and he has a point there. But Bob has things he needs to resolve and wants his dad to help him, so Bob has a point, too.

With Mom, it took my grandfather's death two years ago to bring us back together. I wasn't speaking with anyone in my family at the time, primarily because of how they dealt with not only the fact that I was gay, but my marriage to Rod and the surrounding publicity. Mom had been writing to me, but her letters were filled with an "I haven't done anything" tone, so I just sent them back. After a while, I didn't even bother opening them and just returned them. This one time, she typed my name and address and didn't put her return address on the envelope, so I didn't know it was from her. Rod happened to have opened the envelope because it was in a large pile of fan mail. He found an obituary of my Pap-pa Clark that Mom had sent. He had died two weeks earlier.

The next day I traveled back to Indiana and stayed in a hotel the first night. Early the next morning I went to Mom's house, and she was happy to see me. She called my Mam-ma, who was staying about thirty miles away, and we drove out to meet her.

During the drive, it was complete silence on "the issue." She was going to pretend like nothing was wrong. So I said, "Mom, where do we stand?" And she said, "Well, I'm willing to let bygones be bygones." I pulled over to the side of the road and told her that bygones were not bygones and that unless we dealt with this I was going to be on the next plane out. She started to cry and said, "I don't understand. When you talk in the magazines and on TV about being gay, it's like you were bragging about it." I explained to her that I was, that I didn't see my being gay as something wrong, and that I was happy with who I was. I said, "Rod is the love of my life. He makes me happy. Why shouldn't I brag?" She said, "I accept that, but how could you turn your back on your family?" We talked some more and drove the rest of the way to see my Mam-ma.

When I saw my Mam-ma, I held her for a long time. This was her time, her loss, and I wasn't going to make an issue about anything. We had a nice talk, and she said that she hoped Rod and I were happy, and that she'd like to meet him someday. I told her that we would be traveling to Florida, which is where she lives, and would see her then.

Mam-ma told my mother that she hadn't thought she'd ever see me again. It made me so sad to hear her say that because there had been such a strong bond between us when I was growing up. And I was angry at society for making it so that I was an outsider to my own family, for making me feel that I had to run away because they couldn't accept me.

I took Mom and Mam-ma back to my mom's house. We stopped at my Pap-pa's grave. It was on a hillside and very beautiful.

While I was home I also saw my sister Lisa. We hadn't talked for several years because she'd interfered in a fight I was having with my mother over whether or not to tell my grandparents I was gay. But that night we hugged and held each other, and I told her why I'd been angry all those years and how I'd missed my nephews, and that I was sorry Rod had never been able to meet them. She said that she was sorry and that she was wrong.

In some ways it was a healing visit, but things were still unresolved with my mother, and on the third day I was there we had a knock-down, drag-out argument. She couldn't understand why I was so angry about how the family had dealt with me and why I was so angry with her. I told her that she had to find a chapter of Parents and Friends of Lesbians and Gays and start dealing with the fact I was gay. I told her that if she didn't, we would never have a relationship again. She said she would, but I knew she wouldn't. I got very angry with her and started to leave, and she said that I was exactly like my father, that I was the curse of her life, just like my father had been. She pushed all my buttons and I cussed her out. Immediately I knew that was a stupid thing to do. I apologized and left her standing there crying.

I couldn't believe that I'd opened myself up to that again. I don't know how many times in the past I'd tried to reach my mom and been disappointed or frustrated or infuriated by her inability to understand me.

Over the next few months my mother didn't mention anything to me about going to a Parents FLAG meeting, so I wrote her a letter in which I said, "You need to get help dealing with my being gay. You've said that you want me in your life, but you only want me on a very superficial level. If you want to have a real relationship, you've got to get help and you promised me you would. Are you going to live up to that promise?"

I was surprised, but Mom went to a few Parents FLAG meetings in Indianapolis. The first time she went, she took my sister, and she actually spoke up. She also took some literature. It also helped that other parents in the group told her how proud she should be of the work Rod and I were doing. Many of them knew about our work.

My relationship with my mom is growing and improving. I have to understand that my mom is not going to be who I want her to be. She can only be herself. And I have to keep in mind that I'm not going to be who she wants me to be either. But things are getting better. She sent us a Christmas present this year for the first time since we've been together. Rod has had several conversations with her by phone, and she has a genuine interest in meeting Rod and getting to know him. I know Rod is looking forward to meeting her as well.

38

Conclusion

We get letters from a lot of people who tell us that we're their role models. But we're not comfortable with that. For one thing, we could have done a lot better job of dealing with our families than we have, and we could have gotten on the road to self-respect sooner, but everyone's path is different.

We wouldn't want someone to read about how we've handled our parents and then turn around and be as harsh as we've been. That just isn't the most productive way of doing things. But we've learned a lot from our experience and our mistakes, so I guess if somebody can look at what we've done and how we live our lives, and they're able to get something positive from it, that's great. It's an honor. And we recognize the responsibility we have to those who look toward us. But we can't let that dictate our lives. We're still normal human beings with all the problems other people have.

We try to live our lives in a way we can be proud of, and we try to use whatever celebrity we have to draw the spotlight onto the issues that are important to us. That's our contribution. So we can go on a show like *Oprah* or *Donahue* and reach large

A Tom Bianchi photo from our upcoming book, *Bob and Rod*.

numbers of people for an hour. But even more critical is the work each and every one of us can do in our own communities on a daily basis. It's so important for a young gay man or lesbian to see a gay or lesbian person or couple living across the street from them, with dignity.

People sometimes tell us how much power we have to change the minds of other people and that they themselves are not very important in that effort. That's so incredibly wrong because everyone has a role to play in helping gay and lesbian young people feel like a part of society and in changing attitudes in their community, local high school, or at work. Our work doesn't end when we finish a *Donahue* or *Oprah* show. We still go back to our neighborhood and our family and try to live our lives openly and with dignity. The world will change only when each and every one of us, gay and non-gay, makes the effort.

We really hope that the work we're doing is not needed in ten years. We hope that the debate about the place of gay people in American society will seem as archaic as segregated lunch counters. But I'm realistic. Things may not change in an evolutionary way and then that may be the time to do something revolutionary. We've been using peaceful, non-violent methods to secure our equal rights, but I don't know if that will get us what we want and deserve as citizens of the United States.

We're very different in our views on this. I don't think we need to arm ourselves for revolution, and I don't think that would be effective. I believe in peaceful solutions, but Bob thinks we need to prepare ourselves to fight, just in case.

I think we should be prepared. We should know martial arts and know how to use a gun. People are attacking and killing us already, and it's obvious that the police aren't doing enough to protect us.

Bob and Rod at the Tavern on the Green for brunch.

I think neighborhood patrols are a great idea and that we should look after each other, but I don't agree that we need armed militias. I think we can accomplish our goals without resorting to violence. Just because someone has a gun to your head doesn't mean that you have to pick up a gun and point it at somebody else's head. That doesn't make it right.

If we're being led away to concentration camps, I'm not going to go peacefully. Just the same, if people are going to bash us, we need to protect ourselves. That's not going to change the violent feelings people have in their hearts toward us, but it may make them think twice before picking up a baseball bat and trying to kill a gay man or lesbian. Some people only understand violence.

DUO ON THE HUDSON

Duo on the Hudson benefit for the Gay Games.

We have to face the fact that there are people out there who are actively working to strip us of our rights, like what happened in Colorado in 1992, with the passage of anti-gay legislation, and similar hateful legislative attempts around the country. Who's to say we're not going to face a national fight at some point in the future? We've got to be prepared.

Whatever happens, I know that we have already played a part in the battle for human rights for everyone, especially gay and lesbian people.

I hope we take our place in history as openly gay individuals and as an openly gay married couple who were completely open.

I don't agree with that at all. I hope we'll go down in history as one of the great gay loves. I think that's the most political statement we could make, that two gay people found each other and loved each other. I believe that would be very empowering for people because I really think that love changes the world.

I guess I have to agree with Rod, that as two people who are in love with each other we've been able to have a much larger impact than if we'd been two individuals working on our own for human rights. People can identify with love, even if it's between two people of the same sex. They know what it feels like to love another person and it breaks down barriers. We hope that by seeing two individuals who had to overcome so much adversity in order to love each other and themselves, gay and non-gay people will keep the hope that love is always possible.

It's an especially powerful message for people who have been told that they can never have love in their lives.

It's funny, my friend Michael always said that he just wanted to find a man he could love, that he wanted a station wagon, a house in the country, 2.1 kids, and a dog. I told him, "Michael, grow up. You're queer. You're not going to have those things, so get over it." I really didn't believe that I could have those things because I'd been taught by society and I saw for myself that it was hard to live with dignity as a gay person. I couldn't imagine living my life like that, which is one of the reasons I ran from Bob for so many months. Bob made me think it was possible

Publicity photos of Bob and Rod. (*Art Zeller*)

to have all those things I thought I never could, but I didn't want to believe it was possible. I didn't want to be disappointed.

The other day Michael said to me, "You didn't even believe in any of that, and now you have everything I wanted." Almost— we still don't have children.

Long before I met Rod, my fantasy was to find a person with whom I was very much in love on an emotional, intellectual, physical, and spiritual level. And I thought it would be wonderful if we spent all of our time together, and worked together, played together, and slept together. So I've gotten my dream.

We've both gotten our dream.

APPENDIX

BE TRUE TO YOURSELF FOUNDATION
3213 W. Wheeler Street
Suite 261
Seattle, WA 98199

The Be True to Yourself Foundation is a 501 (c)(3) non-profit funding organization established to support projects which create an environment where Gay, Lesbian and Bi-sexual youth can thrive, prosper, develop self-esteem, be safe, and live free of oppression and discrimination as contributing citizens of society.